MW00587369

RUNAWAY TRAIN

RUNAWAY TRAIN

Or,
The Story
of My Life
So Far

Eric Roberts
with Sam Kashner

ST. MARTIN'S PRESS NEW YORK

First published in the United States by St. Martin's Press,
an imprint of St. Martin's Publishing Group

www.stmartins.com

The Library of Congress Cataloging-in-Publication Data is available upon request.

ISBN 978-1-250-27532-5 (hardcover)
ISBN 978-1-250-37172-0 (signed edition)
ISBN 978-1-250-27533-2 (ebook)

Our books may be purchased in bulk for promotional, educational,
or business use. Please contact your local bookseller or the
Macmillan Corporate and Premium Sales Department at 1-800-221-7945,
extension 5442, or by email at MacmillanSpecialMarkets@macmillan.com.

First Edition: 2024

10 9 8 7 6 5 4 3 2 1

For Eliza, who picked up the pieces

Find what you love and let it kill you.

—*CHARLES BUKOWSKI*

Get it together, Eric.

—*ELIZA ROBERTS*

CONTENTS

My father taught me to lie.
We don't learn by what our parents teach.
We learn by what our parents do.

You won't find this book on the reading list of anyone else with the last name of Roberts.
You might not even find it on my reading list.

It isn't going to be the book my father would write.
It isn't going to be the whole truth.
But the truth makes the best stories.
And it's time . . .

■

I love books as much as I love acting. But I have too much respect for books to have ever considered writing one. Until now. Then I remembered something Steve Martin once said about writing his first play. I forgot Steve's exact words but they were something like, "What have you got to lose? There's no one telling you that you shouldn't try it. There's no law against being a novice—you might even get good at it." So you hold in your hands the autobiography of the chaos theory of life.

Read it and weep.

RUNAWAY TRAIN

I. Born Broken—1956–1974

It's all about the journey home.

—Eric Roberts

People don't take trains anymore—they take drugs to get where they're going.

I've done both. My life has been a runaway train. It's never been on time. I even received a supporting actor Oscar nomination in 1985 for a movie called *Runaway Train*, but I lost to Don Ameche in a movie called *Cocoon*. He was seventy-seven; I was twenty-eight. As of this writing, I have ten more years to go to catch up with Don Ameche. There's still hope! But who will remember any of us who sing or dance or recite for our supper? We're shadows on a wall, figures from a magic lantern. We disappear at your will.

Here's *my* footprint in the snow.

I've been a shit and I've been unapproachably great. The singer and actress Rihanna once said I was "too fine to kill," but I've been walking wounded most of my life. This is a book of scar tissue, the scars I can live with and the scars that I hide. I need to brush up on my Dante, but if you can get to Paradise only by going through Hell, I should be there by now.

One more thing you should know: a devastating car accident I suffered decades ago punched a lot of holes in my memory, and this book that you hold in your hands is what's left. I don't need Ancestry.com to learn what fucked me up. I just need to tell you about my father.

During the long Covid winter of our discontent, and knowing I had signed on to confess my sins in a memoir, I started reading a towering number of books, many of them by people I know. As admirable as many of them were, they all seemed to have sailed the same sea: the abusive childhood; the early, often humiliating years of struggle; great success; and then the pain of fame. To me, the memoirs begged a crucial question: Does there have to be damage for a gem to shine brightly? Is there even such a thing as a nice, kind, benevolent, sweet childhood, where you feel safe and loved? Among actors and artists, probably not.

Funny, but I never quarreled with being famous, or whatever you would call the little notoriety I had. I always loved being "famous," because it isn't anything real or meaningful. For me, it was just another form of getting high, the only difference being the drug is other people and their reaction to you. When I lost that, there wasn't a painful withdrawal. I got used to it pretty quickly. If anything, I got high on the secondhand smoke from my sister Julia Roberts's unimaginable fame and success. But that, as you will see, dear reader, became a darker tale.

But here's a happy memory I have of Julia: when she was little, I used to carry her around on my shoulders. She saw her young world from up there, but later, it was the world that held her up and celebrated her as its darling. It's hard when admiration and envy sit down together at the family table. Sparks will fly, and the house may burn down.

My parents were Walter Grady Roberts and Betty Lou Bredemus. (Why do Southerners always have three names, like felons or serial killers?) They were often drinking and depressed, a 1950s couple in an era when drinking and depression were just par for the course. I came out of them, so I have that in my DNA, though I basically raised myself.

Mom was born Betty Lou Bredemus in 1935. I think she was born in Minneapolis but I'm not quite sure. Daddy was a football player in college and maybe even early pro, and he was big—over two hundred pounds, so they were sort of an incongruous looking couple, at least in height. When I was a very little boy, Mom once showed me a postcard of a Gatsby-like mansion that my maternal grandmother—Betty's mom—had been raised in. It was now owned and run by the state of Wisconsin as a tourist attraction. I don't know where their money came from, but they had plenty of it until the Great Depression. They lost it all in the stock market crash of '29.

Maybe it was a "Bredemus thing," but Mom never talked about her original family. I only met her brother, my uncle Jim, twice in my life. The first time was when I was five, and Mom and I took a train from Atlanta to St. Paul, Minnesota, to visit Grandmother Bredemus, who lived with her brother, my great-uncle Cliff. I remember that was the most exciting trip I could have thought possible—the train station; the uniformed porters all shouting and smiling, offering to help with our luggage; all those grown-up travelers, dressed nicely like my mom with someplace important to get to. And of course, the train! To a little boy who'd yet to travel, the train was magic—big and loud and goin' somewhere.

I met Uncle Jim for the first time on that trip. The next time we'd meet, ten years later, it was awkward and sad for both of us. But I'll get to that later.

I'm not exactly sure how my folks met and what their early relationship was like, except that they were two physically beautiful people who met when they were nineteen and twenty-one. They married a year later while stationed at Keesler Air Force Base in Biloxi, Mississippi, where I was born. They were both doing time in the USAF for college tuition. When that ended, they moved to New Orleans so my dad could attend Tulane University for two years.

Walter had been the youngest writer hired for *The United States Steel Hour*, an early, live TV drama. The head writer who had hired Walter right out of Tulane was a flamboyantly gay gentleman whose politics leaned so far left that he was blacklisted, as was everyone he'd been closely associated with, including Walter. Though Daddy was as political as a three-legged stool, after being blacklisted, story has it that he ended up running guns to Cuba. I don't know how true that was, but we did end up living on a boat in my early days. We spent two or three years in the chartered boat business, on a one-hundred-foot sailboat. In fact, my earliest memories are of living on that boat.

One of those memories, now bittersweet, concerns a beautiful little Cuban girl selling shells with her mother near where our boat was docked. I ran up to Daddy one morning, pleading for some money to buy my way into that little girl's heart. Daddy gave me some coins, so I ran back and bought one of her shells. I told the little girl how beautiful I thought she was, but she looked right through me without answering. I was crushed. Shell in hand, I walked back to the boat, full of disappointment.

"She doesn't speak English," Daddy explained. "She didn't understand a word you said."

Well, I've filed that early memory away as a treasure—one of those little rescues that made my daddy into my idol. I would discover that my mom would never rescue me from anything—not even herself.

The next four years would be spent drifting, settling in Decatur, Georgia, where we lived in a house. Next door was another young family with twin girls, three years older than myself. Those two loved to torment me! They wore knit caps and reeked of their mother's perfume. I was scared of them! They were girls. They were aggressive. They were tall.

But once they chased down the ice cream truck for me, screaming at the top of their lungs to get it to stop so I could buy a popsicle, so I was glad I knew them. In fact, I never forgot them.

Back then, Daddy was not just my hero, he was the most fascinating guy a four-year-old could ever look up to. He was tall—six feet. He was so handsome that strangers on the street did double takes when they saw him. He had a beautiful baritone voice and spoke with a perfectly standard American accent. It was one helluva package. A passerby would never have guessed that Walter grew up in poverty and had been raised as a dunk-you-in-the-river country Methodist.

I once asked my daddy after they had my two baby sisters—Julia and Lisa—why'd you marry Mom?

"Cuz she was the most gorgeous woman I ever saw."

So then I asked, "Why'd you wait nine and eleven years after me to have my sisters?"

And he said, "Well, every time we almost got divorced, she'd get pregnant." So that was that story in a nutshell.

My mom had my color hair (before the white showed up)—a kind of earthy brown—and big, bright, blue eyes and really pretty teeth. My mom was a beauty queen, and Daddy looked like a handsome Italian guy. He was dark and had a big buffalo head, like the profile on the Indian nickel. He wasn't Italian, but he did have some Native American blood from his mother's side, whereas his father—my granddaddy—was every bit a white guy, and proud of it. A really, really, white guy. He was also a redneck. On visits, we only went to their house, as they seldom came to our house except on holidays. This was the fraternal set; the maternal set lived in Wisconsin and Minnesota, and I wasn't around them as much.

By the way, perhaps I should say here that most Southern men call their fathers "Daddy" throughout their lives. It drives my wife, Eliza, crazy that I still refer to Walter as "Daddy," but ingrained habits die hard. So Walter Jr. was my daddy, and Grandpa Thomas was my granddaddy. That's just the way it was.

I have happy early memories. I remember that whenever my parents were going out and getting dressed up, I would go into their bedroom and sit on their bed and watch them get ready. I used to love to watch my mother become this incredible beauty. I mean, she was always good looking, but then this transformation would happen. I would go gaga over how my mom looked. Wow! I remember feeling that every time I sat there watching them get beautiful, that was a treat for me.

I don't remember ever having a babysitter.

I have a dim memory that, early on, we were living on a boat. Whether that's true or not, frankly, I'm not sure, but I do remember that they were going out, and I was mad that I wasn't going with them. I ran after them, but a deckhand Daddy had hired onto the boat held me back. I remember he stayed with me, and that's the only time I remember anybody ever doing that. All the other times, nobody ever babysat. I'm sixty-eight now, so that was a long time ago.

I grew up, mostly, in Atlanta. *That* I remember very well.

When I grew up, Atlanta was very white, very middle-to-upper-middle class in some sections, and very Christian. Daddy hated all those things. My mom didn't, but she got weird about church. She was raised in an Episcopalian household, but she never went to church until after she and Daddy got divorced in 1971, when I was barely sixteen. Her second husband, Michael Motes, wrote for a Catholic newspaper, so she became Catholic. I think she even got baptized—she did the whole nine yards.

I grew up pretty close to my extended family. I was especially close to my cousin Adam Bowles, whom I always loved. Adam looks just like me, but he's ten years younger. He lives in a place called Tiger, Georgia, named after a Cherokee chief named Tiger Tail. The name was probably given to him by white settlers, or, as legend has it, it came from the cries of roaming mountain lions.

Adam's father—my uncle Elbert—put in a pond right behind their house. He got down there and cleared out an area, then got some guys with bulldozers and loaders to cut out about half to three-quarters of an acre. It was fed by a creek. He stocked it full of catfish, and we used to go swimming there all the time during the summer—and sometimes we fell through the ice during the winter. Swimming with my cousin in that pond is one of the pleasant memories from my childhood. Even after my uncle sold his place and a new bunch of houses were put in, the pond was still there.

I probably wouldn't have been able to do *The Righteous Gemstones* if Adam weren't my cousin. I even saved some of Adam's messages on my answering machine, so I could get that Georgia accent right, because my sisters and I mostly lost our accents somewhere along the way. I have to admit, I used Adam to model some of my characters on. I also asked Adam if he could remember incidents from our growing up together, as my father gave me so many different family stories to tell that some of them became second nature to me—but were they true?

There's one story about my daddy's family I know is true, because I was there.

Walter's mother, my grandmother, was part Cherokee Indian who had been "rescued" by missionaries. Her two younger brothers escaped into the woods and raised themselves, like Huckleberry Finn. Their names were hard-to-pronounce Indian names, so as far back as either of them could remember, they were called Dump and Buddy. They would both die, almost sixty years later, from cirrhosis of the liver.

I vividly remember meeting the oldest brother, my great-uncle Buddy, when I was five years old. Walter took me to meet him.

After a long drive into the country, we parked at the end of a dirt road and walked into the woods. We followed an echo of a trail that led us to a clearing. In the middle sat a Trailways bus on cement blocks.

Daddy knocked on the folding doors, and out came the whitest woman I'd ever seen, and she could not have weighed less than 250 pounds. She became positively giddy seeing Walter, and she looked into my little boy's face as if seeing a treasure.

"Hell-lo, beautiful boy! I'm your aunt Ginnell."

She was my great-aunt through marriage, but she probably thought that was too complicated to explain to a young boy. She screamed for Buddy to come out and meet us, smiling at me with a frightening set of unkempt teeth. Buddy came spilling out with a stumble that looked almost athletically graceful.

"Walter Roberts! My sister's baby boy."

They invited us in to stay for grub.

"We got catfish in the fryer," Uncle Buddy said, but first he had to check on the "new still." Would we like to come along?

Daddy said, "Sure, why not?"

Aunt Ginnell seemed happy to have the extra time to tidy up for her unexpected guests, so off we went on my first backwoods adventure.

Buddy was famous for moonshining, both with his customers and with the authorities. His still was quite the business, complete with booby traps, but in fact, there were actually *two* stills. The first and very visible one—the "new still"—was not even functional. It just *looked* real. Buddy called it his "red herring." It was in a clearing about a half mile off the trail and about three-quarters of a mile from the real one.

"I keep about ten gallons of 'shine' at the new still, in case the no-dick, law boys find it. That way, they'd be satisfied they'd really found something," he explained.

The genuine still was quite the little franchise. It was laid with booby traps that would have impressed the Viet Cong. On the entrance side to the real still was a six-foot-deep trench, covered by camouflage netting that supported leaves and branches. That left a walkway about eighteen inches wide into the camp where the still was; but if you didn't know it was there, you'd never find it. At the bottom of the trench were many leftover pieces of lumber with size sixteen common nails driven through them. Those were covered with what looked to me like cake frosting.

Uncle Buddy explained, "That's old cookin' oil. You end up down there, you ain't gettin' out."

The camp was really nice, for a guy who lived in a Trailways bus. It had everything you needed—lawn chairs, old and ratty but set out with a table made of a wooden crate that had red plastic nailed to the top as a tablecloth. Buddy's barbecue was a rusty oil drum cut in half and mounted over ashes in a circle of rocks. His refuge from bad weather was a three-sided shack, which held a well-padded cot, a radio that ran off batteries, two kerosene lamps, and a pile of girly magazines as tall as I was.

Now, when you use the word *shack*, you tend to think rickety. This wasn't. The open side faced the camp, while the other three sides were complete with "slide holes"—two-inch wide, twenty-four-inch long spaces for a rifle barrel to poke through.

"You wanna see 'em comin' so you can get 'em goin'," Uncle Buddy explained.

That was one of Buddy's many proverbial sayings, along with classics like my personal favorite, "It's good if ya like it, 'cause it is if ya do."

I could tell, even at five, how fond Uncle Buddy was of Walter. Loved him! Took pride in being related to him, even just knowing him. Walter was the first person in his family to finish grammar school, let alone go to college—and that was in addition to being a straight-A student.

Uncle Buddy and Walter talked and reminisced for the better part of an hour, laughing together and finding comfort in each other's stories. That's how I began to learn more about our family's history.

I discovered that my grandpa Tom (aka Walter Sr.) did not like Dump or Buddy—and it was mutual—but they all loved my grandma Beatrice—Walter's mom—so everyone behaved whenever they got together for holidays and the occasional birthday. I also learned that day at the still that Grandpa Thomas had issues with my mom, because Betty was a "Yankee." Can you believe it? This was 1961, ninety-six years after that awful, bitter war had ended. Grandpa Thomas was still affected by the fact that his Southern Prince of a son hooked up with—let alone married—a Yankee. And there was something else—something spoken of as "the broken promise" between father and son.

When we returned to Uncle Buddy's double-decker Trailways, we all sat down in a four-by-six dining area and ate catfish, greens, homemade cornbread, and sweet iced tea. I remember the fish being very bony, so Uncle Buddy showed me how to bone a cooked fish before you eat it. That was a meal I would never forget.

I had no way of knowing this at the time, but that day visiting my great-aunt and great-uncle, Buddy's deep, slurred Southern accent would lock into my brain and be used for the rest of my professional life, whenever I was required to use a

Southern dialect. So between my cousin Adam and my great-uncle Buddy, I had it covered.

As Daddy and I drove away that day, I could not stop asking questions. "Why didn't Grandpa like Mom?" "What was the 'broken promise'?"

Even at five I knew that grown-ups kept secrets. Apparently, Grandpa didn't like anybody very much, except for white, Southern, American Protestant males like himself. Everyone else was "up to no good." But the real problem, I learned, was that Grandpa Thomas just did not like his son, Walter, very much, either.

Maybe that was because of the broken promise Walter had made to his dad, to help him set up a big amusement park on a nice chunk of land that he'd purchased in 1960 for less than a hundred bucks an acre.

He'd asked Walter to return from New Orleans, where Walter was attending Tulane, to help him get the park up and running. I never learned the details, but father and son parted ways over the fact that they agreed on basically nothing. Maybe Grandpa Thomas resented the fact that Walter was getting an education, at Tulane no less. In any case, the bitterness between them grew, and they never comfortably reconciled.

But Grandpa Thomas was always hard on his only son, as he would later be on me. Because of Walter's interest in theater, art, and reading, my grandparents saw no future for him. To them he was a pointless, arty, well-read pain in the ass.

When Walter was around five or six years old, he went for a walk in the woods with his dad. They came to a gorge with water rushing through it. A log, about three to four feet in diameter, connected the two sides of the gorge.

Now, nobody knew it at the time, but Walter had no depth perception. He saw everything as flat—two dimensional as opposed to three. So when Grandpa Thomas told Walter to cross over on that log, it scared him to death, as he couldn't tell how deep the gorge really was. He threw himself to the ground, screaming and crying and begging not to be forced to cross.

Grandpa Thomas was a large man of 240 pounds. He went and cut a branch off a tree and proceeded to switch his little boy across the gorge. Walter never forgot it; and after he told me about it, the story had a profound effect on me. I held that against my grandfather for the rest of my life.

I began my education in Decatur, Georgia. I remember that I went from Ar'Lyn Worth, a truly great private school for kindergarten and first grade, to a below-average public school, Clairemont, for second and third grades. I also remember moving from Decatur to Atlanta a couple of months after I turned eight. We lived in a tiny apartment at the corner of Peachtree and West Peachtree for just under a year.

I was always small for my age. I thought that I was condemned to a life of shrimpiness, as both of my grandmothers were under five feet tall. But in my dreams, I was always a standard six feet tall, and grown-up. I would dream about Miss Smith, my first-grade teacher. I had a huge crush on her. In my dreams, Miss Smith and I would meet on a small romantic bridge, embrace, look into each other's eyes, and slowly kiss. In reality, I was six years old and short for my age. (I stayed short until I turned eighteen. That year, I grew from five foot four to just under five eleven. It was a good year.)

I well remember the apartment house on Peachtree Street,

because that's where I became a brother. In fact, I remember the countdown to brotherhood as if it were yesterday. I was nine, and I had plans! First, I was going to teach this new little person to read, feeling that it was the most important thing anyone could learn. Then, of course, I'd give him or her pointers on acting and horseback riding—I felt I excelled at both. I had lots of plans for my new little sister, Lisa Roberts, born August 7, 1965.

Lisa was the best baby! She was quiet—not a crier at all. She was a happy baby, easy to entertain. The only hassle with Lisa was that she arrived two months early, so when she was born, she had trouble breathing. She had asthma, in fact. It didn't help that Mom smoked right up till Lisa's birth, but everybody smoked back then.

Mom had been rehearsing kids for a children's play called *The Bremen Town Musicians*. I specifically remember Mom taking a big drag off one of her Viceroys and then basically going into labor. Those were the days when people believed that the placenta protected the unborn from all toxins.

So Lisa's stay in the hospital was several days longer than usual, which was disturbing to my nine-year-old self, especially as I was not allowed in the pediatric ward. Overhearing grown-ups' phone conversations and given vague explanations, I was very worried about my premature little sister. In fact, I looked up the word *premature*, which only made matters worse when I started having images of the baby being born without body parts. But when she was brought home, all such fears were dispelled, and it was love at first sight. I could not get enough of this tiny creature—extra tiny, being a preemie. And so sweet! From the very first moment I met Lisa, I could see there was something innately good about her.

Two years later, Julia was brought home from the hospital. "Look, it's a real baby" were Lisa's first words when she saw the newborn. I was eleven, so I became responsible for everything that baby Julia did, or liked, or didn't do, for the next three or four years of our lives.

Our first six years in Atlanta were really cool. You could talk to anybody, anywhere, about anything. Later, I became aware of the racial divide. I became aware that my father was on one side and the rest of his family were on the other. Wow. There were arguments and disagreements over that, and I admired Walter for his open-mindedness. Back then, Daddy was my hero.

With my mom, Walter founded an acting school for children. It grew out of a job Walter once had as a publicist for the Children's Civic Theater in Atlanta. In fact, the founder of that theater, Edith Russell Harrington, felt that Daddy had stolen her contact list and had used it to launch his Actors and Writers Workshop, along similar lines. The Workshop allowed my dad to indulge his lifelong interest in directing and writing, and my mom's long-deferred interest in acting finally was put to use teaching speech and making costumes. You might say that Daddy gave me the start to my profession and my love of acting, another thing I admired him for.

The classes were held in our house in Atlanta—a great, big old Victorian thing with high ceilings and huge rooms—at 849 Juniper Street, with a wraparound porch. We moved there when our apartment became too cramped for our family of five.

For those of you who don't know Atlanta, Juniper Street is between Piedmont and Peachtree, and between Eighth and Tenth streets. Built around 1890, the house had ten rooms. The workshop classes were on the first floor, and we lived on the top two floors. Upstairs were four big rooms, a kitchen, and breakfast nook, and lots of bathrooms upstairs and down. The cobblestone driveway made me think of horses and buggies.

When we first moved in, however, it was overwhelming because the house had not been lived in as a single-family home for some thirty or forty years. The scraping and painting began, and Daddy enlisted us, Grandpa Tom, and some of his acting students to help. It seemed endless, until the house actually began to recapture its former elegance. The main staircase—five feet wide with two flights—the waist-to-ceiling windows, and the window seats all sparkled. (There was a narrow, back staircase that I thought was made especially for me.) Two big rooms in the back of the house were used as a laundry room and a costume room for our plays. I was proud of where we lived. That house became my world, and I loved it. In its early years, the Actors and Writers Workshop was a success. I remember one day in 1965, Coretta Scott King showed up with all four of her and Martin Luther King Jr.'s children—Yolanda (Yoki), Martin (Marty), Dexter, and Bernice (Bunny). She had heard that acting classes were being taught for children in the only integrated theater school in Atlanta, so she was interested. There didn't seem to be any racial issues with this group that I was aware of. After a while, the King Foundation even helped fund my father's school.

Walter had a big influence on the King children. Yoki adored him but was a little frightened of his booming voice and his somewhat rough manner. Yoki was good friends with Donzaleigh and Juandalynn Abernathy, children of the civil rights activist and leader Ralph Abernathy. In fact, Juandalynn believed that the only reason Yoki went to Grady High School was because Walter lived down the street, and he'd sent *me* to Grady High School.

Juandalynn took Walter's acting classes, but Yoki, who was six or seven, was too young at the time, so she would have to sit on the floor and watch. Classes were in the dining room, which had floor-to-ceiling pocket doors that separated the living room and dining room. When the pocket doors were open, there was an amazing view through tall, beveled-glass windows out to the huge trees in our backyard.

Those classes Daddy held were integrated at a time when segregation ruled Atlanta. I have to say I was proud of my father that he had no intention of following those rules. Back then, he seemed to love everybody. He hugged the King kids and the Abernathy kids, and he attended plays they put on for their parents and attended their ballet recitals at Spelman College.

I remember Saturday mornings during Juandalynn's acting class, I would often sit in the kitchen with Yoki and make her peanut butter and jelly sandwiches on the Formica table. The sisters would have come directly from early-morning ballet classes at Spelman, so by the time acting classes started, Yoki was hungry! Or I'd take her outside and keep her occupied. She was so eager to participate in her older sister's acting class, but that was distracting to Dad. To his credit, he took those classes very seriously.

I think, back then, I wasn't at all intimidating to the King and Abernathy kids. Instead of the typical, white-boy crew cut every other teenage boy wore in Atlanta, I already wore my hair much longer. I didn't look like a redneck.

From the ages of six to twelve, I can say that I was happy. I wasn't aware of how much Dad had to struggle to make ends meet. He relied a lot on grants, and in the summer of 1968, we took a "show mobile"—really just a flatbed truck—around to poorer neighborhoods where we performed plays.

Our world didn't seem segregated back then. I met the King children when I was about eight and a half. By the age of twelve, I knew racial attitudes were all fucked up. Because racial mixing was so okay in my house, I thought it was okay everywhere, even though my paternal grandpa, Tom Roberts, was racist, or what I politely just called a "redneck." He and my father didn't see eye to eye on anything in the world—except food. They both liked the same food.

Around the age of seven, I began to know that I would pursue acting as my life's profession. I sensed that it meant I would be remembered if I were good enough. The simple, stark fear of being forgotten mapped my course toward acting. Acting—really good acting—would always be remembered.

Even before I'd started school, I could name a dozen grown-up movies as well as the actors who starred in them. The summer after I turned four, I appeared in my very first play as the Mute Clown, a toy in a children's Christmas play called *Toys for Tots.* It was so much fun! We ended up performing the play twenty-four times—eight times a week for three weeks. All the performances went perfectly, except for opening night. At seven, I was already a veteran, having acted in several plays, thanks to my parents' acting workshop.

The set of this little Christmas play was very simple—a door at upstage center and a toy box at downstage left. I don't remember why, but on opening night, after the last technical rehearsal, the toy box was moved from downstage left to upstage right. At the end of Act One, the toys all head for the toy box and jump in. I didn't notice that it had been moved, so I went flying downstage left and landed in the space between the first row and the stage. I ended up with a black eye and a bruised forehead.

During intermission, I calmed down and iced my injuries, so the show—and I—really did go on. The lady who was stage manager kept telling me what a "trouper" I was—the first time I heard that word—as she iced my face. Now, whenever I hear that word (used a lot by theater people), I always feel it's said to make somebody feel okay about making a mistake. I've never liked being called a "trouper."

After I debuted as the Mute Clown, I played a servant boy in *Othello*, then I played the youngest son in *J.B.* by Archibald MacLeish (with several lines of dialogue!), followed by the Gate Keeper in a play written by Walter called *The Emperor's Nightingale.*

That same year, 1963, when I was seven, I was part of the Actors and Writers Workshop repertory company. We were given a half-hour spot, from ten to ten thirty every Saturday morning, on Atlanta's local Channel 11. The show was *Bum Bum and His Buddies*. Bum Bum was a clown who would introduce a story every week, dressed in a bowler hat and a tux that was about two sizes too big. With spats, of course, and classic smiley-clown makeup.

Guess who played Bum Bum? Betty Roberts—my mother!

I thought it was pretty cool. She was good at it, too—likable, rubber-jointed, sexless, all the things one expects from a clown. You'd never have known that under that getup was a beautiful woman. Mom would have been twenty-eight at the time and at the height of her beauty. Think of a blonde, blue-eyed, fair-skinned Julia Roberts.

Well, *Bum Bum and His Buddies* brought me my first good review, followed by a nomination for best supporting actor from the local critics for playing Richard, a crippled boy, in a teleplay called *Little Pioneers.* The script was taken from an old newspaper article from the 1890s about two brothers and two sisters left home alone while their father goes to town to sell a cow. Everything is fine until two American Indians stumble onto their property, so the kids think they're under attack. They can't sneak away because Richard, my character, would not have been able to keep up with his siblings, so they decide to stay and fight. In one emotional scene in *Little Pioneers*, my siblings know they can't take me with them. "What if you have to run?" I ask, as I start to cry. In the last technical rehearsal, my tears were so realistic that the run-through was stopped to check that I was all right.

I had found my way to real tears. Everybody—the cast, the director, my mom—was not only delighted but also impressed. I had discovered a way into real, living breathing emotion as opposed to pretended, acted feelings. I thought I had come upon a unique technique that was my little secret—emotional recall. It worked every time. I was not only beginning to feel like an actor but I was also becoming one. The academic and technical aspects of acting had become second nature to me by the age of seven. I found I could *feel* things while acting, as if they were really happening. Later that year, I played John Henry West in Carson McCullers's *The Member of the Wedding*, and again, I'd found a way to *be* this character, not *pretend* to be.

Of course, that leads to the question: what has a seven-year-old experienced that, upon recollection, could make him sob his heart out?

That was a little secret I shared with Mom.

Dad had high ambitions for his little theater, hoping it would become a major cultural center for children's theater in Atlanta, but he just couldn't make it work financially. In a last-ditch attempt to put the Actors and Writers Workshop squarely on the map, he staged an ambitious production of *The Owl and the Pussycat,* with Yolanda King playing a prostitute and a white boy playing the writer who falls in love with her. As liberal as Atlanta seemed compared to the rest of Georgia, a biracial love story was a bridge too far in 1970, and Dad had to close down the workshop because the race mixing in that production was just too much for Atlanta parents.

So the family moved to 432 Eighth Street. Dad had to take a full-time job selling vacuum cleaners at Rich's department store—a huge comedown from operating his own theater. For a guy as proud as Walter, it was humiliating. Mom worked, too, as a secretary for the Catholic Archdiocese newspaper, the *Georgia Bulletin.*

By 1969, Daddy and Mom were quarreling a lot, permanently on the way out of their marriage. Their divorce was final on January 28, 1971. The sprawling old Victorian on Juniper was later torn down. Nonetheless, those were probably the last happy years for the Roberts family, at least from my perspective.

Even though our family was doing well in those early years, I had trouble making friends. In fact, except for my wife, Eliza (more on that later), I've been mostly friendless much of my life. I've had a couple of really close acquaintances, like Christopher Walken, but Eliza is the only friend I've had for any length of time.

I surely never had friends growing up. And I know why—I had a terrible stutter.

I was ostracized by the other kids, especially for the first three years I was in grammar school, which is kind of your foundation for how and when to *make* friends. At my first school where I went to kindergarten and first grade, we all had to read out loud, so I was laughed at a lot whenever it was my turn to read.

Even today, I get really broken up when I think about that sixty-year-old memory of those kids laughing at me in class. I still get ripped apart. It had such a terrible effect on me. I know now that's part of what drove me to get out, to achieve something on my own, even to become an actor. I found out that when I memorized shit, I didn't stutter! It was like finding the pot of gold. It was a gift, like getting kissed on the mouth by a beautiful girl when you expected a handshake.

I remember discovering I could conquer my stutter when I first memorized a monologue. I don't remember what the monologue was, but I remember walking around, reciting it to myself. I realized I could say it to anybody and not stutter, so I started reciting it to everybody: "Hey, hey, listen! Listen, listen to this." And I'd recite it perfectly. Wow. It was a big deal to me, a huge revelation to know that's how I could beat my stutter, that's how it could be done.

But this goes back to the idea of raising myself. Nobody helped me with my issues, explaining, "Here's what we'll do with that, Eric." Nobody took me by the hand to comfort me, to say,

"You'll grow out of it, it'll be okay." I found it all by myself. I nurtured it all by myself, and I got the happiness out of it all by myself.

Beating that stutter really did change my life.

As rough as the kids were, some of my early teachers were really great to me. But it wasn't until sixth grade that I had a teacher who I felt taught me anything. Her name was Miss Shivers, and she was the first Black elementary school counselor in the Atlanta public school system. She was the coolest teacher I ever had.

When she started teaching in our predominantly white school, I remember the principal called all the parents to make sure it was okay with them. My dad, bless him, threw a temper tantum on the phone because he was mad that he had to be asked, just because Miss Shivers was Black.

"Of course she should teach! Of course Eric will be in her class!" he yelled over the phone. He was mad that it was even brought up like that. I was only ten at the time, but I remember it to this day.

Starting out, I wasn't just ostracized by my schoolmates. My grandpa Thomas totally ostracized me, not just for my stutter but also because he saw me as a little sissy theater kid. It's true. Even as a seven-year-old boy, I loved the songs from *Oklahoma!* and was a fan of *West Side Story*. I'd say to my dad, "You know this cool dance from *West Side Story*? You know how they did it in the movie?" And I'd demonstrate. My dad's running an acting school, and my being an actor, didn't go over so well with Grandpa Thomas.

Eight years later, when one of my male cousins was born, my grandfather told me right to my face, "Well, now I got a *boy*." He was really saying, "Now I got a butch grandson," though not in those words. At the time, it wasn't just about sexuality or gender—it was about being a theater kid. He wanted me to be a farm kid, which I was not, even though I exercised his horses for him. So I was fine with it at the time, but I look back on it and think, *What a mean motherfucker!* That's what he was! He was mean and nasty to everybody, not just me.

After all, bullying starts at home. Our younger generations are wondering if they should bring kids into this world. Well, my friends who were born in the fifties thought the same thing, because life is really mixed—it's torture and torment, and then sometimes it's magically magnificent. But the stuff you have to climb through to get there! It makes you wonder whether to become a parent, knowing your kid will suffer too, perhaps even by your own actions.

So here's a story about my teenage years, after my parents divorced, when I just turning sixteen.

Back then, I had a couple motorcycles. Dad didn't like me riding motorcycles, so when I got into trouble, I had to deal with it on my own. Once I got clocked speeding and they put me in jail, even though I was not old enough to be held legally. Another time, I came off the bike—*bam!*—and landed on my ass. I could have handled that, but I landed on a ton of a broken glass and suffered several cuts. I thought I could just throw some alcohol on it and be fine; but then the wounds got infected, so I had to get all the infection dug out and the wounds sewn up. Painful!

Those memories are vivid to me, but you know what? I'm not

sure they really happened that way, or if they happened at all, or if they were stories that my father told me that we incorporated into my life's narrative.

Actually, my cousin Adam remembers a time when the police picked me and a friend up for some teenage mischief. Here's how he tells it: "I remember that Irwin was Eric's best friend coming up. They got caught stealing golf flags one night on a golf course. They was just out drinking beer, smoking pot or something. They got the wild hair so they decided they was going to confiscate them for laughs. And they got caught and locked up. I say, 'locked up,' but it was more like they got grounded. The police picked them up and made them call their parents."

I'm more reliant on Adam's memories than on the stories my daddy told me. The question is, though, why Walter felt he had to make up those tales. Well, for a couple of reasons. My daddy gave me these scripted passages that I was to tell people. And it doesn't stop with just a handful of stories. Every detail of my life was embellished by Walter and scripted for me. "Here's how you do this," he'd say. Maybe he wanted me to appear more butch, to please *his* father? I'm not sure. I was just taught to tell people what was gonna work for the kind of image my dad wanted to project. I was taught that from a very early age, through early adolescence.

Why did my dad need to do that? I can answer that question. Because he came from poverty. Poverty, poverty, poverty. No education. Grandpa Thomas only went as far as the third grade; and because my dad looked Italian, he was discriminated against as a young man in Atlanta. So those scripted stories were to elevate us, to make us into something we weren't. It was to make us interesting, valuable—and undeniably white.

So it's not surprising that, growing up, I had mixed feelings about my dad. Until the last five to eight years of his life, I thought he was a gift from heaven. And then I saw he wasn't. In fact, I realized I was afraid of him. He was the most intimidating presence I've ever been around. I got the same feeling when I was around my grandfather and the horses. If I did something wrong or fucked up in his domain, I was treated as a criminal.

This makes me think about the fourth grade. I was nine years old. I played the trumpet. I took the bus to and from school. I got home on the last day of school and realized, oh God, I left my trumpet on the bus. I went to the bus station: no trumpet. I got punished and was forced to write a thousand ways to make two hundred dollars. I did it. It was agonizing. So when the summer was over and I went back to school in the fall, I discovered the trumpet was in the cloak room all summer long. I didn't leave it on the bus. I hadn't even taken it on the bus. It was still in school, waiting for me.

I believe I had suffered brain trauma even at that age; there was an oddness about me from birth. My mother's violence, a strange kind of passionate violence—that didn't help either. My mom drank. Martinis. Daddy, because of the times, used to get those big old tubs of Valium—250 tablets in a jar—like the kind of things you buy at Costco these days to keep the bomb shelter well stocked. Those little blue pills were five milligrams.

When my parents split up, six-year-old Lisa and four-year-old Julia went with my mom, and I stayed with Dad. I was heartbroken to be separated from my sisters, but Mom insisted. She didn't think she could handle me as a teenage boy. In fact, Mom went so far as to say in court that I once tried to kill her. I never got physical with my mom! Sure, we had screaming matches, but I never got physical with her, ever. The only time I saw that happen was when my dad attacked her. That was bad, and I intervened.

Dad was a big slapper—he slapped me twice a week—but the real beatings came from Mom. She used to hit me with these things called dowels. We had them all over the house; they're about a yard long and they come in all kinds of widths. They were actually used for rod puppets and all kinds of stuff for the theater, so we always had them around. Well, I remember that she used to hit me with those.

I also remember two big fights we had that were two years apart, but they were both such big events that they come into my memory as back-to-back. One was when I was eight and a half and I brought home a puppy.

I was in the third grade, and I'd finally stopped expecting to ever have a baby brother or another sister, which I desperately wanted. Betty and Walter informed me after many requests that I was going to be an only child. I learned to accept this—I even learned to feel special about it, as all my imaginary friends had at least one sibling.

So on the way home from school one day, I saw a sign, FREE PUPPIES. Ya can't beat free, so I decided to have a look. Well, I met five of the cutest little puppies I'd ever seen. They were all two- or three-tone, white with black and/or brown spots, with the exception of one who was all white with little brown freckles across his nose. I named him Freckles on the spot.

I will never forget the pride and satisfaction I felt as I bundled up six-week-old Freckles to take him to his new home. My home.

When I got home that day, puppy in hand, at first my parents were fairly pleasant about it. Freckles could stay, but I would be "totally responsible" for his care and well-being. I was so happy! To an eight-year-old, the words *care* and *well-being* meant endless love, and I so loved that little dog. I felt it was going to be the most fun I'd ever thought of having. Freckles was my first real responsibility, taken on solely by myself.

I fed Freckles anything I wanted, as there was no dog food in the house until Mom went grocery shopping the next day. So after running around for a couple of hours, bonding and playing with each other, Freckles and I ate several Baby Ruth chocolate bars (taken from Grandma and Grandpa's house), and a half dozen slices of Daddy's whole wheat bread. We went to bed happy.

Unfortunately, Freckles got diarrhea during the night.

I vaguely remember waking to the smell, covering my head, and going back to sleep. In the gray light that morning, Mom came into my room to wake me for school and she stepped in the slippery puppy poo.

She fell hard and came up swinging—literally. She pulled me from my bed by my hair and proceeded to drag me through Freckles's diarrhea, screaming all the while that I was a "worthless piece of shit." She told me to clean it up.

"I don't want to smell a thing," she yelled. "IS THAT CLEAR?" She had me put my pajama bottoms into a plastic bag on top of the washing machine.

"You're washing them as soon as you get home from school. And that's AFTER you take that goddamn dog BACK to where you got it. DO YOU UNDERSTAND ME?"

I did. I cleaned up the mess, then showered and got ready for school. Mom also showered, and then, feeling better, complimented me on what a fine cleanup I'd done. Not a word about Freckles and the Baby Ruth bars the night before, not a word about what's involved in housebreaking a puppy. Nothing. Just crime and punishment. But I was getting used to that.

Beatings had become a constant in my life. I never remember not being aware of Mom's moods, and whenever she and Daddy had an argument, I knew she'd be coming for me. The pecking order went: Mom and Daddy fought, then I got my ass kicked. In fact, my earliest memories are of Mom pulling my hair.

On the way to school that crappy day, I returned Freckles to his original home. The people there—a lady and her grown daughter—were very sweet and understanding, which somehow only made it worse. To this day, I'm sad when I think back on it. I looked upon losing Freckles as my first failure.

The next memory that stands out in my mind is when I was ten years old. It was before Julie was born, but after Lisa's birth. My mom and I were having a fight about something, and it ended with her winning the fight. I was stewing and already planning what I would say in the next fight to best her. I was a ten-year-old kid, so what can I say to really get her? I know. I'll tell her I don't even like her. That's what I'll say.

So our next fight, Mom says, "Goddamn you. I don't even like you." Now, she's thirty-two, and I'm ten. She's a grown-up. That was fucked up. After that—and dragging me through my dog's diarrhea—I felt nothing for her really ever again, intellectually or emotionally. I just completely disrespected her existence. It got so bad that after I became famous, I told people that my mother was dead. (I got that idea from Bob Dylan, by the way, who used to make up wild tales about his upbringing—that he ran away as a boy to join the circus.) I just didn't want to talk about her, so I'd say, "No, she's dead." Okay, moving on. Because nobody wants to talk about a dead person.

After Julie was born in October of 1967, I turned eleven, and I showed Dad my bruises from Mom's beating, saying, "This has been going on my whole life."

Dad got all, "What the fuck? I'll take care of it." And she never hit me again, except I recall that one time she took a dowel down and hit me in the leg—she got my knee and she split my knee cap. It was so bad, I had to get a cast.

Problem is, I'm the only one of my siblings who has that memory. In fact, whenever I mention it, it drives my dear sisters out of their minds—especially Julie. They insist it never happened. "It would have shattered your leg," they tell me. Even Eliza, keeper of the golden truth as far as I'm concerned, thinks it unlikely. "Maybe she lifted the dowel up, and you imagined what it would be like if she had hit you," she tells me.

But I also remember that our Acting Workshop was putting on *Charlie Brown* at the time, with me in the lead role, and I had to go onstage doing *You're a Good Man, Charlie Brown* in a wheelchair. I remember that we had to restage it with Snoopy pushing me in the wheelchair. It was a great gimmick and it worked. Even if I misremembered the event, it's a memory that has clung to me through all these years, and that tells you something about the fear I felt toward the two people in all the world entrusted by nature and fate to protect me.

I also asked my cousin Adam about those memories, and this is what he had to say, "There was always friction between Betty and Walter, and Eric was their whipping post. Betty would take her hatred of Walter out on Eric. When she and Walter broke up, she didn't want Eric to come with her—just the girls. I'm not saying it didn't happen. I'm just saying I didn't ever see any loving, good-mom times between them."

I do remember that the abuse eventually ended, either because Daddy intervened, or because I just got too big for Mom to whale on me.

Despite her skepticism about the dowel memory, Eliza believes that many in our parents' generation were abusers—it's just the way they thought they had to raise kids, the same way their fathers raised kids—anything to turn that boy into a man! Slapping, beating, belittling. Yep. I grew up with that, and Walter got even worse from his daddy. And so did Adam's family, though not from Grandpa Thomas.

"I know this isn't what you remember," he once told me, "but Grandpa Roberts walked on the sun as far as I was concerned." Adam thought highly of his own father, my uncle Elbert who was actually very nice to me. The day after school let out for the summer, Walter and Betty would drop us off at their farm in Marietta, where we were living then, and we'd stay there until it was time to go back to school. Adam remembers, "There was so much for Eric to do—we had pasture and animals and all kinds of rooms for them to do whatever they wanted to do. My dad always gave Eric the neatest gifts that he didn't think he would ever have gotten, like a bow and arrow and a bike, which my dad taught him how to ride." And then there was that wonderful swimming and fishing pond that Uncle Elbert put in.

Adam recalls how "Uncle Walter got me my first solo airplane flying lesson. Walter didn't want no part of it—he stayed on the ground. But I got to learn what it was like to be up in a two-seater and be copilot." He also remembers how his mom "never said anything bad about my papa. He just didn't take no crap off nobody. He worked in the concrete field all his life, and he left home when he was in the third grade. He was the oldest of all the kids. His daddy would come home drunk, beat the shit out of his wife, and then he beat the shit out of Papa, and Papa let him do that so he wouldn't go after any of the other kids."

So it runs in families, especially where folks struggle to make a living, are full of rage and disappointment, and live in more isolated communities.

While I was grateful that my mom's beatings stopped, it began to dawn on me that Dad was not a gift, he was a problem. Despite his enlightened views on race, he was not to be admired. As time went on, he revealed more and more of a very dark side, while I did everything I could to please him, though he found ways to undercut me.

I even robbed a pharmacy to get money for Dad when he was broke. That I remember.

Dad often complained about not having enough money and being in debt, so I thought maybe this was an area where I could do something for him. As a teenager, I was still trying to please my dad.

I had a good friend in high school who had a job in the pharmacy at a local drug store, and he told me they had a big safe where they kept the cash that they took to the bank every Monday. I told him about my dad being in debt and how I wanted to help him, and I asked him how much was in the safe.

"Thousands."

We had already talked about robbing the safe on our walks

to and from school, so finally I said, "Let's do it Sunday night at ten p.m."

Sunday night arrived, and I drove us there, where we went to work. Fortunately, he knew how to avoid the alarm system. He told me that the manager of the pharmacy had three numbers of the combination taped on the side of the safe. He dialed the first two numbers and knew the third by heart, but my friend didn't know what the last number was.

I asked him, "Even though we're not safe crackers, could we hear the click of the last number?"

"I don't know."

"You wanna find out?"

Sure enough, the safe opened and there were thousands of dollars in there. My friend took out all the money. We counted it, and it turned out to be $3000, a lot of money in 1973! We took the money and ran, and my friend used some of it to buy new tires for his car. I gave my dad what was left, around $2600. He was grateful, and he didn't ask where it came from.

Why did my friend help me? He barely knew my dad, but he was my best friend so he really did it for me. I think he felt sorry for me because I didn't have the home I was supposed to have, shuttling back and forth from the house with my mother and sisters to the apartment I shared with Dad. Oddly enough, my friend and I were never blamed for the robbery.

Nonetheless, I tried to paint a good picture of Dad to Julia and Lisa. As they were living with Mom, they didn't know what our father was truly like. I painted a picture of him that didn't exist, and it was always a lie, but I wanted to give them something positive. I thought I was being a cool older brother. But Mom was as bad or worse than Dad, and my sisters must have known it because they lived with her.

Things got even worse when Mom married her second husband, Michael Motes, and they moved to the smaller, more conservative town of Smyrna, Georgia. Motes was a small-time journalist for local Christian newspapers and occasionally for the *Atlanta Journal-Constitution.*

Even Julia, who has a kind word for just about everybody—at least professionally—hated him. Motes had once been arrested in a department store for exposing himself. (I later heard from a friend that the arrest record was expunged because somebody related to Michael worked in the police station.) Weirdly enough, we all—even Mom—knew he was basically gay, but that didn't seem to be a problem for her. He was six foot four—long and tall. They had a child together, a girl who looked just like my mother, had my mother's face. Same teeth. Had that beautiful mug of my mom. They named her Nancy. Sadly, she would come to a terrible end, which I'll explain later.

But I had an awful encounter with Motes just before he and Mom were married. I went to my mother's house to pick up some clothes for my sisters because we were all crashing at my dad's one-bedroom apartment, about four or five miles away from my mom's house. I stopped by her house when I thought no one was home, but it turned out they were both there.

Mom ran out to get clothes for Julia and Lisa, leaving me alone with Michael. He suddenly backed me up against the front door, put his hand on my throat, and grabbed my balls. He goes, "I'm gonna marry your mother, then I'm gonna fuck you, too."

I broke away and ran to my dad's apartment. I told him what happened, and we actually called the cops.

We went over to Mom's house, and we arrived at the same time as the cops. My mom's car was gone—and so was Michael.

Even after the divorce, my home situation with Walter was so stressful that I began looking for ways to assuage the pain.

At first, I did it with drugs. Later on, I did it with fame, which is the same thing, by the way. I tried to do it with money. I tried to do it with every kind of power. Otherwise, I did it with sex. I did it with partners. I did it with lying. I did it with making up stories. I did it every way. I tried everything I could think of—things I wouldn't recommend to anybody. None of it worked. So, to me, the psychology of it *is* the lesson. That's the lesson.

As I said, I was always conflicted in my feelings for my dad. I had worshipped him as a kid, and later on, one of the cool things Walter did for me was to set up a stateside audition for the Royal Academy of Dramatic Arts—RADA—in the summer of '74, where I was taken on as a student. I had already done some Shakespeare in Atlanta—*The Taming of the Shrew* and *Othello*—when I was fifteen. Studying at RADA should have been wonderful for a very young man with high ambition to be an actor, but it was around then that my dad started going fucking nuts about my future. He'd complain, "Here's how you present yourself?" Dad didn't really think I could do it on my own.

If I was happy from the age of six to twelve because I'd learned how to conquer my stutter, from twelve to seventeen I knew I had to get away—from my family, from Atlanta, from the South. I knew I had to have a reason to get out, and I had to have a place to go, and I had to create both of those things myself.

I also knew I'd have to get a job to start saving a nest egg for those rainy, unemployed days that lay ahead. At seventeen, I found employment at the Jory Concrete Company where I worked after school, five days a week for fourteen months. I saved damn near every penny for my great escape.

I liked working there, cleaning clamps and washing, loading, and unloading trucks. It was real work, and I found it engaging. I enjoyed talking to the drivers. A couple of them were ex-cons, and I found their stories of prison, convicts, and crime fascinating. Those guys were drinkers, but having grown up with drinkers, I thought nothing of it. Drinking was what grown-ups did, that's all. I didn't know it at the time, of course, but I would use some of their hyper, nervous mannerisms in my future role as an escaped convict in a movie called *Runaway Train*.

Once I had a few bucks to my name, I hiked up my balls and hit the fucking road.

I headed straight to New York City.

II. Escape to New York—1974–1977

Everybody in this world is nearly all by himself.

—Walter Roberts

If I thought moving to New York would put me out of range of my dad's influence, I was wrong.

My father's consciously stated opinion was to be proud and excited for me, to believe in me, to want it all to work out. He'd paid for my RADA classes while working as a vacuum cleaner salesman. He wasn't even one of those parents who's secretly thinking, *My kid could make some serious money for me.* I almost wish it had been that, or something like it. I'm not sure what came first, whether I was there to be exploited or that it was a matter of control, but he and I had created this unit—this "us against the world."

He saw himself as my professor of life. Something like Miyagi from the *The Karate Kid*, where he was the master and I was the disciple. It started with the acting lessons, and then continued even after I left home. I suppose that was one way of coping with his kid's imminent success, a success that was likely to surpass his own.

Walter had a lot of the same lacks in his life that I've had in mine. Through much of my life, I haven't had many friends. I've had fans and I've had haters, people I've harmed and people I've angered, just like my father, whose own father was a real sidewinder, a real son of a bitch. I can see it more clearly now, this multigenerational repetition. Eliza calls it "the drive home." I lived for a long time with an overt fear of Dad's disapproval.

As I mentioned earlier, my paternal grandfather was a horrible dad, and my grandmother was too weak to fix that, so Walter came into life angry, and he came into being a parent even angrier. He could have been all the great things I thought he was, growing up, but the generations have a way of repeating themselves.

That didn't mean he didn't love us, and God knows, he really loved my sisters.

However, my father had no sense of what was appropriate to share with a teenager. If he was upset or angry with my mother, I became his ear, his confidant. I was the one who had to listen. Later, after his divorce from my mom, he would speak to me about his sexual escapades, and they were not about dates and drive-ins—it was hard-core stuff, almost pornographic. He would speak to me about people he hated, and he expected me to hate them, too.

Just as soon as there was some physical distance between us and I felt I had outrun his influence, the letters started coming. Even before I left Atlanta for New York, Daddy started coaching me on my image. "Here's how you present yourself; these are the stories you tell about yourself," he advised, even though almost none of them were true. I was being tutored in "this is how you leave home."

In general, I miss writing and receiving letters, but not his. To this day, I ask people to send me a postcard when they go away, as if I still need to get the foul, cruel memory of my father's letters out of my system.

I've had misgivings about sharing with you any part of these letters from my father. I've been tempted many times to set a match to them, to burn, as it were, a funeral pyre of his terrible life, but something held me back.

Some of Dad's letters were full of expressions of love and flowery support and a father's pride, but many were poison pen letters. Eventually, I slowed down my reading of them. I would skim them or just not even open them, but I wouldn't throw them away. Once I'd started living in New York, I would come back to my apartment after a successful audition or a party, feeling pretty confident about myself, and I would see one of the unopened letters I had left on the chair. It was like he was sitting there, scowling at me, puncturing my self-confidence.

Rereading them now, I see that my father's letters were the stuff of mind control. I don't know how else to explain it. It was a full-time job just to read them: single spaced, badly punctuated if at all, page after page, double sided, usually typewritten, occasionally handwritten in a tiny, cramped script. And they came almost daily to my series of apartments in New York. I thought I had escaped, but not really. Reading them made me physically ill sometimes.

One sample letter shows you his misogyny and his crackpot, old-fashioned ideas:

> For any marriage ideas you may entertain, the seemingly old fashion wife and mistress combo, still seems—to me—the best. Get a wife who can send Christmas cards for you, cook routinely, but knows flowers for the table when company comes, who will wash sheets other than ones she likes and knows her place in any and all situations. . . . We have given women the vote and the orgasm and I'm not sure we were not wrong both times.

Dad knew how to make me feel guilty about not staying in touch with him often enough, as in this letter:

> Dear Eric,
>
> I had somehow expected that I would get a letter yesterday, and didn't, but today, I met the postman on my way out and there it was. A week's about as long as I can go without coming unstrung not knowing what you're up to.
>
> The first part of your letter didn't really surprise me . . . what bothered me at first was that I never expected you (of all the people I know) to get hit very hard by this, and I was afraid you were really down and so far away that I couldn't do anything about it.

As I recall, I was struggling with some depression, so he tried to advise me. He didn't know how much of my depression was due to him and his letters:

> . . . you're suffering from the first real shock of finding out that everybody in this world is nearly all by himself, and that the world doesn't give a shit more about you than it does the next guy . . . and that the next guy always seems somehow to be slightly out in front.
>
> . . . you've got looks, smarts, talent, and most of all, you've had experience that most people your age never have, or never have and survive. You KNOW what's going on. You KNOW what you're up to. You must also realize and KNOW that the feelings of depression you're having are a part of it.

Some of his letters predated my escape to New York. That last bit was his response to my beginning to attend classes at RADA when I was still a teenager, which he had made possible. He writes:

> Actors are shits by the way.
>
> Two kinds of people hang in: fools and wisemen. I'm not altogether sure which I am, but I'm reasonably certain you're not a fool, and I know you can do it.
>
> If the school gives you more than I've been able to, it's a positive . . .
>
> You know I love you, and your sisters love you . . . Believe me. I might lie to you about some shit, but I would never lie to you about something important. . . .

This was Walter being nice, but I just needed to be away from him and his sphere of influence as I tried to make it as an actor in New York.

I wasn't the most equipped person to suddenly make it in the big city. I was slightly more functional than I am now, but not by much. I made a lot of mistakes. For example, in an early job waiting tables, I was terrible—forgetting orders, picking plates up from the table before people were finished eating. I could get the jobs easily enough, but then I'd blow them and get fired.

I first lived in Brooklyn—2601 Glenwood Road, #6-M—which is where a lot of us went because we didn't have any money. It's expensive now, of course. It was a four-story walk-up. I had a mattress on the floor, and for a desk, a door on two New York City sawhorses that I stole from the street. I loved it because it was my beginning—that was my launchpad.

Soon after his divorce, my father remarried a much younger woman named Eileen Sellars (he called her "little e" in his letters). She was in her twenties, Walter was in his thirties. Adam remembers Eileen as "real quiet, and she liked to read and stay by herself. She tried to make everybody happy."

I think Walter really loved her at first, but in a short time, he had come to feel very annoyed with his young wife. He began complaining to me about her being lazy, even stupid, as if I were his best friend and confidant, and not his kid. I tried to tell myself that it was just a period of adjustment he was going through, and it'd pass.

In retrospect, I think Walter might have been jealous of his young wife, a rather thoughtful, intelligent person who loved to read, just as I believe he would have become jealous of my success. (It's an unwritten law of the familial jungle that the son doesn't surpass the father—perhaps that's another reason for my snatching defeat from the crocodile jaws of victory. Dad is always watching. The dead really don't let you live, do they?)

You can tell just from these fragments how he thought he was God's gift to the world—as a writer, a teacher, a lover, a husband. He was, of course, barely any of those things, but in the wee small hours of his night, he was smart enough to know that about himself, and I think that's part of what made him so devious and mean.

Insecurity is often the father of great cruelty. I think this was true of my father. But I suppose we should and could be grateful to him for one thing. He did give us a calling, he brought us into the world of the theater and he did set the stage, as it were, for our livelihood. "The evil that men do lives after them; the good is oft interred with their bones," Marc Antony says in his funeral oration over Julius Caesar. In my father's case, though he ruled over us like a tyrant, in public we interred the bad with his bones, and pretended there was enough good that would live on after him. There was barely enough good to scratch with a fingernail.

Soon his letters about his new wife began to scare me. I had the feeling something bad was going to happen. "What pisses me off with her is the slothful way she does everything," he wrote in one letter, banging on about the way she left crumbs in the chairs and dust everywhere. In another letter he wrote,

> The kitties threw up on the bedroom rug today, but it wasn't a total loss because I set Eileen's bedroom

> slippers in it. I may even learn to love the kitties and forbid her to get rid of them, ever.

I was a little alarmed when Walter wrote me that "e" had suggested they do their wills, adding:

> I'm going to set up a beauty of a will that gives her half of everything, give her a copy, and then do another one that doesn't leave her a thing.

My father was turning into one scary dude. No wonder I left so many of his letters unopened. I was too dutiful a son to throw them away, sight unseen, but at the same time I wanted so desperately to break away that I couldn't bear to read them. It's painful even now to look at these, to feel the meanness and narcissism coming up from the pages like an oppressive heat rising off asphalt.

In another letter, Walter is relentlessly critical of his young wife and mocks the pure delight she takes in her cats:

> She sits and watches the cats eat and giggles. It is the cutest, most clever sight she ever saw. She says things like, "I just like to watch cats sit there." That's really exciting. It's even more exciting to talk about it. She seems to be somewhat intrigued about your possible movie career. That gives you value, if not class I suppose.

After accusing Eileen of having a lack of class, Walter ends by boasting that he "stole four little trees from the Riva Ridge nursery yesterday and put them around the front of the air conditioner in the front yard.

Poor "e." She deserved so much better in this life than Walter Roberts.

Once I hit New York, my classes with RADA behind me, I auditioned for a so-so acting school, The American Academy of Dramatic Arts—and got in. The school was on Madison Avenue between Thirtieth and Thirty-First streets. I think it's still there. It was a great building in a great spot. For the audition, I had to do one dramatic monologue and one comedic monologue. I don't quite remember what I did—it's been fifty years!—but it got me accepted.

I was about to get an education in another area as well, one I hadn't foreseen. One of my teachers at the academy was Manu Tupou, who'd played a young Indian chief in a Richard Harris movie, *A Man Called Horse*, and a Hawaiian prince alongside Max von Sydow and Julie Andrews in *Hawaii*, based on James Michener's bestseller. We sometimes ran scenes at Manu's apartment at 11 West Sixty-Ninth Street in Manhattan, and I stayed there occasionally.

One night, the work went very late, and because I was living in Brooklyn, I crashed at his apartment. I woke up to Manu sucking my cock.

I said, "Excuse me, Manu, this is not cool. I gotta go."

It was upsetting, mostly because I was caught off guard, and Manu was six foot three and about 270 pounds, a very big guy with a very deep voice. I was eighteen, and he was easily twenty years older than me. He was my acting teacher, not to mention the fact that he was aware that my sexuality was with women.

I got out of there as soon as I could without embarrassing him, because I still valued him as a teacher. There was another time, much later, when Manu invited me over in the afternoon to run lines, and he said an old roommate of his and his former roommate's girlfriend were going to be coming over to his apartment. When they got there, I quickly realized that Manu must've had a relationship with this guy, who was there to show off his new girlfriend. I think Manu wanted me there to show me off as his new boyfriend, which I clearly wasn't. I didn't put that all together at first, and then it dawned on me. But I played along because he was a very good teacher and basically a good guy. Call it my sentimental education.

After I passed the audition for the academy, I thought, *Okay, I've arrived. Now I gotta find a job.*

The first job I had was in a bookstore on Broadway. It was heaven sent! It was great, but I blew it—I started stealing books. I just couldn't resist. I've always loved books, so it was like the proverbial kid in the candy store. I would take out the garbage and hide the books; and then when I left the store, I'd get the books out of their hiding place and take them home. They finally found out and they fired me. That killed me 'cause I loved that job. I loved that store. I loved everything about it.

Next, I got a job as a delivery boy. This was when I was living in Brooklyn for $160 a month, in a four-story walk-up. I could afford that even on my delivery boy salary—thems were the days!

I delivered coffee and snacks and lunches for a restaurant about a quarter of a mile downtown from the American Academy on Madison. It had bar stools. I think I'd answered a HELP

WANTED sign in the window. Every morning I was running coffee everywhere. And then running lunch everywhere. I was on foot because I didn't have a bike. But I made great money for the work. I probably made three hundred to four hundred bucks a month, or a hundred bucks a week, enough for my rent and a few bills. I liked the money, but I didn't like the work.

Next, I took a job as a waiter on Restaurant Row, but I was a terrible waiter! It was hard work. You gotta pay attention, but I wasn't interested in working hard or paying attention, so I blamed all my mistakes on the kitchen, or on the customer. "We got this new chef . . . ," I'd say. You know, that kind of thing.

My first few years in New York, I didn't do any drugs and I didn't drink. As a newcomer to the city, I didn't really know anyone, and I couldn't afford alcohol. Drinking costs money and I didn't have enough money left over after paying rent and buying groceries. Drinking is an expensive habit, especially when you're frequently broke. So I didn't drink, but eventually I'd go home to Atlanta and come back with an ounce of pot.

In 1975, I got cast in my first play, Joe Papp's *Rebel Women*, written by Thomas Babe and directed by Jack Hofsiss. It was a Civil War story, and the actor David Dukes played General Sherman, while I played a Confederate scout. Peter Weller and Mandy Patinkin played two of Sherman's lieutenants. It was a good play with a good cast, right there on Astor Place in the East Village. It ran three months, and then got voted one of the ten best plays of the year. For me, it was a good New York debut—that's how I got my actors' Equity card, which was a big deal, a turning event in my nineteen-year-old life.

I made the mistake of telling my dad all about it, and even

sending him a copy of the playscript. As excited as I was to be cast in *Rebel Women* at the Public Theater, my father threw mud all over it. This was one letter I was especially sorry to open:

> When I got home yesterday, there was in my provincial mailbox, a new play from the big city. I opened it excitedly and read it with gradually—actually rapidly—dropping enthusiasm.
>
> Rebel Women is the worst play I've read since an epic about the atomic bombing of Atlanta [by] a lady writer . . . who was willing to underwrite any production I would give it . . . I don't know who Thomas Babe is, but I would be willing to wager that he is a pretentious, deliberately half-assed educated faggot.
>
> In some seriousness, I have not read many plays headed for any kind of production which were so poorly wrought. Is Papp so desperate for material that he must do this? Is his wife blowing the playwright? Is he blowing the playwright? Is the playwright blowing everybody?

I could tell that Dad was still thinking of himself as a great acting teacher—the Lee Strasberg of the Peach State—dispensing advice like those advertisements tucked inside paperback books promoting "the Great Writers Correspondence School." I remember Adam saying, "Eric didn't have a chance of being anything other than what he had become, because of his dad. That was all his dad ever wanted to be: a playwright, an actor, a director, and when he couldn't do it, Eric had to do it in his place."

So why was I still asking him for advice? I don't remember if it was just out of politeness, which he didn't deserve, or that I still trusted his judgment about things having to do with acting and the theater, which is why his comments about *Rebel Women* unraveled me for a while. I felt vindicated when the *New York Times* gave *Rebel Women* a rave review: "tautly staged" with "a gifted cast," written "in a kind of poetry mixed with the vernacular, which gives the play a very special air, a mixture of Southern magnolia scent and the smell of Yankee sweat."

However, Daddy was still capable of giving me good advice and encouragement:

> . . . it seems to me out of all the material I can in good conscience recommend to you from afar, there is only scene three from Glass Menagerie. Several reasons: first the material you choose must be exactly right for you. At your age and with your general appearance you can tuck all your goods and bads into Tom and they will make no lumps or seams . . . It is one of the few pieces of material for a young actor that has genuine emotion and fire in it and does not depart from youth.
>
> I'm also sending you along a copy of some scenes from which I've had kicking around since long ago. You might read through these at your leisure and see what future use, if any, any of them

> would be for you. If Glass Menagerie meets with your approval, work . . . on it, and tape it and send it to me. I will send you some suggestions on it soon as I can locate the microphone for my tape recorder.

Adam had the best take on Walter. "I think Uncle Walter was born either before his time, or too late. He should have been born with Aristotle and all those guys. And he would have fit in with all that Hollywood crap."

Walter followed his encouraging letter with one of the most cringeworthy letters of all time, when he wrote:

> I was talking to your mother about your perhaps doing the film in which she would get to see you naked along with the rest of the world. She said, "ooooh my no, I don't think I want to see that." I told her that we would arrange for the whole family to go see it. We'll tell them it's about a boy and some horses, and they will think it's a Walter Disney film and won't that be sweet, and she cannot tell them anything until it's too late and won't that be fun.

What dark place did that come from?

Thankfully, Joe Papp was very good to me. He was always smiling, saying, "Eric, hi, come here, kid." That's also when I got to know Doug Kenney (who cowrote *Animal House* and the golf comedy *Caddyshack* and was one of the cofounders of *National Lampoon* magazine). He picked me out of the group and was very good to me, taking me to lunch all the time. Kenney would soon have a big influence on me.

After living in Brooklyn for two years, I finally got to Manhattan in 1977, staying briefly at the West Side YMCA on Sixty-Third Street until I moved into a beautiful penthouse apartment at 7 West Seventy-Third Street. I really felt that I had made it, especially when twelve-year-old Lisa and ten-year-old Julia visited me there and were impressed by my posh surroundings. Later I would move to 45 West Seventy-Third. Walking into those two Manhattan apartments was like opening presents on Christmas Eve. So many young actors were living on the Upper West Side then. If you made it big, you might move to a brownstone on the Upper East Side, near Bloomingdale's, but the working actor who wasn't yet discovered or hadn't made his or her splash—was drawn to the Upper West Side. It was like a hive full of ambitious bees vibrating with nervous ambition.

I quit the delivery boy gig when I was briefly hired at Cafe Central. What Studio 54 was to New York City in the late seventies, Cafe Central was to New York in the mid-seventies. A hip, happening place where people loved to congregate—including celebrities like Cher, Andy Warhol, Al Pacino, and a shy, young gay man who would become an important physician and writer, Oliver Sacks. In the early days it was on Amsterdam Avenue, and we would hang there—Chris Walken, Tom Berenger, me. It was nice. It was fun. It was cool. It was a room with eight tables and a bar, that's all. It had the lighting of a small bathroom—you couldn't see shit, though it was all windows. Even though it was tiny, it felt huge 'cause it looked out onto the street.

When Cafe Central first opened, before it moved to its last location, the owner was a wheeler-dealer named Peter Herrero. I remember there was a girl named Sheila who worked for him as a coat check girl. Peter was a cool cat. I miss him, and I always enjoyed his company. I liked his style. Peter loved me because I was not a movie star guy—I was just this guy from Georgia. We had fun there—it was a great place to be. He ran it with an iron hand—you couldn't misbehave. He was on-site a lot, and he would throw your ass out if you so much as mouthed off.

When my sister Julie—aka Julia Roberts—made her first trip to New York to visit me, she stopped by Cafe Central. I had just seen Robin Williams there several days earlier, and that had impressed her.

I told Robin, "My baby sister's gonna be in town this week. Gotta freak her out for me."

"Yeah, no problem. Okay."

So I'm in one of the windows with Julie and we're having a hamburger, and here comes Robin Williams. He walks over, looks at her, opens the door, grabs her hamburger, and bolts out the door. Julie freaks out. "Was that Robin Williams?!"

"I think it was, honey."

"He took my hamburger!"

That was Robin being Mork, because he was already in that hit show *Mork and Mindy*, which was tailor-made for his antic spirit. I was delighted to be able to impress my baby sister!

Though he was an inspired comedian, Robin and I had a couple of serious talks about looks, fame, and money. He had very strong opinions. For example, he told me that people thought a certain thing of me because of how I looked. And I said, "What does that mean?" He goes, "You look arrogant. You look arrogant, dude. People think you are."

"I'm not."

"I know you're not, but people think you are, man, and you gotta fight against that." That was another example of how looks can determine your fate as an actor.

Robin was always giving me advice. To tell the truth, he was a bit pompous about his intelligence. On half a dozen occasions, it would be, "You need to know this, you know that"—that kind of thing. But I liked Robin. I had real affection for him, and our friendship lasted many years. The only kind of disagreement we ever had was much later, in 1986—a kind of "fuck you" at the end of a conversation—over the Academy Awards the year I was nominated for Best Supporting Actor in *Runaway Train.*

We're in the new Cafe Central, by then located on Columbus Avenue. It was just me and Robin in the joint. Robin asked me, "You wanna win?"

"Fucking yes, I wanna win!"

And he goes, "You've let them take you down their road, man!"

He gave me his big speech about how "they" had made me think like them—the establishment that runs this fucking business. "They're not artists!" He said I was an artist, but I wasn't acting like one because I wanted to win.

But no matter what he said, I still wanted to win the fucking award.

Many months after the Oscars, I ran into him. "Can you believe they gave it to Don Ameche!"

Robin wasn't immune to the allure of movie fame and success, however. In the last phase of his life, he felt he was almost as recognized as Robert De Niro, and he kind of acted like it. But I thought he was cool. In fact, I liked everything about the Robin I knew, and I was devastated when he took his own life.

Bruce Willis was a bartender at Cafe Central. Back then, he worked under the name "Bruno," a sort of *nom de bartending.* He graduated into that TV show with Cybill Shepherd, *Moonlighting*, just as the restaurant moved to its new location, so we all waved goodbye. We knew he'd be a big success. He had star quality and was a favorite bartender all along the entire East Coast. I thought he was cool, funny, entertaining to be around, even though I was surprised he got that part. He had come out of nowhere to land it.

It seemed we were all actors at Cafe Central, and we were all *almost* successful. I had been in a Joe Papp production, so I was known around town.

But there's always a dark side, a cautionary tale to this business. I remember a very good buddy of mine, an actor named James Hayden—Jimmy Hayden. Back then, Jimmy and I had very heavy talks about life and acting and women. He was portraying a heroin addict in the off-Broadway play *American Buffalo*, starring Al Pacino, when he died of a heroin overdose. A lot of New York actors knew and loved him. Later, when I made *The Pope of Greenwich Village* with Mickey Rourke, he dedicated his performance to Jimmy Hayden.

He was an actor's actor, the real deal.

That was my first loss as a grown-up, losing someone I knew as a peer. It was shocking because we all loved him—and he was a good actor, by the way. He and I would go in the back of Cafe Central and smoke dope with the kitchen staff. For me, his death was the first sobering thing about drugs. By then, I was back to doing drugs whenever anybody had it—especially coke. In the seventies and eighties, coke seemed to be everywhere, a half-accepted, wink-wink secret indulged in at all levels of society. That's where it started for me, at Cafe Central, and you'd think it would have ended there, too, after Jimmy's death. He was my first sobering realization you can die from this shit.

To keep body and soul together (or apart, as Dorothy Parker once quipped), I took a role in 1977 in a soap opera, *Another World.* The soap ran on NBC for thirty-five years, but I was on it for only a few months.

"You take me to another world," I think was the tag line, where prominent Bay City families endure the usual soap opera storylines such as murder, amnesia, evil twins, etc. (The funny thing is, I've had most of those things happen to me in REAL life!) I originated the role of Ted Bancroft. I've forgotten what Ted's problems were, but several actors who came after me played Ted and, I'm sure, suffered magnificently in the part.

One reason I lasted only a few months was because I clashed with the director when I complained about some of the dialogue written for my character, and I'd ad-libbed some changes.

"Are you an actor or a writer?" he said, confronting me.

"But my character wouldn't say these lines."

"Are you an actor or a writer?" he repeated.

I tried to defend my actions, but he wasn't having it, so I got the ax. Rather than have me die in a fatal car accident to explain Ted's sudden departure, he hired another actor to replace me—and then another. As I said, the soap lasted thirty-five years.

Apparently, viewers were loyal to the characters, not the actors who played them.

Of course, the other reason I was fired was because I was using cocaine, and that became obvious to a lot of people. I don't know everything that I did wrong, but to do a soap opera, you really have to have your shit together. You have to know your lines. You can't be inconsistent in your personality or your moods. I simply didn't have that kind of discipline then.

So, I figured they probably let me go because I was terrible, but what I was, was terribly troubled. It turned out getting fired was a good thing for me, as it freed me up for what would begin to truly launch my acting career.

For starters, things really sped up for me when I found a manager.

As luck would have it, right around the corner from the American Academy of Dramatic Arts, I met Marion Dougherty, a legendary casting director. In fact, she was the most successful, most famous, most career-changing, industry-changing casting director there's ever been. She discovered Robert Redford. Name a George Roy Hill film—like *Butch Cassidy and the Sundance Kid*—she cast it.

She came to one of the plays at the American Academy, saw me there, and left me a note with her office address on it. It read, "Do not lose this address. Come to my office." So I did, and once I got there, she told me, "You're a natural. You don't belong in that acting school. It's not even a good school." (It's funny how you can spend your whole childhood and adolescence taking acting lessons and appearing in plays, just to achieve the quality of being "a natural.")

Marion told me that she went by the school twice a year just to catch a play, which is how she noticed me. She said, "You need to meet one of my casting associates, Juliet Taylor. You need to talk to her." Juliet—another legend who would end up casting all of Woody Allen's great movies—sent me on an audition, but I didn't get the role.

Nonetheless, Marion introduced me to Bill Treusch, who represented Chris Walken, Sissy Spacek, Tom Berenger, and my ill-fated friend Jimmy Hayden. Berenger had been a steward on a plane when Bill saw him and said, "You should be an actor." That's all it took—right place, right looks, right time. Would it happen for me?

I headed to Bill Treusch's office at 104th Street, way uptown. Treusch was a handsome guy with curly hair and tall—five eleven or so. We met, we talked for about an hour, and Bill said, "Well, I'd like to try managing you."

"I don't know what that means, but I'm game."

He signed me the day I met him. Never saw me work, but he took Marion's and Juliet's recommendations and took me on. Treusch not only had an eye for talent, but for assistants as well. Scott Rudin, who would become a wildly successful producer (*The Girl with the Dragon Tattoo*, *Zoolander*, *No Country for Old Men*) worked for Treusch back then. Little did I know at the time, but I was in the company of a future EGOT winner—one of a handful of people who've won Emmy, Grammy, Oscar, and Tony awards.

I was really naive back then; in fact, I thought it was all kind of stupid. That's how I felt about it—*is this the big time?*—because it didn't feel like the big time. It felt like amateur hour. I'm only an amateur, I thought, so this *must* be amateur hour. I didn't buy what was really happening to me. Besides, I felt more at home with Marion and Juliet. Another woman, Gretchen Rennell, who went to work on *Children of a Lesser God*, worked in their office, and all those cool women eventually became icons in the business. They loved real actors, and they thought I was one.

As for Bill, at first I thought that he just liked my looks. I never thought I was handsome at all up until after I was married, many years later. I didn't think I was ugly, but that was never on my mind as a *thing*, until my relationship with Kelly Cunningham, but I'll tell you about that later. You know who *is* gorgeous, for a guy—Robert Redford. And Brad Pitt. I remember seeing Brad being interviewed on the talk show *Between Two Ferns with Zach Galifianakis.* It was one of Zach's comic interviews in which he's really insulting to the person he's interviewing. He's sitting with Brad Pitt, reading from his clipboard, and he says, "Do you think people concentrate too much on your looks, instead of thinking that you're a really shitty actor?" Of course, that wasn't even true. Not only is he a good actor, Brad Pitt is the most normal cool cat, a nice guy, and a bona fide superstar. He acts just like one of the guys. I mean, everywhere—no exceptions. He has grace, even when he's being mobbed by fans.

It just didn't occur to me that *I* was a good-looking actor, which maybe is how I caught Marion Dougherty's and Juliet Taylor's attention, which got the whole ball rolling. And maybe that's why Treusch decided to manage me on the spot. He really launched my film career, and I'll always be grateful for that.

When Bill took me on, that began a series of substitute father figures who—like Walter—did not always have my best interests at heart. But early on, Treusch and I were the happiest team ever. He was my mentor and I really respected him. I looked up to him—I thought he was an instinctive genius. I loved being in his roster of actors. He was lovely as a person, very approachable, and he let me know right away that he was gay. That was cool with me.

As I mentioned, getting fired from *Another World* was the best thing to happen to me, because the following week Treusch got me an audition for a big movie for Paramount Pictures, playing the son and heir of a modern-day Gypsy clan living in New York. It would be a game changer for me, justifying the years of apprenticeship, acting classes, RADA, theater, and my own belief that I could make it. If only I could make it.

Reader, I got the part.

III. *King of the Gypsies*—1977–1982

It's ALMOST his time.

—*Tagline for* King of the Gypsies

This is the movie that changed my fortunes.

In Frank Pierson's 1978 film adaptation of the book by Peter Maas, I was thrown in with amazing actors—Sterling Hayden, Judd Hirsch, Brooke Shields, Shelley Winters, Susan Sarandon. I was the only one who was a film rookie. I worked my ass off all night, getting about three hours' sleep from anxiety, then getting up and going again. I was a twenty-one-year-old, wet-behind-the-ears actor suddenly thrust in the big time. I was scared to death.

I played Dave Stepanowicz, the conflicted grandson of Zharko Stepanowicz, the patriarch of a group of Gypsies living outside the law in New York City. That role was played by Sterling Hayden. As king of the Gypsies, he's dying and he wants to leave his leadership position to his grandson—me, Dave—passing over his son, Groffo, played by Judd Hirsch. My character doesn't want the position, and my father, Groffo, tries to have me killed in resentment over being passed over. The usual family drama!

Nervous as I was in that company, I was thrilled to meet Sterling Hayden. He was big, he was handsome, he had that voice. *The Killing* is one of my favorite movies. He was also nasty, sardonic, and smart. I just loved him.

We first met during a night shoot when the second assistant director knocked on my dressing room door to say, "Mr. Hayden would like to talk to you."

I walked into his trailer. Right away, I smelled hashish very strongly. I saw the smoke in the air and I recognized it. So I'm in this little trailer filled with hashish, and there's Hayden, smoking a hash pipe.

The first thing Hayden said to me was, "Want to get high?"

"I can't work if I'm stoned," I told him. "I don't talk well when I'm fucked up."

He goes, "You do get fucked up, don't you?"

I said, "On occasion."

"Okay, let's get down to business. What scene are we shooting tonight?"

"Scene 87."

"I don't give a shit about the fuckin' number," he answered. "What *happens* in the scene?"

"It's kind of a pivotal scene, Mr. Hayden. I run away from home, and you've come to find me, and you have your thugs grab me and bring me back because you want to hand your kingdom over to me and not to your son."

Hayden asked me if I was good at improvisation, because that's what he wanted to do. We ended up improvising the whole scene. I felt like I was skydiving—but with a parachute. I wasn't scared—I was thrilled. Later, after the movie wrapped, Hayden said to me, "You're in for a big ride, you know. They're gonna try to get you to move to Hollywood. Do *not* do it."

I'm like, "Okay, okay," because he was adamant. That was the last piece of advice he gave me.

As well as I got on with Hayden, I always thought Judd Hirsch didn't like me very much. But maybe he was just staying in character, playing the father who resents being passed over in favor of his son. In those days, actors often thought it necessary to remain in character even when not performing.

I had two scenes in *Gypsies* when I really had to dig deep—go Method, go sense-memory, go Stanislavsky. Those scenes involved tears and anger. One scene was this one:

My character's mother and sister—played by Susan Sarandon and Brooke Shields—come to find me and take me back into the Gypsy fold, only to find me with a girl. I'm enraged at realizing that I'll have to leave my outside life to go back to the family. My girl is serving them tea, so I throw the tea set at them in an unscripted act of rage. (I had already confirmed with the props manager that there was a duplicate tea set.) Pierson loved it and everyone was happy.

The other deep scene is when Sterling Hayden tells my character that my dad is a fool, thus I would have to come back to the fold and take over as the Gypsy king. I remember that it was my first-ever night shoot, and it was a cold night—and I *had* a cold, so I was fairly miserable. The scene took a lot out of me, but I loved playing it.

Hayden was brilliant. He was off script, improvising his ass off. I was having to work very hard as an actor just to stay with him, because he was going all kinds of places that I didn't expect to go. In that scene, I really had to use my training as an actor to get through it. I got tears in my eyes. I got angry in that scene. Even now when I put myself back there, I feel very sad for that character who had to give up everything to return, reluctantly, to his family.

Looking back, I see that Hayden was another father figure who provided the encouragement and emotional support that Walter, for all his complicated reasons, just could not provide. But, like Bill Treusch—as I would discover later—Hayden wasn't always the best role model, offering me weed during the filming of *Gypsies*. However, I felt that both men were there for me.

In many ways, Bill Treusch was a lot more like my dad than Sterling Hayden was. They were both covert guys. Though he'd come out to me, Bill's homosexuality was covert, so was his use of cocaine (years later I found out we had the same dealer, a Frenchwoman named Simone). My father was often covert, often up to some mysterious mischief, so they both had that secretive quality.

Treusch was a more sophisticated version of my dad, who was very intelligent and well read, but not very worldly. Treusch was indeed special—a gifted, brilliant, interesting, unique guy from Baldwin, Long Island—but he just drank it all away. Like my relationship with my dad, my relationship with my manager was checkered. But he was there and helped to bring about the high points in my career. It was Bill who took me to Sunset Boulevard at the end of the press tour for *King of the Gypsies* to see a giant billboard that announced, *KING OF THE* GYPSIES*: IT'S ALMOST HIS TIME. I actually cried when I saw that, because it referred to my character in the movie, and to me. I felt I had arrived.

But I also think he gave me some terrible advice along the way. Once *King of the Gypsies* wrapped, Treusch took me to meet Dino De Laurentiis at his penthouse apartment on Central Park South. He told me, "Dino is gonna offer you a three-picture deal, but he makes movies like *Mandingo*, so I'm gonna invite you to say no."

"But he made *Gypsies*! *Gypsies* was a good script. We have a winner here!"

"He'll make you a B-movie star. We have to say no."

So we said no, and De Laurentiis never spoke to me again.

Paramount then offered me a three-picture deal, but once again, Treusch advised me to turn it down, saying, "They're gonna make you into Robbie Benson, an adolescent superstar, and then you're gonna be stuck."

"It's a lot of money," I pleaded. "I come from poverty!" But Treusch got me to turn down that offer as well. And, in 1985, he encouraged me to turn down the lead role in *9½ Weeks*, which made Mickey Rourke a superstar in France. I kinda wish I had taken on that one, but I thought Mickey was awesome in that movie.

Despite those setbacks, I stayed with Treusch from the 1970s through the late 1980s. I think I finally just fired him. Sissy Spacek fired him first, based on some kind of money deal that went wrong, and then it was a slow avalanche of firings. By then, he was drinking more and more until he finally became dysfunctional. Of course, if cocaine and I were only casually dating during *Another World*, by the time of the press tour for *Gypsies*, it had become a torrid affair.

Looking back, I can see that there was another reason I embraced cocaine so desperately. It wasn't just the stress of finally being in an important movie, or the stress of the press junket, or the discomfort of getting all those upsetting letters from Walter. It did, however, involve him in a way I can't quite come to terms with, even now, decades later.

Soon after I'd left for New York, Walter hatched a crazy scheme to scam Eileen out of money by appealing to her belief in astrology, and he wanted my help. Here's how the scam, which he called "Star Fire," was supposed to work:

> What I plan is this. I will prepare the introductory material to send her. It will contain a test to help us interpret the person and how they have used their fate to date. . . . A cover letter will begin . . . Dear Mrs. Roberts, recently you requested some chart readings, and we therefore feel that you might be interested in a new service we have offered to many cosmically aware modern young people like yourself. . . .

The plan was to charge her a "smallish quarterly fee," and Walter wanted my help so he could use a New York postmark and thus remove any suspicion that it was all coming from him. He had thought everything through, down to how the transfer of funds would be handled.

"Don't worry about what we're doing," he reassured me.

> I'll give you very specific info when the time comes. Right now, all I need is the account number of your bank account. Better yet, send me one of your current checks, so I can take off of it whatever is necessary. . . . Of course, it's the kind of stupid thing she would probably spend money on without reservation.

Still in thrall to my father and wanting to please him, I went along with Walter's scheme. In many ways, I was still young, dumb, and far from home. But what his scam could not predict was the terrible fate that awaited "little e." This is probably as good a time as any to tell you what really happened that day on Lake Lanier.

On one of my visits to Atlanta, Daddy had arranged a canoe trip for him and Eileen on Lake Lanier, a popular recreation site about fifty miles northeast of Atlanta, and he asked me to go along. I agreed. Before taking the canoe out, we visited Eileen's mother, and she reminded her daughter to wear her life preserver. Every year there were about five drownings on that lake, and Eileen didn't know how to swim.

"She doesn't really need one," I said. "She has me."

I was a strong swimmer, and maybe that's why, at the last moment, Daddy stayed at the houseboat where we launched the canoe, and he sent me out alone with Eileen. Was he afraid of his own motives and wanted me to be there to save her if anything happened?

Here's how my cousin Adam remembers it: "What happened on Lake Lanier? Well, a boat came by and swamped them, and she fell out of the canoe." The canoe capsized and we both hit the water. Eileen flailed around while I tried to save her, but she drowned, like Shelley Winters in *A Place in the Sun*. You might say that's a parallel between me and Monty Clift, except his trauma was fictional and mine was all too real.

The official death report was accidental drowning, but I have been haunted by it ever since. Was I meant to be the patsy for my dad, who made no bones about wanting to be rid of Eileen? I was not able to save her, and so, reluctantly and without intent, did I end up being the means by which my father got rid of his second wife? She had gotten into that canoe because she had trusted me.

When I was in the water, I must have panicked because I couldn't rescue her. I was desperate to. If I could foil Walter's plot, it was one way to separate myself from my father, forever. In that moment of confusion, I even considered killing my father. I didn't know what to do, and all this was happening just as I was about to become a movie star.

Adam was at Eileen's funeral, and he remembers that I "was a wreck, and so was Walter." I don't remember this exactly, but Walter put a miniature bouquet that he'd brought into the coffin. I've always wondered: Did Walter care for Eileen and lament her death after all, or were those tears of guilt and remorse, not love?

Later, on a documentary TV series called *The Haunting Of*, I said that Eileen was the only woman Walter had ever loved. That was in 2016, and I wasn't prepared then to share the real story about my father.

Not long after Eileen's death, and right around the time of *Gypsies*, Dad was diagnosed with esophageal cancer. I don't know how long he was sick before he knew he was sick, or how long he was sick before he told us. When I heard about it, I did some research on cancer of the esophagus, and how it is all over the place in terms of diagnosis. It's not always terminal, but it was for my dad. Like many sons with conflicted relationships with a parent, it hit me hard, and I made sure to be there for him when he was dying.

I did talk him down from the ledge a few times. He was still angry at my mother, Betty, and I could tell that he wanted me to take his side against her—even then, after all the blood that had run under the bridge. I generally did not like to talk about her, already having drawn the line at poisoning the waters for my sisters. I had my issues with Mom, but I didn't like him ranting against her either, and I spoke up. I hoped that he was just raging against the dying of the light; but then again, his light had been dying for a long time, it seemed.

I did even more agreeing with him than usual, because he was ill. I probably should have said, "Dad, you just gotta let me have my own life," but I didn't. The grief he would've felt then, at the end of his life, would have been too much, and I couldn't do that to him.

Looking back, I think I wanted so badly to be a success, just to be able to say, "Look, Dad, look what I did. Look what I was able to pull off." But he died just weeks before *King of the Gypsies* opened in New York and Los Angeles. He never lived to see it, or the giant billboard looming over Sunset Boulevard with the tagline: IT'S ALMOST HIS TIME.

Still, I'm sure he would have found fault with something in the movie, or in my performance. In his letters, he often wrote about different movies and shows. He was very insulting about people who I thought were great. I remember in one letter he said something about how this young filmmaker named Steven Spielberg was going nowhere.

When he died, Walter was just shy of his forty-fourth birthday. I was twenty-one.

In retrospect, I have to admit that he could be very inspiring, but he was also the most condescending motherfucker I've ever met, with the exception of his father, my grandfather, who was that way toward him. I just couldn't forget how he put me down from the time I was cognizant until the day he died. But when I was a young boy, I thought he was the smartest man I had ever known—things you remember when your father is dying.

I didn't want to hate my father. Shortly after he died, in interviews promoting my early movies, *King of the Gypsies*, *Star 80*, and soon after, *The Pope of Greenwich Village*, I would blow up any tiny act of kindness by my father into something grand. But it was clear to me he was not a good person; he was, in fact, a very screwed-up individual and not safe for me, or anyone, to have as a father.

Nonetheless, I was devastated by his death. At the same time, it was probably better for all of us that he passed, so he could no longer do us any harm. Had he lived, I'd like to think that when he saw our success, especially my sister Julia's great ride, that he would have been thrilled and supportive, that he would have been delighted to be relieved of any financial worry, that he would have even been capable of putting his arm around our mother, and she could've put her arm around him, to gaze at each other as if to say, "Betty, look at our kids."

But I know that's just a fantasy. My fear is that he would have tried to intervene, control, object, resist, go against the grain, find fault, all because of his own insecurities.

We will never know, of course, but his reactions to my early success were very mixed. He did stand outside of Rich's department store in Smyrna, Georgia, where he sold vacuum cleaners after his acting workshop failed, and where they had all the TVs lined up in the window. He'd watch me on *Another World*, and proudly say to people passing in the street, "Hey, that's my kid!"

But at the same time, if I was putting together an audition for a play, he would tell me it was a terrible play and that I shouldn't do it.

Nonetheless, I paid for his funeral, and I drove my sisters to the funeral service. It was hard, but I got them there. After he was cremated, I took his ashes home in the cardboard box the funeral home provided. I ended up leaving his ashes at the house of a friend I had grown up with. I think they're still in his safe.

Years later, long after my dad's funeral and after *King of the Gypsies* wrapped, Sterling Hayden, who played the crooked cop in *The Godfather*, lay in a hospital room, dying of prostate cancer. I visited him in the hospital. By then, I was probably more numb to his condition than I would've been otherwise, because I'd watched my father die. But I was pained when he said to me, "Don't come back anymore."

"Why?" I asked.

He goes, "Because I need to die."

That's when I started to feel both losses. Losing one of the father figures I would collect over my career, after losing my biological dad, hit me hard.

I starred in *Paul's Case* in 1979, which aired on PBS in 1980. Again, Treusch didn't want me to do it, saying, "You're not PBS material." But this time I didn't take his advice. I loved Willa Cather, so I took on the role.

The program was part of an educational series called *The American Short Story Collection*, each hour-long episode helmed by a different director. *Paul's Case* was about a working-class boy in Pittsburgh at the turn of the century, entranced by music and art, who steals some money in order to run off to New York. I loved doing it because I felt that I *was* Paul, champing at the bit to escape my life and head for the glamorous big city.

I think that the movie, and my character, spoke to a lot of people.

One IMDb contributor who goes by the name "eftstudios1" wrote in response to seeing *Paul's Case* on PBS: "Eric Roberts embodied the young man Paul. . . . He had the dark, brooding, depth of soul Willa Cather's boy had." Thank you, eftstudios1! At the time, I was renting a room in Treusch's house in Westport, Connecticut. Chris Walken was living up there as well. I remember sitting on the porch with Bill late one evening when the phone rang.

It was the acclaimed actress Sandy Dennis.

She tells Treusch, "I've just watched on TV this actor in *Paul's Case*, and, oh, my God, Bill, I haven't seen an actor that good since—"

"Oh," Bill says, "it so happens that that actor is here with me right now. He's sitting here and his name is Eric Roberts."

"Bring him over. I want to make him dinner. I want to know this guy."

Bill took me over to Sandy's house and we had dinner. We talked and talked. I checked out her library and was thrilled to find that she must have had over four thousand books, many of them precious first editions, and books with fascinating provenances—a book of plays by Eugene O'Neill once owned by Katharine Hepburn.

We began trading books, and we formed our own two-person book club. There's something romantic right off the bat when people share the same passion for something, as we did for books and for acting.

We became friends very fast. One day I jumped her bones and we started a relationship. It's corny now to think of it, but I asked her, "May I kiss you?" and she said, "Why on earth?"—she was quite a bit older. I thought it was such a cute thing to say, "Why on earth?" She was just such a cool chick.

Reader, I kissed her, and so began our affair.

Not only was she a cool chick but Sandy was also a brilliant actor. She won her Best Actress in a Supporting Role Oscar for her brilliant portrayal of the mousy wife, Honey, in *Who's Afraid of Virginia Woolf?* in 1967. She was the only person, other than Richard Harris, who I loved talking to about acting. I don't usually like talking about acting. It's like talking about sex. We all know the mechanics, but when you find someone who has a completely different technique from you, it's oh my God, let's hang out, let's talk about this shit! And it's insightful, too, because acting is hard. It's fucking work, dude. You've gotta dig for it and dig for it, and when you do, it's like sliding a hand into a glove. The acting glove.

Later, I got to know the director Robert Altman through Sandy, though not well, but I loved watching him work. It was the early eighties, and he was directing Sandy and Cher and Kathy Bates in both a Broadway production and a film adaptation called *Come Back to the 5 and Dime, Jimmy Dean, Jimmy Dean*. It was the story of four friends who reconnect on the twentieth anniversary of James Dean's death. Cher became a close friend of Sandy's. I could tell they really liked each other—they were so silly and girly together.

I would sit in the back of the theater with Altman, and the first thing he ever said to me was, "If I ask you a question, answer me honestly."

"Okay."

Then he said, "Can you hear them?"

I said, "Not a word."

And he agreed, "I can't hear a fucking word."

Altman really loved actors, and that's not true of most directors. Most directors don't, and for all the right reasons. Actors are pains in the ass, we're all a bunch of babies who want attention. I really liked Altman and he was good to me, though he never put me in a movie. And we had our admiration of Sandy Dennis in common.

He once said to me, "Sandy is a gorgeous human being."

"I know."

Sandy would have a major, brilliant career, winning accolades for *Up the Down Staircase*, *Sweet November*, and Alan

Alda's movie *The Four Seasons.* She was hilarious in *The Out-of-Towners*, with Jack Lemmon.

When she won the Oscar, she didn't even go to the awards ceremony. Instead, she was doing something on Broadway, so on that night she went to Frankie & Johnny's, a restaurant in the theater district that was popular with actors. I later found out that she thought she might win the Academy Award, but she didn't care. (Robin Williams would have been proud of her!)

So she's at Frankie & Johnny's, eating dinner, when she heard on the TV above the bar, "And the winner is—Sandy Dennis for *Who's Afraid of Virginia Woolf?*" Her response? "Champagne for everybody!" That's how she did it. As I said, a cool chick.

Not surprisingly, I suppose, our May-December romance couldn't last, but not just for that reason.

Sandy rented a huge mansion on seven acres in Connecticut—twelve rooms with a guest house and a garage. Sandy's mother, Yvonne Dennis, lived with her. She was a little eccentric, very outspoken, not intimidated by anything. She'd had Sandy and her brother when she was very young. Yvonne was very up-front—maybe too up-front—certainly unusual for a woman born and raised in the early 1900s.

Sandy's live-in housekeeper was a wonderful woman named Mary, who was there five days a week. Mary was one of my favorite people outside of show business. She discovered that I liked to cook, and we would sometimes prepare meals together. Sandy, on the other hand, was like Dorothy Parker—she couldn't boil water. Or if she could, she preferred not to.

Despite our nineteen-year age difference, ours was a tender

relationship, but there was one big problem: when we first got together, Sandy had thirty cats. In a twelve-room house, thirty cats can look like five or six. (I remember reading that the novelist Shirley Jackson, who wrote "The Lottery" and *The Haunting of Hill House*, kept dozens of cats, all black. Her husband hated it, so she named them all Blackie and said she only had five or six cats.) But when you get up to a hundred cats, as Sandy did, every room has three or four, and then there are the ones outside. It became so overwhelming and such a full-time job looking after them that I really couldn't take it anymore.

So I came up with a plan. "You're going to start an animal shelter," I suggested, "and we'll end up keeping half a dozen, but we'll find all these other cats good homes. Great idea, huh?"

"No, I don't want to do that," Sandy said.

"But why? That's what you should be doing with all these cats."

She just wouldn't do it, so I broke up with her over that. I said, "I can't live like this. It was all right when I first met you and there were only thirty-five of them, but now we're up to a hundred."

"This is not as weird as you make it sound."

"It is, Sandy. This is weird. I can't do it."

When she wouldn't give up the cats, I told her I had to leave.

After this stressful talk, Sandy went upstairs to her bedroom. I stood at the bottom of the stairs like Bette Davis in *The Little Foxes*, waiting for what would happen next, though I didn't know exactly what I expected. I just stared at the black-and-white-tiled floor that leads to the front door, and then I saw Sandy standing at the top of the stairs.

She threw down this two-hundred-year-old burnished walnut jewelry box with all her things in it. I had given her this beautiful antique, and over the five years we were together, much jewelry. I loved giving Sandy presents. She loved jewelry and I loved getting it for her, but the jewelry box was something special. It cost me many thousands of dollars, and I had even less money than I do now. But she hurled this thing down the stairs. *Bam!* It shattered all over the tiled floor. I found her engagement ring and put it on my little finger and left.

That was the end of our relationship.

In the final analysis, she chose her cats over me. Years later, I asked a friend of mine, "Why do you think she did that, why did she make that choice?"

He said, "Because she knew you were eventually going to leave her, so she wasn't going to give up her cats for you. You were eventually going to walk out the door. After all, you were twenty-four when you met her—Sandy was in her forties! When she got old, you were just going to be middle aged." But even now, I sometimes think, *How could she know that, how could anyone know something like that?*

Truth be told, the other issue in our relationship beyond the cats and the age difference was that I was increasingly into using cocaine, which Sandy hated.

After we broke up, I moved to California, but I flew back East at one point, because I heard she was in the hospital. She was dying. I was going to see her, but a mutual friend, Charles Gordone, the playwright whose play *No Place to Be Somebody* won the Pulitzer Prize for Drama in 1970, talked me out of it.

"Don't do it, buddy. Don't do it. You're going to see somebody when they're sick and dying and you're going to feel bad. Don't hurt yourself."

So I didn't go. I took his advice, and I'm glad I did because my memory of her is totally free of that, totally free of that image of her dying.

There was, as there so often is, more to the story. I learned later that Sandy had sent out the word that she didn't want to see me. I think part of it might have been she didn't want me to see her like that. I mean, she was always afraid of becoming "an old lady." That she had ovarian cancer was a big thing for her, because she thought she couldn't get pregnant. And then suddenly, when she was with me, she did.

What had happened was that Sandy had lived with the great jazz musician Gerry Mulligan in the late 1960s and early 1970s and they got pregnant, but it was an ectopic pregnancy and so she lost the baby. She had half her tubes tied after that and was convinced she would never become pregnant again. She never used birth control, never became pregnant, and then—with me—it happened. I found out later that she'd had an abortion in London. I guess the timing wasn't right for her, and I wasn't anyone's idea of an ideal husband.

She died in March of 1992. She was just fifty-four years old. A terrible loss.

About a year into my relationship with Sandy, before our big fight, I had just gotten back from filming *Miss Lonelyhearts*, based on the novel by Nathanael West, who also wrote *The Day of the Locust.* Montgomery Clift had starred in the first film adaptation (along with Maureen Stapleton, curiously enough, who later ran off with Eliza's father, David Rayfiel, who abandoned Eliza and her mother).

I'm very proud of *Miss Lonelyhearts*. It was essentially a student film, made by a star student of the American Film Institute named Michael Dinner (he would later direct for TV and garner many award nominations, winning an Emmy for *The Wonder Years*). We did this great piece together—one of my favorites of all the work I've ever done. I wish more people could have seen it. (Years later, I also appeared in *Justified* for Michael Dinner.)

So I had just gotten back from filming. One weekend in June, in 1981, Treusch and I were cooking something. I left his Connecticut house in the afternoon. "See you, buddy." And I went over to Sandy's. But I was all coked up, and Sandy could tell right away.

She said, "Get the fuck out of here." So I did. I went out to my car, which was a Jeep CJ-5 without the doors on it. It was summertime, so the doors were off.

So it was the evening of June 4, and I saw Sandy's big blond German shepherd, who was also named Sandy, who liked me. She jumped into the car with me. I backed out of the driveway and started down the road, and then Sandy, the dog, started to act up, so I took my hands off the steering wheel to keep her from jumping out. Suddenly I saw a tree coming straight at us, and that's all I remember.

After being in a coma for three days, I woke up in the hospital. I'm missing some teeth, and I hurt all over. I'm like, "Dude, I'm fucking injured!" I buzz for the nurse, and she's named Mary, just like Sandy's housekeeper whom I adored. She's Black and overweight, just like the other Mary. For a minute, I figure I must be back at Sandy's.

"What happened to me?"

"Honey, you tried to climb a tree in a CJ-5."

I remembered the dog was with me, so I asked about her right away. She needed thirteen stitches in her shoulder but she got to go home, which is more than I could say about myself.

Sandy later told me that as soon as she'd heard sirens, she knew it was me and that something terrible had happened.

The coma only lasted seventy-two hours, but they kept me under very heavy sedation when I came out of it. The EMTs said there had been a box of crystal meth on the seat of the Jeep when they found me, so the question was: did I go into a sudden drug-and-alcohol-induced coma that caused me to crash into the tree? Or was the coma a result of the crash? That was what the doctors asked themselves.

They noted that when I finally was discharged from the hospital a month later, I left with a heavy prescription drug dependency. They were all looking for someone to blame for giving me so many highly addictive drugs, but they really didn't know at the time how to best care for brain-injured patients. I *was* brain-injured, and it caused terrible gaps in my memory.

Glenn Walken, Christopher Walken's younger brother and a friend of mine who had been a Green Beret, came to visit me in the hospital. He had seen ugliness and terrible injury in war, and he said to Chris Walken, also visiting, "He's not gonna make it, dude." My temperament didn't help my recovery. I made one of the nurses so angry that she yanked the cotton out of my nose in a violent way. I don't remember my behavior being so bad, but obviously it was.

One pleasant moment in all this was during one of Sandy's visits. I was sitting there in my room, waiting for her to walk in. We were still together then, and before long we were making love in my hospital room. Sexual healing, I suppose. I'm glad I still have that memory.

The one thing I do remember is the mental fog I experienced after the accident. It's so frightening to an actor who thinks, *I have to go back to work and learn shit and become other people, but I don't even know who* I *am.* I'd forgotten so much; it really scared me. It was like the whole library in my head had been reassembled, as if all the books had been thrown onto the floor and the shelves were empty. I didn't know where anything belonged. My speech was messed up. I was in rehab for two months and I had to learn how to walk and talk again. It was really hard.

Two strange things happened to me while I was in the hospital that I can't explain, but I don't think they were caused by the heavy sedation I was under.

While I was still in a coma, I had the sensation of hovering over my hospital bed. I could see my face and I was so close I could actually feel my breath. I started rising and I rose so high that the bed shrank to the size of my thumbnail. But I guess it wasn't my time, because somehow I chose to come back to my body. One of my doctors later told me that my heart had stopped, twice, and it sounded like what I'd experienced was what's referred to as "a rising," though he made me swear not to quote him on that. Doctors aren't supposed to believe in those kinds of things.

After that experience, I was lying in my hospital bed and became aware that I couldn't remember anything. I thought I was ruined as an actor because acting is all about talking and remembering, and I couldn't do either very well. In this business, you cannot be damaged goods. I remember thinking that I might as well just die, because all I knew how to do in this life was act, and I'd never be able to do that again.

That's when the second strange thing happened. I saw two people walk into my room, but apparently, I was the only person who saw them. They were a little couple who both looked as if they'd just gotten off a train, having traveled a thousand miles. I remember thinking that they reminded me of my grandparents on my mother's side, and that they knew me.

I asked them where they came from, and they told me, "Romania."

"You came here all the way from Romania?"

And they said yes, that they were here to help me. They told me that I had to start taking a different drug, which was both a youth serum and a memory enhancer. They explained that it was illegal, but it could be gotten under the counter in most drugstores.

I asked them to write it down for me, which they did before leaving.

The strangest thing is that nobody else saw this couple. I asked the nurses, but nobody saw them or had any idea who I was talking about.

About a week or so after I was released from the hospital, I decided to go to the pharmacy and ask about that medication. I went to my drugstore and was told by the pharmacist that it was indeed illegal, but he sold it to me anyway. I took the pills and I got my memory back. Thanks to this ghostly Romanian couple, I got my life back.

RIGHT: Staring into space on the set of *King of the Gypsies*. How did I get here? The work is hard. The pressure is relentless. Goddamn it if I'm gonna let myself or anyone else down. (Credit: Paramount Pictures/TopFoto)

ABOVE LEFT: My paternal granddaddy, Walter Thomas Roberts, and my grandma, Beatrice Beal Roberts (she was more comfortable with her feet on the ground), with some of my aunts atop Granddaddy's horses. I got my love of horses from him, but I sure treated them better than that mean man ever did. (Credit: Roberts Collection)

ABOVE RIGHT: I always thought my mother, Betty Roberts, was a beauty queen. My parents split up in 1971, just as I was about to turn fifteen. It's never easy. (Credit: Roberts Collection)

TOP LEFT: Here's the evil, thwarted genius himself—my father, Walter Roberts. Not really a genius, but a frustrated writer and theater director. I'm a little ashamed to admit it, but some part of me loved the son of a bitch. (Credit: Roberts Collection)

RIGHT: What big brother doesn't proudly give his little siblings shoulder rides? That's Julia, seeing the world from above, with me keeping her secure and safe. (Credit: Roberts Collection)

LOWER LEFT: My first apartment, in Brooklyn. "Open concept" they call it now. It was just one room, but I loved that place. I looked ten at the age of nearly twenty—that was a blessing and a curse back then. (Credit: Roberts Collection)

ABOVE: A moment captured in *Gypsies*. Notice Shelley Winters, just one of the wonderful actors in that movie, along with Susan Sarandon, Brooke Shields, Judd Hirsch, and the incomparable Sterling Hayden. (Credit: © Globe Photos/Zuma Press/Alamy)

RIGHT: Milo O'Shea and me in *Mass Appeal*, directed by Geraldine Fitzgerald, who almost sabotaged my career. (Credit: Everett Collection)

BOTTOM RIGHT: With the amazing, pixelated actress Sandy Dennis, one of the loves of my life. I made her choose between me and her dozens of cats. Guess who won? (Credit: Robin Platzer/ Twin Images)

TOP: With Bob Fosse and Carroll Baker on the set of *Star 80*. I was in thrall to Fosse, a dangerous place to be. (Credit: Warner Bros./ Moviestore Collection Ltd/Alamy)

BOTTOM LEFT: *Miss Lonelyhearts*, inspired by a novella by Nathanael West. To this day, one of my favorite roles. Grandma Roberts loved that one, too. (Credit: Everett Collection)

BOTTOM RIGHT: Very proud of having done *To Heal a Nation*, and having opposed the Vietnam War from the start. Standing in front of the incredibly moving Vietnam Veterans Memorial in Washington, D.C. (Credit: © NBC/Everett Collection)

In Cannes with Russian director Andrei Konchalovsky and the Israeli film producer Menahem Golan, for *Runaway Train*. I'm still proud of that 1985 movie, which got me an Academy Award nomination for Best Supporting Actor. (Credit: AP Images)

With the legendary casting agent Sheila Jaffe. We go way back, although I think I fell from grace with her and her casting partner, Georgianne Walken (married to my pal Chris Walken). (Credit: Ron Galella/Ron Galella Collection/Getty Images)

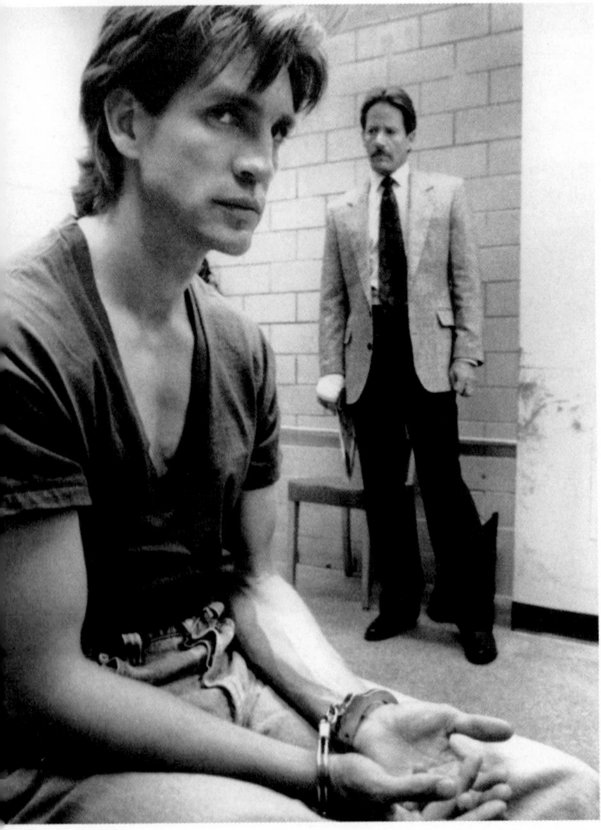

TOP LEFT: With the very sweet Patrick Swayze at the 1987 premiere of *Dirty Dancing*. Wish he'd not left us so soon. (Credit: DMI/The *Life* Picture Collection/Shutterstock)

ABOVE: A moment with Mickey Rourke, my costar in *The Pope of Greenwich Village*, whose shout-out when he won the 2009 Independent Spirit Award for *The Wrestler* meant the world to me. (Credit: DMI/The *Life* Picture Collection/Shutterstock)

LEFT: *Fugitive Among Us*, a 1992 Movie of the Week with actors Lauren Holly and Peter Strauss (pictured, right). A police detective played by Strauss becomes obsessed with capturing an escaped drifter—that would be me. (Credit: © ABC/Everett Collection)

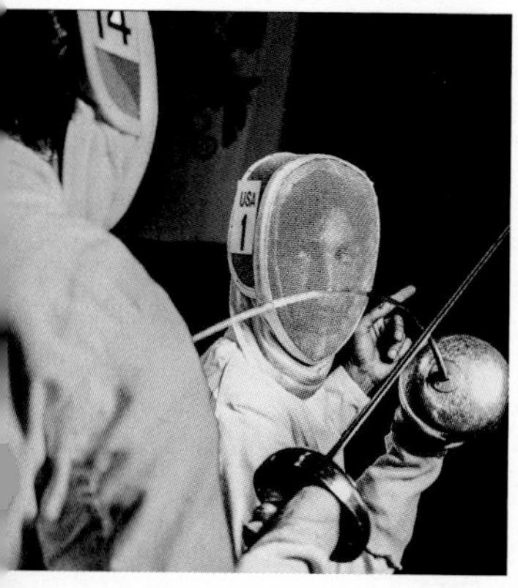

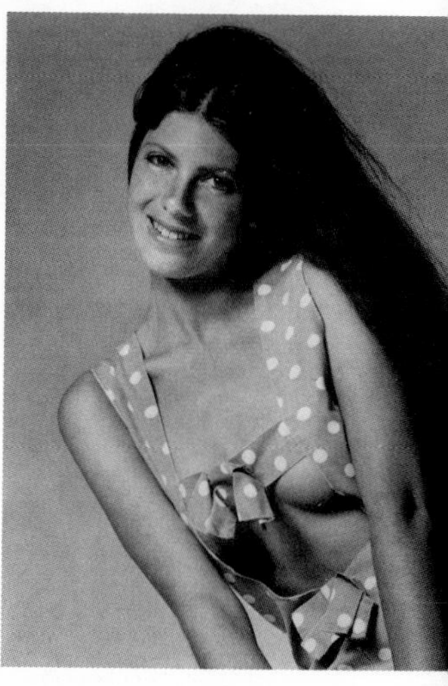

ABOVE LEFT: On the set of *By the Sword*, a 1991 movie about world-class fencers that I really liked and enjoyed doing. Some photographers are like directors—you'd work with them anywhere, anytime. I felt that way about Greg Gorman. (Credit: © Greg Gorman)

ABOVE RIGHT: Greg Gorman works his magic: Here I am with Billy Idol and Robert Wagner. Eliza and I had such fun the day of that photo shoot. (Credit: © Greg Gorman)

RIGHT: Here's a teenaged Eliza. You can't tell from the pic, but her hair was and still burns bright red. Always beautiful! (Credit: Roberts Collection)

BELOW: Eliza (then Garrett) on the set of *Schlock*, starring opposite her *Animal House* director, John Landis (that's Landis in the gorilla suit). Driving home with the head of the costume still on, plus his glasses over his ape face, caused a few near accidents on the 405. (Credit: Roberts Collection)

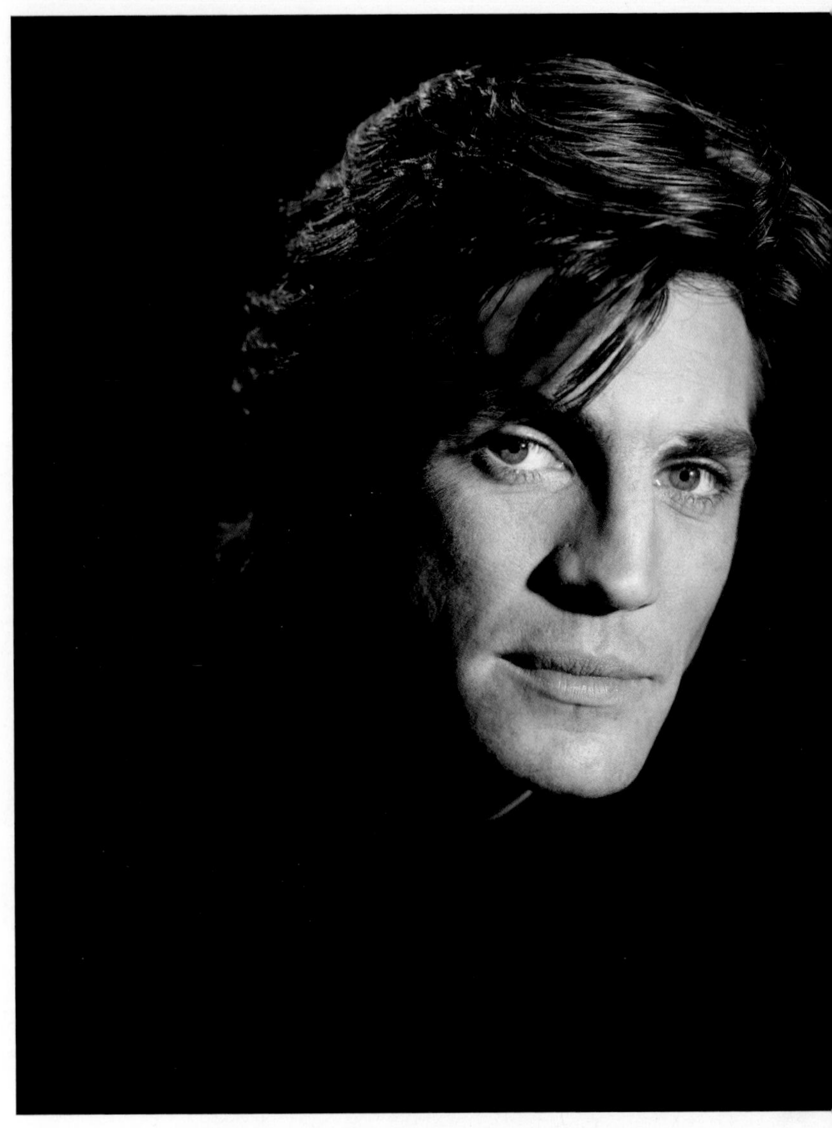

Portrait taken by Greg Gorman, who sure knows how to make a fella look pretty. (Credit: © Greg Gorman)

To this day, I have a real love for them and a real gratitude. I do think they were not three-dimensional, tangible people as we know them. I feel a little silly when I talk about it, but the truth is, after the accident, I started seeing spirits, or ghosts, or entities, or whatever you want to call them; and to some degree, I have ever since. I believe Eliza and I have an entity here in our house in Los Angeles, a young woman I've glimpsed half a dozen times but encountered only once. I have to say that ever since that car accident in 1981, I have on several occasions experienced paranormal activity.

I was asked to go on *The Haunting Of*, hosted by a psychic named Kim Russo. (I was also on *Celebrity Ghost Stories*, so I'm probably the only actor in Los Angeles who's appeared on both *Celebrity Ghost Stories* and *Celebrity Rehab*, which is funny because it's been a long time since I felt like a celebrity.)

The show—which you can see on YouTube—went something like this. A psychic medium named Kim Russo came to our house to scope out any spirits inhabiting it. As soon as she arrived on our doorstep, she said, "There's something unsettling going on here. I'm feeling this inner turmoil . . . Oh my God. There's a lot of spirits trying to get your attention."

She went on to say that she was sensing "a very strong presence of a woman. Has anybody ever seen a female entity in this house?" She went on to say that she'd felt her presence in the car as soon as she arrived at our house.

Leading Russo into the kitchen, I described how I once walked in, went over to the sink, turned on the water, got a glass, looked over to my left, and suddenly saw a light mist of smoke that assumed the outline of a woman. She didn't speak to me, but I felt there was a communication.

"Oh my God," Russo said. "This is the lady from the car. Hard to tell her age, but she looks like she may be thirty to forty years old. . . . In my vision, there was a car parked in the middle of nowhere. I just see an open area right around the car. And I see her sleeping with her young child in the back seat. I'm just getting flashes of her."

She also told me that there were other spirits trying to get my attention. "I think some of the spirits who are trying to come through are people that were in your life," she said. "Family members, friends, relatives . . . You have a grandma named Betty?"

"Beatrice. That would be Beatrice." My mom's name was Betty.

"I sense the nurturing nature of this woman. Comforting, loving."

"She was probably the nicest person I ever knew."

As comforting as that was, Russo went on to tell me that she thought the spirit haunting my kitchen was the woman she had perceived in the car with her child, and that years earlier she had murdered her child and killed herself. There had been a case like that in the area, decades ago. Russo explained that she was seeking forgiveness from the living, which is why she was haunting my house.

Almost a month had passed since the accident when I ran into Chris Walken. Chris said, "Your nose is so much better since the accident; you have a better nose now."

It was good to hear, because I had been told that after the crash, my nose was flat as a pancake on my face and the doctors had to lift it up. *Bang.* Lifted it right up. Eliza later told me that some cosmetic surgeons explained to her that one of the things that we are most drawn to in faces is symmetry, but there was nothing symmetrical about me. I was more symmetrical before the accident.

Which brings me back to *Miss Lonelyhearts* and Montgomery Clift.

Clift was a beautiful, genius actor, mostly in the 1950s, in movies like *Red River*, *A Place in the Sun*, *From Here to Eternity*, *The Misfits*. But a terrible accident happened after an evening dining at Elizabeth Taylor's home (they both were filming *Raintree County*). His car veered off the twisting road of Laurel Canyon and smashed into a telephone pole. He nearly died; in fact, Elizabeth was credited with saving his life, pulling the teeth out of his throat that were choking him. After the accident, the left side of Monty's face was paralyzed—a terrible thing for an actor—and it left him with a visible limp. As a result, he fell into a very dark place, going deeper into painkillers and booze addiction. (The Clash even wrote a song about him, "The Right Profile," that describes Monty's beautiful, broken face.)

The fact that we'd both played the Miss Lonelyhearts columnist, twenty-five years apart, and both suffered devastating car crashes shortly after wasn't lost on me. It's also ironic that he had been visiting Elizabeth Taylor, who won an Oscar as Best Actress in *Who's Afraid of Virginia Woolf?*, and I had been seeing Sandy Dennis, who won for Best Supporting Actress in the same film.

Thinking about it, I saw there were other parallels. We were both child actors (Clift was thirteen when he made his acting debut on Broadway in *Fly Away Home*; I acted in my dad's plays as a teenager and made my film debut at age twenty-two in *King of the Gypsies*). Though I never identified with it, we were both considered "beautiful men" in our prime. Clift's devastating car accident pretty much ended that, and mine might have if I hadn't had a good surgeon. Clift's face was partially paralyzed on one side as a result of the crash; my appearance also changed. Clift was famous for throwing tantrums, and I was known for difficult, contrary behavior. Finally, both of our lives and careers were darkened by struggles with multiple addictions—for Clift, booze and pills. For me, mostly coke and weed.

I'd like to say my accident sobered me up, but it didn't. Ten months later, Treusch threw a surprise party for my twenty-sixth birthday. He presented me with a quarter ounce of cocaine as a birthday present. During the party, I noticed Bill talking to people, including Juliet Taylor, a prominent casting director. From what I could make out, Bill was telling them how fucked up I was on the very drug that he was feeding me! I guess it only goes to show how truly messed up I really was, that I didn't have the courage or the awareness to fire him on the spot.

I never understood how it benefited Bill, to have an actor who was too high to work, but it was the only way he could control me. Acting itself was so freeing, I suppose he had to find a way to rein me in, to keep me under the lock and key of cocaine.

IV. Lisa and "Hulie" (aka Julia)

Why can't you call me
by my name?

—Julia

I'm probably one of the few straight men on planet Earth not physically attracted to Julia Roberts, and that's certainly a good thing. But don't read me wrong. I adore my sister—for our shared history, for the history we never got to share, for the undeniably lovely and loyal person she became, and for her faith in the person she was hoping I would become. Sorry, Jules.

Julia Fiona Roberts. But when she was a little girl, when you asked her, "What's your name," she'd say, "Hulie." So we all started calling her Hulie, 'cause that was what she called herself, until she was in high school. Of the three of us kids—me, Julie, and Lisa—Julie was always the funniest, and the most daring. Lisa and I did everything for her, probably because she was the baby of the family—and she knew it. She liked it!

Both Walter and Betty doted on her. I think it really ripped up Walter to lose custody of both of his daughters. He actually wrote tenderly about them, and me, in one of his otherwise toxic letters:

> While I was talking with Lisa over the telephone, Mother took Jul for a walk. Mother said they were walking along talking and Julia suddenly said: I don't see why it is that we can't all visit each other and not have any problems. I love Daddy and I love Mommy and they are both good to me. They never spank me . . . I would like to go see everybody, but there's always problems.

I felt that way too about wanting to be reunited with my sisters. But, of course, that wouldn't happen, for all kinds of reasons—perhaps one reason being that Julia and I were too much alike.

We are both children of the South, though our own civil war was fought between ourselves. But that's all blood under the bridge now.

We both devoted our lives to a profession where you can't help but leave parts of yourself on the playing field. After *Pretty Woman*, she endured the most unimaginable kind of fame, and she did so with gratitude and grace. My fame flamed out early, but I didn't act to become famous. In fact, I became an actor to become anonymous, to make myself disappear from myself. It didn't work out that way. Eventually, I became famous for all the wrong things.

Julia's smile is incandescent. That's one way we differ: I've been told my smile is like a cobra coiled up in a basket ready to strike.

We both buried our parents and a half sister.

We both lost people we loved and loved people who lost us—to fame, to drugs, to work, to life, revolving like a magic lantern. (I had one of those in my room when I was a boy. The world moved, projected along the wall, while I sat mesmerized. It was like an offering from the future—the first movie, if you will—that I had ever seen.)

After our parents' divorce, Julia and Lisa eventually left Atlanta with our mom and moved to the small town of Smyrna. Adam remembers that "when it was just Betty and the girls, Lisa got parenting experience real quick while Betty was trying to make a living."

I used to stay in my room in the apartment I shared with Dad and say a prayer that we might all be together again—but happier than before.

I still feel that way. It's funny how some prayers never grow old.

Not everyone is so willing to promote the careers of family members, even the gifted ones. Eliza comes from a show business family. Her biological father, David Rayfiel, couldn't have been more successful as a screenwriter, but he never did shit for any of Eliza's family, not even his gifted grandson, Keaton Simons, a singer-songwriter. I know it sounds boastful, but when I can get away with it, I make it a deal breaker to find a place for my stepson's songs in the movies I'm in.

Eliza observed that "it's fascinating when you see that in families, where one person after another is so dynamic and radiant, you're like, wow. With Eric and Julia, it's pretty cool because it wasn't a typical showbiz family. It really started with Eric's generation and it came out of nowhere."

So I'm always stunned when I hear about people—talented people—being turned away by their own blood. There's a famous old show business story about Louis B. Mayer, the boss of MGM and one of the great Jewish moguls of the movie industry, who in many respects, was more Old World than New. LB, as they called him, was always in the habit of hiring family members to various jobs at the studio. One day, some of MGM's lawyers came in to see LB; they explained to him that if he went on hiring his relatives at the studio, people might begin to accuse him of nepotism.

"You mean they have a word for that?" Mayer asked, incredulously. Whether there's a word for it or not, that's how I feel about helping family.

My wife started out as an actress and became a casting director, an acting coach, and a manager, though she never gave up acting. As I mentioned earlier, she was Brunella in *National Lampoon's Animal House*, one of the wide-eyed innocents who gets taken for a ride by Delta frats. She also appeared in a remake of *A Star Is Born*, the one with Barbra Streisand and Kris Kristofferson, and others. In fact, she's busier now than ever as an actress.

As a casting director, she would go through all the usual suspects, through all the top agents, and when no one jumped out at her as being the right fit, she'd start looking at family, at siblings, at the kids of actors, even if they'd never had a single credit in their lives. I don't see a single thing wrong with it. You still have to show your stuff, you still have to shine. Sissy Spacek, one of the greatest actresses of my generation, and her husband,

Jack Fisk, a hugely talented art director who became a production designer, busted their asses for their daughter, Schuyler. She deserved it, she's such a talented person. There's only so much you can do to help your child, but sometimes it's more than worth it, as it was in Schuyler's case.

When you have a gorgeous younger sister who didn't come from an established show business family but from a local, Southern version of show business, that didn't mean she wasn't going to make it. It didn't mean that at all, but it didn't hurt her that I was willing to open up my mouth whenever I could and say, "Give her a shot."

Now one of the things I'd like to apologize for in this book is for publicly saying on more than one occasion, "If it wasn't for me, there would be no Julia Roberts." That's not only unfortunate, but it's also untrue. And I hope Julie will accept this more public apology. It was an asinine thing to have said. I was proud of her, but it was pride turned on its head, to my own advantage.

I know that, growing up, Julie thought of becoming a veterinarian and all those other things that young kids dream about, but as Eliza said, "You can't look like that and not become a movie star." Plus, she's a very driven woman. Someone would have plucked her out of the crowd in a place like New York without my help. On the other hand, I was born to do this. I moved to New York City when I wasn't even old enough to drink a beer in public. If Julie had stayed in Atlanta, she'd probably have married a wealthy dude and lived a very different life. So I will take credit, once I had broken away from my father (or thought I had) and moved to New York City, for telling my sisters, "Come on up, girls; the water's fine." That's when, it seems to me, she saw my life as a young actor in New York, and saw what I was doing for my livelihood, and she wanted to try it.

They did come up, and they lived with me for a time in my penthouse apartment on West Seventy-Third Street. Little did they know that I would become so difficult to be around. That's why Julie and Lisa soon wanted a place of their own. I was already deep into drugs. They lived with me for the better part of a year, and then I got them their own place. I wanted it that way. I was a drug addict, let's face it, and I wanted to be alone with my drugs. I got them a really nice apartment in the West Village. I paid for it for a year. But I wanted them out as much as, I'm sure, they wanted to leave. The truth is, I needed my privacy because I was such a fucked-up guy who wanted to do fucked-up things, but I had enough sense to take care of them, to get them out of my apartment and out of harm's way.

But here is where the shit started hitting the fan, and it was this. In early interviews, whenever I was asked about my mother, who was the only one of my parents alive when I first became famous, I would say that my mother was dead.

"How'd she die?" reporters would ask.

"I don't wanna talk about it," I'd say.

This made my sisters wonder, *What the fuck is wrong with him?* I was still angry with my mom. I had read somewhere that she was going to teach acting. She must have thought, *Eric's famous, now I'm going to teach acting.* The only problem with that was, I was going around the country promoting my movie, telling reporters my mom was dead. I'm only now beginning to realize the impact it must have had on Julie and Lisa, who were eleven and thirteen years old, who were living with our mom, but hearing their big brother—who now had the ear of the world, as it were—saying in public that their mom is dead.

It was the great undoing of my relationship with my sisters. That I was unconcerned about them and focused only on my mom reading that I'd killed her off was such a selfish thing to have done. When you become famous at twenty-one, when you're on billboards, when journalists from *The New York Times* are interviewing you, it's heady stuff, dude. And don't forget, I'm even more of a child because I felt like a country-fucking-bumpkin in the big city, even though by then I didn't sound like one. I came from people who talk like, "What the fuck, motherfucker, goddamn! Did you just shoot 'im, because I just shot 'im right in the face." Those are my peeps. So when you are flush with the freedom of having escaped from that, and from brutal parents, you feel invincible. At least for a while.

And then there's my other baby sister, Lisa, who sometimes got overlooked in the shadows of her older brother and younger sister.

It was around 1984, and I remember coming home from Australia, having just finished *The Coca-Cola Kid*. Lisa was living with me in a house I owned in Connecticut. Julie hadn't come up yet. I'll never forget how, as I walked through the front door, Lisa came running toward me as if it was Christmas morning, and we hugged each other, and I don't think I ever felt more missed or more loved in my life.

When Julie became Julia, this unimaginable superstar, I suddenly became a more established guy you could depend on for a successful performance—but as an *actor*, not a movie star. Lisa, unfortunately, became somewhat overlooked, the lost middle kid. Yet, of the three of us, in my view she was the better actor, back when she first entered the family business. I would watch her perform and turn to Eliza in wonder. I couldn't believe how good she was. More important, she was the most patient and the most giving of all of us. So the crime, if there was a crime among the three of us, was committed against her in that she may have felt she couldn't compete with me and especially with Julia.

That's not to say there weren't any good times. After Julia was established, but before *Steel Magnolias*, I went to L.A. on some kind of business meeting. At the time, Julia and Liam Neeson were living together, and they offered me their place to stay. That was probably the nicest time I would ever spend with my youngest sister. I wasn't just basking in the California sun, but in the happiness of being with Julia and Liam. I made friends with Liam immediately. What a guy! I just loved him. He was sweet, gentle, and so smart—such a lovely person, and such a talented actor. I thought, *Wow, my sister has a really cool cat for a boyfriend. Julia has really grown up.* It felt like we were a family again.

I didn't know then what happened to break that up, but I do know it was the last time Julia ever extended anything like that to me. The welcome mat was turned upside down after those beautiful few days in Los Angeles. Of course, now I understand why. I was still doing cocaine, and the inconsistency of my moods must have reminded both of my sisters of Walter, besides my being a pain in ass to be around.

Drug addicts are the most inconsistent people on the planet, and I was one of them, from roughly 1978 to 1992. How could I share any kind of love with anyone when my primary relationship was with my narcotics? Everybody—and I mean everybody—comes in second, or third, or fourth. Drugs became my wife, my mistress, my best friend. And I didn't start to heal until the day I finally woke up and became ashamed of myself. Only then did the healing begin.

After *Pretty Woman* came out in 1990, I remember being on the phone with Julia in upstate New York. I forget what we were talking about—we were having a mild disagreement about something—and I said, "Julie, listen to me."

And she goes, "My name is not Julie. My name is Julia."

And I started laughing. I said, "Who are you talking to?"

Bam! She hung up.

I realized then that I had to get in line and give her respect as an actor—that's what she wanted from me. What did I want from her? Besides her friendship and love, I'd like to know what she thinks of *me* as an actor. Eliza assures me that Julia told her she respected my acting talent, and Mom would often write to them when I appeared in something that impressed her. But that's never been expressed to me directly. When *King of the Gypsies* came out, I never heard a word from Mom. Oh, that's right—I'd told everyone she was dead.

Like any actor starting out in New York or Los Angeles, Julia had her share of auditioning and not getting the part. Her first acting gig was in an episode of *Miami Vice*, followed by a terrible movie for NBC called *Satisfaction*, back when the networks were just starting to get into the movie business. What she and I both had going for us was that, in the seventies and eighties, producers didn't need to have a big name attached to a movie in order to get it made—not like they do now. If so, neither one of us would have gotten our big break—for me, *King of the Gypsies*, for Julia, *Pretty Woman.* There were big stars who wanted those roles, and they would have gotten them whether they were right for the parts or not. It helped that no one thought *Pretty Woman* was going to do any business, even its director, Garry Marshall. After all, he was from TV, and the attitude at the time was, let him make his little movie with this no-name actress. Who gives a shit. That was a lifetime—and $20 million a picture—ago.

Pretty Woman, of course, was the movie that put Julia over the top. It's interesting that she became "America's sweetheart" by playing a hooker; but to me, that's America in a nutshell—the puritan and the profane go hand in hand.

Everyone loved that movie and Julia's role in it. I was working with George C. Scott (who'd won an Oscar for *Patton* in 1971) at the time, and he told me in his gruff voice that he thought her movie was going to go through the roof. It did. I watched it happen: Oh my god, Julia's becoming a superstar!

Was I jealous of my baby sister? Not really. For one thing, we were never going to be up for the same parts. And I felt I helped her in every way I could. I knew she wanted to act, and I always delighted when she got a part. I had no idea what was going to happen to her. I didn't have a real sense of "stardom" anyway, not for myself or for anyone. So when suddenly this rare and rarefied thing occurred, this worldwide phenomenon of Julia's stardom, it shoved me into the public eye in a different way.

First, there were all kinds of suspicions cast upon us—even outlandish and creepy rumors of incest. I don't exactly know where that started, but it's right up there with Richard Gere putting a gerbil up his ass—another ridiculous urban legend. It could have been a dumb idea of what Southerners were capable of—a mean-spirited swipe at the South. But beyond that, it seemed as if there wasn't room in the public imagination for both Julia and me—that we were in competition with each other.

I still get fan mail from people who write things like, "If I have to choose, you're still my favorite, but I love her." And people who actually say to me, "Oh, you act too? Isn't that cute? Julia Roberts's big brother decided to try acting." I think it's funny and can laugh at it, but it makes Eliza want to pull up my IMDb page, which lists every movie and television show I've been in for the past fifty years.

I remember I was shooting a movie on the same lot as *Flatliners*, Julia's next movie after *Pretty Woman*. I was playing Al Capone in a fat suit, and Julia invited me to lunch so I could meet her then boyfriend and costar, Kiefer Sutherland. We had a great time, but I couldn't help noticing that Kiefer acted very competitive with me. Later, I took Julia aside and asked her about it, and she goes, "He just thinks you're a good actor."

Julia and I were still friends back then. It's a shame we lost it, because we really liked each other and had the same sense of humor, the same mannerisms, the same everything. We were very much alike. I blame myself, mostly due to my long journey through drugs and how that brought out the worst in me—and how it scared people who felt they didn't know me anymore—but there were other currents as well.

When you rule the world, which she kind of did for a while, and a member of your family is slow to acknowledge that, you hold it against them. I never paid enough homage to her. I still saw her as my baby sister, and I knew that she—like me—came from white trash, yet she became one of the biggest stars that ever breathed. And she knew it, bless her heart. What a trajectory!

As I mentioned, Julia is a movie star and I'm an actor. There's a difference. That's how people look at us, and that's how I look at us, and I'm fine with that. When people ask me, "Do you have a problem with your sister's success?" I tell them no. We'll never be up for the same part. I'm not waiting for her kind of paycheck, or stardom, or her help. I'm not waiting for that stuff. When Eliza comes home and tells me, "I just saw your sister's movie," if it's good, I'll say, "Oh, yeah, take me to see that one."

I think I first really fell out with Julia when she appeared to side with my ex-partner Kelly Cunningham, over custody of our daughter, Emma, who was born in 1991. More on that later.

I first met Kelly in 1987 on the set of a *Saturday Night Live* broadcast. It was an amazing evening. Dennis Hopper was the host, and Roy Orbison, with his dark shades and German Iron Cross, was the musical guest—he was mesmerizing! Who knew that his "Crying" would turn out to be our anthem for what lay ahead?

Kelly Cunningham was very pretty. She really got a kick out of my world, and it was fun to see it through her eyes. I bought us a home on Grinnell Street in Rhinecliff, in upstate New York on the Hudson River. I loved this piece of earth. It was the first thing that truly belonged to me, bought and paid for by no one but me.

Rhinecliff, a hamlet within the town of Rhinebeck, was so small—its population was only a few hundred people. But it was in an historic spot, men having died there during the American Revolution. Just down the hill, about 250 yards to the north, was a tavern. On weekend evenings, you'd hear badly covered rock classics floating up through the air.

Later on, when I was with Eliza, our friend, the actor Jeffrey Dean Morgan (who played Negan in *The Walking Dead*), didn't have money for rent (or anything else), so we virtually gave him our Rhinecliff house to use whenever we were away on location. Well, the zombie world was very, very good to Jeff—he now owns a zillion acres in Rhinebeck, and he even bought the candy store with Paul Rudd, another terrific actor. So Rhinecliff and Rhinebeck are magical places that don't even know they're magical.

Kelly made our house on Grinnell Street a beautiful home. Once we had Emma, who was born at the Rhinebeck Birthing Center, Kelly made Emma's room really gorgeous. In addition, Kelly was an absolute genius at preserving memories, keeping photo albums, framing movie posters, and creating gorgeous origami Christmas decorations. I only wish there had been more pleasant memories to preserve.

Ours was a very significant relationship. We went through a lot, and she saw me at my absolute worst—yet she stayed, for a time, though I'm sure she questioned whether or not she should. We both wanted a child—maybe I did more than she—but we both wanted to become parents.

The pregnancy was very exciting. I fell madly in love with Emma the first minute I saw her. We'd even tried to bring on labor so it could happen exactly on the due date. It was a natural birth. I sang "Happy Birthday" to her belly a lot. When Emma finally made her appearance, she wasn't quite quiet and mellow, but when I started singing "Happy Birthday" to her, she must have recognized my voice because she calmed right down.

I kept trying to show off that I knew how to take care of kids because I was so much older than my sisters, but I didn't really know what I was doing. Also, I was bingeing on drugs during the pregnancy and right after the birth—not the kind of behavior that will make you father of the year. Nonetheless, I loved my little daughter with the strength of Hercules, despite my own weaknesses.

However, I couldn't handle the realities of an infant coming into my life, and I couldn't handle being a parent! I'm still not a father figure. Emma, on the other hand, certainly knows what that role is—now grown up and a mom herself. She's that person to her first child, Rhodes. As close as I am to Eliza's daughter, Prairie, and her wife, April's, kids (my "bonus grandchildren"), I certainly know how to engage and play and read Maurice Sendak, but no one in their right mind is going to bring me on for full-time childcare.

Speaking of reading, I'd like to think that Emma inherited her mad love of books from me. Many of the books that Eliza and I have read or listened to came as recommendations from Emma. She even designed her own bookshelves.

Emma gave permission for us to interact a little bit with her on her Instagram page. It's always good to ask, because we're engaging in a very public way. This is often what private life has come to in this upside-down, misruled world so dominated by social media.

So Kelly and I were together for three years, finally breaking up in October 1991, separating soon after Emma was born. That was many years ago. Since then, Emma has made her name as an actress—she was hilarious in *We Are the Millers*, and terrific in *American Horror Story* and in James Franco's *Palo Alto*.

I'm often asked if I have concerns about my daughter being in this business of acting. I love this business. I didn't realize, of course, how much it beats you up, but Emma's much stronger than I was at that age and time. She has more tools at her disposal to build a safe place around herself than I ever did. On the same day I might go from shooting Chris Nolan's *The Dark Knight* to appearing in *Witless Protection*, starring Larry the Cable Guy. There are times I've done three movies in one day. Often, these jobs involve literally showing up on an indie set for two hours and saying a few lines, so I'm very proud of Emma *and* Julia for what they've achieved.

When I became an established actor, one of the first things I did was go to the William Morris Agency and say, "Which one of you is going to represent my sister Julia?" That was before her first solid film, *Mystic Pizza*.

Julia was good in *Mystic Pizza*, great in *Pretty Woman*, but not so much in *Steel Magnolias*, in my opinion, even though it brought Julia her first Academy Award nomination. I don't want to sound like an actor talking, or a jealous sibling, but I don't think her performance held up in that movie. When I saw her in *Steel Magnolias*, I thought, *Okay. Good. She's almost a good actor, and one day she's gonna be one.*

In fact, I think all those brilliant women—Sally Fields, Dolly Parton, Olympia Dukakis, Shirley MacLaine, Daryl Hannah—overacted their asses off in *Steel Magnolias*. Nobody's great in that movie. They all chewed a lot of scenery, and we know that if an actor cries on film, they go to the top of the class. They get the Oscar nod because crying gets a lot of credit. It's the big joke in all acting classes, even in the great Lee Strasberg's Actors Studio. Crying and dying bring home the bacon!

I also think another reason she got an Oscar nod for *Steel Magnolias* was her authenticity as a sweet, small-town Southern girl. That's what she was, after all, or at least that's how she started off. I don't know if she had a dialect coach try to eradicate her Southern accent, but if so, luckily for her it didn't take. I think that's a big part of her appeal—along with her boffo good looks and killer smile—her Southern accent and mannerisms. Beauty like that can be off-putting, especially for other women, but Julia's down-home manner made her seem like your best friend. There's a certain colorful and enchanting quality to Southern speech. I get it, even though I rail at the "rednecks" who tormented me when I was a boy, and my macho, racist grandpa who was so cruel to me.

On the other hand, Julia was fantastic in *Stepmom*, with the sublime Susan Sarandon, who's acted with both Julia and me. I felt that was an important movie, and I get misty every time I see it.

So, in 1990 a new actress bursts on the scene: Eric Roberts's younger sister, and she's an unquestionable star. Fast-forward to 1993, and there's a veteran actor on the scene: Julia Roberts's older brother. That's where I remain today. And I imagine I will remain as Julia's brother and Emma Roberts's dad for the rest of my life. I'd like to make good on that, to move aside proudly and with grace. That's part of the reason for writing this book.

Whenever I've read a memoir—particularly the memoir of a prominent person—I've wondered *why* they're writing it. Why are they telling all this to me, a rank stranger? It can't be just for the money. Something else is going on, something deeper. I'm not smart enough to know what that is, but one obvious answer is that if you don't speak for yourself, someone else is going to speak for you. As the great, late Dr. John used to sing in "Such a Night": "You know if I don't do it, somebody else will." I always loved that song.

In the old Hollywood days, the studios used to make up a bio for every movie star, and you had very little say in what they wrote about you. Some movie stars back in the day were almost relieved to have those phony stories pinned to them, because they were often better than what really happened. Shirley Temple is the perfect example: her parents preferred the official story of the luckiest and cutest girl in the world, though that image would become a straitjacket for her as she grew older.

But other movie stars hated walking around with a fake story about their lives. In a way, it's what my daddy tried to do with me—send me out in the world with a big, fat false narrative.

Of the three of us, in our family, Julia has been able to maintain a lot of privacy and to touch ever so lightly on any stories about our upbringing, and to keep things as positive as possible. I have a lot of respect for that. It couldn't have been easy. But what I don't think she realizes is how that has added to the pain of my own memories of childhood.

Don't forget that I came into this vale of tears eleven years before Julia was born. Though we had the same parents, we didn't have the same childhood. Often you have things you feel like screaming about but no one can hear you, mostly because it doesn't reconcile with the reason you feel like screaming. I hesitated for years to talk about my own life, mostly because of my concern and compassion for the people who would be most affected by my telling my story, especially Julia, who maintains a certain image around the world.

It's true that she's done some work where she's played characters who've been through rough times—it even brought her an Oscar, for *Erin Brockovich*, but for the most part, she's been America's sweetheart. I don't even think she asked for that, but being dealt that hand, she was very obliging in making sure that everything looked as rosy and cheerful as possible.

I, on the other hand, have never been thought of as an American sweetheart. If you've seen any of the movies I've been in, you might even think, *There's something going on with that guy in real life that's a bit troubling.* Again, do you have to be crazy to play crazy?

I've always felt somewhat guilty for messing with Julia's image, that the boiling pot of my own life and work might spill over, scalding the image that Julia has been able to maintain through all these years. I think about the abused kid who's been beaten up at home and has to practice saying, "I fell down the stairs," or "I fell out of the car," or "I bumped into the wall in the middle of the night." Anyone who knows anything about abuse knows that your obligation to cover the abuse is the most abusive part—the secret can be the most abusive part of the abuse.

So I feel strongly, my darling sisters, that I can't continue doing that. I have a daughter, Emma, and I would much rather be able to tell her about what a wonderful father and a great guy Walter was, but he wasn't. He had his own brutal upbringing, so I guess you could say he had a legitimate claim to his own cruelty. I'm trying to understand and explain the source of my own bad behavior.

The first thing to do in saving your own life is to speak up, no matter what. I'm not going to say that I'm doing this for other people who may be in a similar position, but I am going to say that when something bad happens and you've encountered a person who has harmed you, you need to tell that story.

Just before my car accident I appeared in the 1981 drama *Raggedy Man*, a movie with the irresistible Sissy Spacek, directed by her husband, Jack Fisk.

Spacek was really cool to work with, but there were a few missteps, on my part of course! One day we were filming this scene where our characters are dancing together and then, suddenly, we stop and I give her a big kiss, and then it cuts to where we've obviously made love.

So, we were dancing, we go to the kiss, and I kiss her on the mouth, and she pulls back, says, "Cut! Only my husband puts his tongue in my mouth!"

And because her husband, Jack Fisk, is the director, he's standing right there. Oh boy, Eric, how could you do that? How could you fuck up like that?

But Jack's smiling. Otherwise, the scene was going really well, but we did it over again. I did not put my tongue in her mouth this time, of course. I love that woman and I love her husband! (Just why Jack didn't become a star director, name above the title, I'll never know.)

Raggedy Man was turning out to be one of the best little movies, until the studio took it away from Fisk and turned it into another movie altogether—a kind of a horror film. I guess they thought it was too slow or something and had to have some kind of commercial value like horror, 'cause that's what happened to it. But the movie Jack made, I was so proud to be in it. And the movie that got released, I was proud of my performance, but I was not proud of the movie. They changed Jack's ending. Jack's movie was fantastic, but the movie that got released was not the same movie. It broke my heart.

After my car accident, things took a dicey turn. In 1981 I took a role in the two-character, comedic play *Mass Appeal* with Milo O'Shea, directed by Geraldine Fitzgerald. I'd appeared in the off-Broadway production, but now it was doing out-of-town productions on its way to Broadway. Because I'd performed it off-Broadway before my accident, I still knew all the lines, so my memory was not an issue. But I clashed with Fitzgerald about how to play my character, a young seminarian named Rio.

We were in a pre-Broadway run in Boston when Geraldine kept saying, "You're not playing Rio right."

I said, "I'm playing how I'm playing it." After all, it had worked very well in our off-Broadway run.

She goes, "No, I changed it when we brought it to Ireland."

And I said again, "I'm playing it like I played it before."

And she said, "No."

And then after a lot of back-and-forth, I said, "I'm leaving."

Fitzgerald had won by pushing me out so she could hire an actor to do her version of Rio. I had gotten a lot of accolades for playing it my way, but she wanted me to be a "golly gee whiz" sort of character, whereas I played him passionate, mad, angry. I made him a thinker, and then I made him Christlike.

Here's how *The New York Times* reported my leaving the play, in October of 1981:

> Because of medical problems resulting from injuries suffered in an automobile accident in June, Eric Roberts has withdrawn from Bill C. Davis's comedy "Mass Appeal," which is in previews in Boston. The play's scheduled opening in New York at the Booth Theater on Oct. 29 has been postponed.
>
> A new opening date and a replacement for Mr. Roberts are to be announced shortly. . . . Mr. Roberts co-starred with Milo O'Shea in the highly acclaimed original production of "Mass Appeal" two seasons ago at the Manhattan Theater Club. He opened opposite Mr. O'Shea in Boston Tuesday night and received favorable reviews, but decided to leave the production the next day because he was having problems with his speech and mobility on the stage. He had been in a coma for three days and had broken both ankles in the automobile accident.

After I quit the play, Geraldine Fitzgerald told everybody that I wasn't fully healed from my car accident. That was partly true. I know I suffered some brain damage, and it's possible I fucked up the part of Rio because of lingering trauma from my car accident. I still had big empty spaces in my head.

For a while, the phone calls stopped. No one called me—except Bob Fosse, who said, "I want you to come in and audition." This was in 1982, and I was about to take on a role that would change the trajectory of my career—for good or for ill.

V. *Star 80*—1983

Do you need to be crazy
to play crazy?

—Eric Roberts

As a kid growing up in Georgia and as a young actor in New York, my two favorite directors were Hal Ashby and Bob Fosse. It's hard to believe that Hal Ashby's been gone for thirty-five years, and that he was only fifty-nine years old when he died. His name is less well known now, but his movies are immortal.

Harold and Maude costarred the great Ruth Gordon, who wrote one of the most charming memoirs about this strangely beautiful profession of acting that I've ever read. *Harold and Maude* is a story almost as unlikely as my own. It's the tale of a twenty-year-old, played by the irresistibly shy, bespectacled actor Bud Cort, a young man obsessed with thoughts of suicide whose life is turned upside down by falling in love with Ruth Gordon, a magnificently oddball eighty-year-old.

I suppose the reason the movie made such a lasting impression on me is the idea of how love really is salvation and rescue. Ashby went on to make many other wonderful films, such as

Being There with the genius Peter Sellers and *The Last Detail* with Jack Nicholson, Randy Quaid, and an actress from Bill Treusch's stable, the Pre-Raphaelite-looking Carol Kane. Let's not forget *Coming Home*, one of the most powerful anti-war films ever made, costarring Jane Fonda and my *Runaway Train* cohort Jon Voight.

I would have loved to have played in any of Mr. Ashby's films, even the Warren Beatty role in *Shampoo*, or Woody Guthrie in *Bound for Glory*. What a beautiful gift to the world those movies were, even if I didn't get to be a part of any of them.

I would soon have my chance to work with one of those two directors—Bob Fosse.

Fosse was a horse of a different color. In fact, he was more like a pantomime horse, made up of two different people inside the same animal. He was a creature of the American musical theater, directing legendary shows such as *Pajama Game*, *Damn Yankees*, and *How to Succeed In Business Without Really Trying*, and while he kept his hand and his genius in musical theater—directing *Pippin* and the it-will-run-forever musical *Chicago*—it was the siren song of the movies that began to draw his attention away from the stage to the soundstage. He brilliantly directed *Cabaret* and *Lenny* (about the great and deeply troubled comedian Lenny Bruce) and *All That Jazz*, which was a kind of Fosse fever dream about his own career.

As a young man, I would have traded a few years of my life to have been in a Bob Fosse movie or any of Hal Ashby's films.

Though Hal Ashby and I never came together, when I heard that Fosse was doing this movie called *Star 80*, a tragic story that I had first read about when it appeared on the cover of *The Village Voice* in November of 1980, I wanted in.

Titled "Death of a Playmate" by Teresa Carpenter, the article told the terrible story of Dorothy Stratten. Dorothy was a *Playboy* playmate originally from Vancouver, British Columbia, who went to Hollywood at the urging of her boyfriend and then husband, a small-time hustler by the name of Paul Snider. He first saw the beautiful and naive Dorothy at a Dairy Queen; and besides falling for her, he saw Dorothy as his passport to a bigger and more glamorous life in the bubbling cauldron of American entertainment.

It all ended horribly when, on August 14, 1980, Dorothy Stratten and her by-then-estranged husband were found dead on his bedroom floor. It didn't take the police very long to determine that Snider had shot Stratten in the head before turning the rifle on himself. This grim tale would win Carpenter a Pulitzer Prize and it would soon send Bob Fosse on a treasure hunt for the right actor to play Paul Snider.

Fosse had already chosen Mariel Hemingway for the role of Dorothy Stratten. Mariel had been so fresh and pretty in Woody Allen's *Manhattan* the year before Dorothy Stratten met her terrible fate. Mariel is a wonderful actress, but I wondered what the long-term effects might have been portraying an abused, murdered woman. I know that people say, "It's all just acting," but to do it right, you do give a piece of yourself away and put it into someone else, the person you're portraying. And after fifty years of this work, I can safely say you don't always get those pieces back. I think it's why so many actors feel so empty at the twilight of their careers—there's just nothing left of who they started out to be.

Now Fosse had to find the right actor to play Paul Snider. He was auditioning everybody, meeting actors both high and low—unknown actors, TV actors, big movie stars, everybody. Fosse was voracious in his search, like an engine that was always going, always putting out sparks and heat. After all, I soon realized, he was a methamphetamine addict and everything was RIGHT NOW! It was everything at once!

The studio, Warner Bros., and the Ladd Company had wanted Fosse to go with Richard Gere, and in all honesty, Fosse liked the idea. Richard Gere is one good actor, and he was a pretty hot property after *American Gigolo*. If I had to guess, I'd say the studio would have preferred Richard. I found out much later that Fosse had his heart set on Robert De Niro, but I don't believe that got very far at all.

Sam Shepard, surprisingly, also read for Paul Snider. I knew Sam from *Raggedy Man*. We both loved Sissy Spacek. During *Raggedy Man*, Sam made a little home for himself in a barn near where we were filming. I used to climb the hill and visit him there. Two country boys talking, laughing, twirling a strand of hay in our mouths. I had always longed to do one of Sam's plays. I felt I was born to be in work like *Buried Child*, *Fool for Love*, *True West*, or *Killer's Head*, which is about the thoughts of a man sitting in the electric chair. Richard Gere played him a long time ago when he was a young actor in New York, long before his movie stardom.

Later, I would lose a part I wanted to Richard Gere, in Taylor Hackford's magnificent film, *An Officer and a Gentleman*—but more on that later. There are so many crossed wires in an actor's life, it can become hard to separate them. With all those entanglements, your life can resemble a country radio, like the one that was in my grandfather's house, rewired and put together a thousand times.

I had just quit *Mass Appeal*, so I was unemployed. When I got that call from Fosse, I thought, *Okay, I gotta read for this.* Bill Treusch got me the script. I read it, did not like it, did not like the character, thought he was way too one-dimensional, and I didn't wanna play this obviously bad asshole as an obviously bad asshole. I thought the writing, at least as far as Paul was concerned, was too much on the nose. He was just a dick from A to Z. The part just screamed, "I am a dick!" from every page.

But when I met Fosse (who didn't know I'd already read the script), we talked for a long time and he had me read for part.

He gave me some pages and said, "I want you to memorize 'em for me, come back, and we're gonna go again."

I said, "Cool. Okay."

I don't remember what those scenes were, or if he was just watching me be an actor. I ended up going back five times, and every time we'd read and we'd read—it was not even an audition anymore. It was more like an actor session with Fosse. I'd be in there for ninety minutes or maybe longer. On the fifth time he asked me, "Will you do me a favor?"

I said, "Sure, what's up?"

"Walk around this room."

So I walked around the room clockwise, and then counterclockwise.

I knew Fosse was a dancer and a revered choreographer, but Snider was certainly no dancer, so I wasn't certain what was going on, but of course, I did it. I practically skipped around the room. Then he said, "Have a seat."

I sat down as if waiting for a judge to hand down his verdict.

"I was told you were crippled."

I said, "No!"

"Want to make my movie?"

"Oh, dude, yes."

Fosse looked at me for a while, then said, "I was told you were a cripple and I'm looking at you. You're obviously not a cripple. You have a little limp."

I said, "Yeah, I do."

"The first time I noticed it was when I was actually looking for it. Interesting."

"Who told you I was a cripple?"

He wouldn't tell me, but I figured it was Geraldine. I explained, "I quit her play."

Fosse cracked up. "Yeah, they'll get mad if you quit their plays." And that was all he said about it.

Fosse kept calling me back, and he asked more questions of me than a census taker. Where did I go to school, did I have any hobbies (yeah, dude, acting!). On one of my callbacks, we read through the entire script. After that, I thought I had this in the bag, but Richard Gere was still in the picture.

Fosse summoned me one more time. He wanted to read through one of the more difficult scenes, a scene he himself had been grappling with and doing a lot of rewrites for. It was a very hard and challenging scene. It's where Paul visits the Playboy mansion for the very first time. He's clearly in heaven, but he's also clearly out of his depth (which is saying something, as the mansion itself was a kind of lower depths—never my scene in real life). I had to show Snider's desperate nature and his clearly ineffectual, smarmy charm. I guess it worked. Fosse gave me the part.

As Dorothy Stratten had the dubious honor of being a "Playmate of the Year" in Hugh Hefner's *Playboy* magazine, he had approval over everything. I met him, and he seemed like a weird dude to me. I liked him, I thought he was clever, but I also thought he was ridiculous. You know, he sold the Playboy mansion for $44 million, with the prerequisite that he'd be allowed to die there in his bedroom. And the guy who bought it said okay, so Hef lived there three more years and died in his bedroom, surrounded by three very young blondes who cared for him but, I'm guessing, took him for a lot of money.

In preparing to play Paul Snider, I struggled to find a way to make this character multidimensional. In one scene, as the disaster unfolds, I look into the mirror and say about Dorothy, "She broke my heart." It's one of the few places where we can feel any sympathy for the poor bastard. I also felt there had to be some reason why Dorothy, this lovely innocent from western Canada, fell in love with him. So I met with his brother, Peter, who was in L.A. at the time, and through him I got a better idea of what drove Snider. We spent only a day or two together, but I formed a mental image of Paul Snider as overdressed, overbrushed, over-cologned, over-ready for everything, though he didn't make a bad first impression.

But those two days I spent with Peter were rough! He didn't really like the idea of me playing his brother, or even of this picture being made, so he began stalking and threatening me.

Early in the shoot, he called me and asked me to meet him at the Comstock Hotel, then called "the Coms," near Westwood, where I was staying during the film shoot.

I agreed, and soon I heard banging on my door. It was Peter. I let him in and said, "Have a seat," then dashed into the bathroom to finish dressing. When the phone suddenly rang, I called out to Peter to please answer it for me.

"I'm not gonna answer your fucking phone."

When I came out of the bathroom, Peter said, "So you're making this movie for Mr. Fosse?"

I said yes.

"Hell, if you make it, I will consider putting you in my version of the same story." He obviously shared the same insecurities and resentments as his brother, Paul.

I told him I would think about it. And then he left, and we never spoke again.

But I did get an important clue to the character. Dorothy must have been dazzled by Snider at first—his fancy appearance and his promises of fame and wealth—until she later met someone like Peter Bogdanovich, someone with a first-class mind and real accomplishments, with more sophisticated taste. Dorothy was smart enough to know the difference, and when that happened, Paul was a fried egg—he was doomed.

To further prepare for the part, Fosse was my Virgil through the dark life of L.A. strip clubs. He thought I should know this world to better know who Paul Snider was. Fosse was smart about the psychology of the sex worker. I remember his saying that they often have the same problems in life that molested children have. That shook me to my core. I never enjoyed such places. I felt bad for the women who had to parade themselves before these gawking men just so they could feed their kids and take care of their families. I always felt uncomfortable during those visits with Fosse, and then he would do this really underhanded thing of suddenly disappearing, leaving me there to chat up the strippers on my own. I know that people say the dancers are the empowered ones in strip clubs, that they're in control, but if that were true, why did every one of those places need half a dozen bouncers to keep the women safe? I just didn't dig it, ever.

Throughout the shoot, I felt apprehensive for Fosse, for Mariel Hemingway, for myself, for everyone on the set of *Star 80*. We all knew what the ending of the movie was going to be, and none of us wanted to go there. We all were hoping Snider would put down the rifle and let Dorothy go home. I know Fosse struggled with that. I struggled with it in my usual way—I became impossible to be around. Maybe Snider had gotten too deeply under my skin. For whatever reason, I began manifesting him to the point that it was imperiling the entire production and infuriating Fosse.

I would yell at people for no reason, lock myself in the trailer, and violently kick the door from the inside. I knew that Fosse was bothered. I could tell because he'd become especially nice. He was like that only because he found himself inside a tiger cage with a wild animal. At the same time, he would always find ways of reminding me who I was: I wasn't Eric Roberts. I was Paul Snider, and don't you forget it. He would even show up at my house in the middle of the night and bang on the door, yelling up to the bedroom.

One of the more devious things that Fosse did to Mariel and myself was telling me to drop the protective belt just before shooting our sex scene. I was thrown back to the past, when I simply did everything my father told me to do even if somewhere deep inside, I knew it was wrong. Here we go again: Fosse was becoming another dangerous father figure to me.

He offered up some lame excuse to Mariel, but we were both terribly uncomfortable. Of course, that's exactly what Fosse had intended, to show Dorothy's discomfort. I'm quite a prude about things like that, but I did as I was told.

At the same time, I did find ways to rebel against Fosse's authority, but it only succeeded in alienating everyone around me—makeup artists, hairdressers, grips, there was no one I didn't piss off during much of the making of *Star 80*. But I can't blame it all on Paul Snider, or even on Bob Fosse.

Then again, Fosse knew what he was doing. My behavior had put me right where he wanted me, where Snider found himself in Hollywood, in Hefner's own twisted universe, the kind of isolation that would end in Snider's lashing out and destroying his world—and Dorothy with it.

Another scene haunts me from making that movie, though it ended up giving me the key to the character.

We'd spent three months doing our research before we ever shot a frame. We were together every day for ninety days, day in and day out. Fosse was so fucking wired all the time. At one point, we were filming on the soundstage at Zoetrope Studios, which was owned by Francis Ford Coppola, the great filmmaker behind *The Godfather*, and I blew one of my lines. I called out, "Cut!"

Fosse lost his mind. "What the fuck is wrong with you? You don't call 'cut' on a Bob Fosse set, unless you're Bob Fosse."

He walked across the set. I'm in my Fruit of the Loom underwear with a guitar in my hand. I walked over to him, barefoot, some thirty yards away from the crew.

"Look at me," he said.

I said, "I'm looking at you."

He said again, "Look at *me*."

I said, "I'm looking at you, man."

He goes, "Okay, you're playing *me* as if I weren't successful. Do you understand?"

I understood all too well. I watched his little dancer's ass twitching back and forth as he walked away. For the rest of the movie, I didn't take my eyes off Bob Fosse. Every mannerism of Fosse, I licked up like a cat at a saucer of milk. As a result, I still marvel at my performance. I'm just not capable of that all by myself—I owe every inflection, every innuendo, every body movement to Bob Fosse. I think my portrayal of Paul Snider was more Bob Fosse than Roy Scheider playing Fosse in *All That Jazz!* I thought he was a genius—it's a much overused and abused word, especially in the movie business—but he was.

Perhaps the cruelest thing that Fosse could have done to me was something he thought he *had* to do. He asked me to spend the night with him at 10881 Clarkson Road, in the apartment where Paul Snider murdered Dorothy Stratten.

"Can you do it?"

"Yeah, I can do it."

It was Walter Roberts all over again. I couldn't refuse this man I admired, feared, and loved.

We stayed up most of the night and talked about the ending, the ending of our movie, the ending of these two lives. Fosse had filled the apartment with furniture to make it look as close to the way things had been on that terrible August night in 1980. Fosse, incredibly enough, fell asleep, but I was restless and the noise from the freeway kept me awake most of the night. Frankly, that was fucked up and weird, but Fosse did that shit all the time.

When it came time to shoot the scene, Fosse had choreographed it as though it were a ballet, a *danse macabre*. Fosse talked us through every moment, every gesture, leaving nothing to improvisation or to chance. Between awful coughing jags that plagued him throughout the movie, he guided us through the terrible minutes of this catastrophe. The scene was staged using the police photographs—an overhead view of the carnage, with me as Snider on the floor, blood around my head.

The movie was finally over, but Paul Snider wasn't quite finished with me yet.

Cis Rundle was then known as Hugh Hefner's right hand at *Playboy*. Incredibly, Cis's first day on the job was the very day Dorothy was murdered. It was Cis who brought Hefner the news. For some reason, Cis had become Dorothy for me.

I would wait for her to get off work, though I must have looked like a ghost standing in front of her. I even found myself sitting in her house alone watching TV, waiting for her, uninvited.

I would discover later that Fosse suggested Cis get a restraining order against me, but she never did. She felt too sorry for me, I guess. I suppose, looking back on it now, that I was at loose ends after *Star 80.* My nervous system along with my reason had shut down.

I still had a Paul Snider–like virus in my system, and Cis Rundle was my way of holding on to Dorothy, and, in a pathetic way, to Paul Snider himself.

It's a bit of a blur now, but when it was all over, I remember asking Cis if she would mind driving me to the Westwood Village Park cemetery, which is located, appropriately enough, behind a multiplex movie theater on Wilshire Boulevard. It's where Marilyn Monroe is buried. (Hugh Hefner bought the crypt next to Marilyn, so he finally got his wish to be near her, even if it was more necrophilia than romance.)

Cis stayed in the car while I bounded over to the cemetery. When I came to Dorothy's headstone, I dropped to my knees and started weeping. It all came out of me at that moment: inhabiting such a dark and disturbed soul, giving myself over to Fosse like I hadn't done since the days with my father, and just the terrible tragedy of Dorothy, her young life snuffed out too soon.

I reached in my pocket for my wallet and took out my membership card to SAG, the Screen Actors Guild, and I tore it up. I just let the wind blow the pieces away.

You know that expression, that more tears are shed over answered prayers than over unanswered ones? There's so much truth to that. I experienced it with *Star 80.* Snider's anger and dissolution seemed to have fused with my own, at least for a while.

For months after the movie's release, I would be walking down some of my favorite streets in Manhattan and I began to notice women crossing the street to avoid me. The first dozen or so times this happened, I felt weird, but then I asked Chris Walken, "Why is that? I'm sure they're avoiding me."

"Because you're fuckin' spooky, dude," Chris said.

It was the beginning of my being cast as a troubled and possibly dangerous guy. It seemed to plant the flag of misconception deep into the ground of my career that I was simply playing myself in the movies. My performance as the desperate, bottom-feeding Paul Snider in *Star 80* showed the world what a convincing psychopath I could be. I've played crazy as much as the most crazy-playing actors. Apparently, I portray crazy convincingly, but do you need to be crazy to play crazy? I think that was the role that typecast me as a psychopath—a role and an image I couldn't shake.

VI. *The Pope of Greenwich Village*—1984

It was risky to cast me.

—Eric Roberts

Pope of Greenwich Village? That came around 1983, '84. That's when I got caught up with the Italians in Little Italy.

It's 1983, and there was an actor in the White House, Ronald Reagan. I was in Hartford, Connecticut, appearing in Tennessee Williams's *The Glass Menagerie* when Treusch sent me the script for *The Pope of Greenwich Village*, accompanied by a note from the producers offering me one of two lead roles—either Paulie or Charlie, who are Italian cousins who run afoul of the mob after pulling off a heist.

I not only read the script but I also took three weeks and studied it like a Talmudic scholar. I chose to play Paulie, the younger and edgier cousin. But the producers, Gene Kirkwood and Hawk Koch, had other ideas. They were hoping I'd play Charlie because they didn't think I looked tough enough to play Paulie, the hotheaded, wannabe mobster.

But that was the point. I didn't *want* to look tough. I told the producers that I wanted to play Paulie as a momma's boy who yearns to be a tough guy. I felt I knew guys like this—guys who wanted to be fierce to cover up being wounded. Paulie thinks a great deal of himself, but he's also scared of life. He's not a brave man. He's a weak little man with a very small penis.

So I lost thirty pounds in a hurry. In those days, the weight just melted off me. I had my hair permed and got ready to play Paulie as a hyped-up, reckless dumbass who ends up getting his thumb sliced off by a pair of Bedbug Eddie's mobster henchmen.

Messrs. Kirkwood and Koch were not pleased with my dramatic weight loss or my interpretation of the role.

"That's not what's written," they told me.

I'm like, "Have you read the book? Read the book. You're gonna be happy, so just let me fly."

My costar, Mickey Rourke, who would play Charlie, the more serious and grown-up cousin, didn't like my interpretation either, not at first. That's not how any of them saw my role.

By August, my permed hair and I were skating on thin ice. We had five days of rehearsal before we started shooting. I was ready to go. I knew every word of dialogue, not just my own. I spent my off-camera time in character, hanging out a lot in Little Italy. I wanted to know all the lingo, all the body language. In fact, I spent so much time in Little Italy that after we finished *Pope*, I never had to pay for another cup of espresso again. One thing I learned about Italian mobsters—they *like* to be portrayed in the movies. We found that out with the *Godfather* films, though Mario Puzo, who wrote those movies and the book they were based on, sweated a few bullets before he realized that.

All my research paid off. I took eight months to get ready to play Paulie, and I was thrilled to be there.

Three days in, the director asked me to resign.

Who was the director? None other than Michael Cimino of *Heaven's Gate* fame—or infamy. Cimino's career was derailed by that movie's disastrous reception in 1980. An epic retelling of the Johnson County range wars in Wyoming, *Heaven's Gate* went so over budget the movie collapsed under its own weight. (People are beginning to reconsider the movie, though, and some think it's a masterpiece.) However, Cimino is rightly revered for directing *The Deer Hunter*, a harrowing, unforgettable film about the lives of four men newly returned from the war in Vietnam. I would've been honored to be in either one of those films. But I guess it was not meant to be, because another director, Ron Maxwell was hired to take Cimino's place. There was one day, I'll never forget, it was early on, Maxwell sent Mickey off somewhere and asked me to stay after and talk to him, so I did.

He says, "Ah, thank God we're alone. Why are you so skinny?"

I said, "I wanna be a walking spaz attack."

"Why do you perm your hair?"

I said same thing, and I shake my hair.

He goes. "What the fuck is a walking spaz attack?"

"It's feeling constantly threatened. It's John Belushi, only skinny."

"But this guy, Paulie, is a tough thug."

"But that's not how I'm playing it. I see him as a wannabe mobster, but he's never gonna make it."

Maxwell goes, "No, no, no, no, no!"

He's having a fit, and I could tell he thought I was ruining the character. That's when he asked me to resign. If you've ever seen the air go out of a Macy's parade balloon, that was me. I was flattened. This time, I didn't understand why I was fired.

By then, I was so invested, I knew I wasn't going to just walk away. I realized he meant it, so I said, "Let me think about it."

He gave me till the next day to either change my interpretation or resign from the movie.

During the shoot, we were all staying at the Mayflower Hotel near Columbus Circle in New York. I walked around the hotel thinking, *This is kinda fucked up.* I didn't know what to do, so I asked my manager. Treusch would know what to do—any advice he ever gave me I took completely because he was the guy, I thought, who knew his shit. After all, he'd discovered Chris Walken, he discovered Carol Kane, he discovered Sissy Spacek, he discovered me! If I had an issue, I'd go to him.

But first, I went up to Mickey's room in the Mayflower Hotel and knocked on his door.

Mickey seemed happy to see me. "What's up?"

"Maxwell asked me to resign."

"What?"

Mickey picked up the phone and called the producers, and they fired Maxwell on the spot! Practically before we hung up the phone, they hired Stuart Rosenberg to take over as director. Lucky for me, Stuart—who had directed *Cool Hand Luke* and *The Amityville Horror*—saw what I was going for with Paulie, and he let me run with it. Sometimes that's all it takes, someone with a little faith. I think it worked out. To this day, people seem to relate to Paulie as an unforgettable character, a driving piston of big dreams and bad ideas, especially when they see him trying to impress his cool, savvy and far more heroic cousin Charlie. It's a dynamic a lot of people have lived through.

In fact, I think my most favorite character I've ever played is Paulie. He's always unpredictable, and his lack of emotional depth of any kind is pretty stunning. I think my willingness to be as weak and afraid as he is in that movie is actually powerful.

Jump cut to many years later. There's a lot of talk about doing a sequel, a *Pope 2*, even though it was not a hit in the theaters the first time around—because I don't think they released it properly. It just didn't get a great release, but it eventually became a cult classic on video—I mean huge. How could it not—from that thrilling opening of Frank Sinatra singing "Summer Wind" stirring up every humid, human yearning, to Paulie's final, shocking humiliation—it's a beautiful movie.

But I got a call from somebody who was involved in the first *Pope* who said, "You think that Koch and Kirkwood and Rourke are your friends? They are not. Mickey told everybody that you were playing Paulie as a gay man and you were gonna ruin the movie. He was trying to get you out of it."

So that was the story behind the story! I was freaked out. I decided to go back to Little Italy and find one of the wiseguys that Mickey really admired. I still knew all of Mickey's contacts from those days.

I found him, and I went up to him, and I said, "I need a favor."

He said, "Anything."

"Here's what I need from you. I need you to go to Mickey and tell him Eric knows everything. Tell Mickey to make it right. I don't need an apology; just make it right. It's all over and has been for years, but before we're into *Pope 2*, please make it right."

Well, he did. The next month Mickey won the Independent

Spirit Award for his truly great performance in *The Wrestler*, and the first thing he did when he went up to receive the award was to send a shout-out to me. "Eric Roberts is the greatest actor!"

The sequel to *The Pope of Greenwich Village* never happened, but Mickey and I are still friends. And I have to admit, we were pretty great together, Mickey and I, even though I found out that Mickey might have known of Cimino's intention to fire me. But when push came to shove, he did the right thing.

In fact, Mickey is my role model for an actor who turned it all around and got the major recognition he deserved later in life. A hell of an actor, immensely watchable, he's given some incredible performances. You can see the sparkle in Mickey. I've been known to say that on *The Pope of Greenwich Village*, and in movies like *Diner* and *Body Heat*, you just sit there watching him and go, "Say, who was that!" He's a raw, turned-inside-out person, like the Invisible Man—those clear plastic models they used in order to teach us anatomy, where you see all the guts—you see Mickey's guts. But if you look closely at Mickey's Invisible Man, you would see that he has the biggest heart in the world. And his affection for me means so much.

I just wish Mickey had had more confidence about his looks. A lot of pretty boys—Rob Lowe, me, I guess—we start to look like old women as we age, while those character guys, like Mickey and Sean Penn, keep getting better looking. That happens with male faces, but that's not necessarily true with female faces. Take Mick Jagger, for example. Character. He now has a beautiful character actor's face. Mick is just gorgeous. Character ages them up.

Playing Paul Snider and Paulie (not only did they have the same name but they also were both dangerously charismatic sociopaths) in some way sealed my fate. Producers stopped thinking of me as a leading man. I was just too convincing in the roles of colossal fuckups living on the edge.

So when I was asked by Marty Scorsese to audition for the role of Jesus in *The Last Temptation of Christ*, I thought, *Here's my chance to break out of the straitjacket of typecasting—and work with a master.* We had about five auditions and the coolest screen test I've ever had, with Harvey Keitel. Harvey's an especially good actor for other actors to audition or work with.

Scorsese offered me the part, but, Reader, on the advice of my manager, I turned it down.

Why? Treusch said to me, "I gotta tell you, nobody gets away with playing Jesus."

It's hard to believe now, but that comment made sense to me at the time. Treusch pointed out that Max von Sydow didn't get away with it (though he continued to have a distinguished, if somewhat smaller, career). Jeffrey Hunter didn't get away with it. Treusch explained that playing Jesus was a kind of curse. I don't know if he was onto something or not, but my turning down the part destroyed the relationship I might have had with Scorsese. *Last Temptation* was his baby from the time he was a film student! He thought he'd found his Jesus in me, so when I turned it down, he got pissed off, and I don't blame him.

"Why'd you fucking audition?" he asked.

I said, "I wanted to come to your attention."

"You came to my attention."

I could've been in other movies with him, I'm sure, had I

played Jesus in *Last Temptation*. But he offered me his baby and I said no, and that was fucked up. The movies we could have made together! Damn. I think he holds a grudge against me to this day.

Why do people hold grudges? Show business is the most personal business there is. You have your hopes and dreams pinned on things, on places and events and circumstances, and you're rolled into a script. It's gonna be a movie, and suddenly somebody pulls their finger out of the dike and it springs a leak. And it's all very personal. Maybe somebody's assistant says, "He's got a square butt," and then you don't get the job because the director heard her say that. Negative tipping points, feelings hurt, and folks insulted at the drop of an ill-advised comment. It's fucked up, and it keeps you on a tight rope.

But I've discovered that in the movie business, you can't hold too many grudges. It's a business where your livelihood really does depend upon the kindness of strangers. Grudges, like a Louis Vuitton trunk, is one luxury I can't afford.

So, Bill Treusch, the man I most admired and listened to after Walter, gave me the good advice to stay with Paulie and stay in the picture. But he had me throw away my chance to work with Martin Scorsese. I came to wonder if I should be putting my whole trust in this father figure, especially when I found out he was abusing cocaine as much as I was.

All in all, with *Star 80* and *The Pope of Greenwich Village*, the 1980s were a good decade for me careerwise, and I topped that off by replacing John Malkovich on Broadway in Lanford Wilson's wonderful play *Burn This*.

In the old days—the eighties!—we all used to start out in

theater and tiptoe into film. People had begun to notice me when I was in Joe Papp's *Rebel Women* back in 1975, as I mentioned earlier. Theater was a springboard, but you didn't dare do television, much less commercials or voices for animation. It's changed a lot since then. As I became more known as a screen actor, I started to be in demand for plays.

Burn This opened off-Broadway in February 1987 and moved to the Plymouth Theatre on Broadway later that year, with John Malkovich in the starring role. When he left the show, the director, Marshall W. Mason, needed a replacement. (Mason was the founder and artistic director of the CRC, the Circle Repertory Company.) I was on that list, and they offered me the lead role of Pale, a cocaine-snorting, hyperactive restaurant manager—not a stretch for me! Pale is the brother of Robbie, a gay dancer who drowns in a boating accident—which also resonated with me. The wonderful actresses Lisa Emery and Joan Allen played Robbie's roommates in a SoHo loft. One of them, Anna (Lisa Emery), becomes involved with my character.

The director told me, "It's up to you whether you come and see John perform the role or not."

I decided not to watch Malkovich until after the rehearsal period, once I was really locked into how I would play the character, so I wouldn't be tempted to be overly influenced by him. But I did manage to see John in the role, and he was amazing. That part, by the way, would have a great lineage, reinterpreted through the years by a series of terrific actors, including Scott Glenn, right after me, followed by Peter Sarsgaard, Edward Norton, and Adam Driver.

It was risky to cast me. I had the passion and was willing to go big and do that great opening monologue as Pale, playing it to the hilt, but I was not sober at the time. One night I showed up drunk, and late—which I usually never did. However, I got there just in time, and getting on that stage sobered me up. I'm not recommending it, but I think it may have been one of my better performances. In any case, I won the 1987 Theatre World Award for my performance, the first replacement cast member to win that award.

There was something incredible about winning that award and getting recognized for that play. I started to hear from people who really wanted to see it but couldn't get a ticket, including Eliza and her mother, Lila Paris Garrett, whom I had yet to meet.

Being in that play and winning that award were among the greatest artistic experiences of my life. I never grew tired of it, especially working with such a wonderful cast. I even tried to get a revival of the play to happen while I was still young enough to play Pale. Doing a play as demanding as *Burn This*, knowing all those words cold, working with that caliber of actors in a theater with a live audience—I've never matched the sheer high of it, before, during, or since. After the strain of *Star 80* and *The Pope of Greenwich Village*, the play rekindled my love of acting.

My only regret is that my future wife, Eliza, didn't see me in it.

VII. Long-Ass Marriage

Redheads are descended from cats.

—Mark Twain

I don't really like most of my past, but I like my years with Eliza.

I met her in May of 1989. I captured her thirty-one years ago. Made it official twenty-nine years ago. I can safely say that she changed my life. Hell, she *gave* me my life, which has become much happier the longer I follow her lead.

With her blue eyes and auburn-red hair, Eliza has always been beautiful to me.

When I think back on when we met, seated beside each other on the MGM Grand Air flight with my cat, Tender, in a carrier on my lap, what struck me most was Eliza's hair. It was carrot-red—not that carrots are really red, but natural red hair is more of a burnt orange. (We have a granddaughter now, Magnolia, who has brought that hair color back into our lives. One of the most beautiful things in the world.) I flipped out when I read later—maybe it was Mark Twain—that redheads were descended from cats! Dante Gabriel Rossetti would have wanted to paint Eliza's wild, Pre-Raphaelite hair.

I spotted her the minute she got on the plane. The MGM Grand was the first airline to allow animals to sit with their passengers, as I was glad that I had Tender with me. And I was also glad that I had a giant bottle of Evian on my open tray table because I felt it would make a good impression on this fresh-faced, blue-eyed redhead seated next to me. Ever since I had a crush on Miss Kitty in *Gunsmoke* when I was a little boy, I was always attracted to redheads. But the first thing I noticed were her eyes. I knew she was my dream girl.

She hid a script she'd planned to read on the flight under the seat, trying to avoid having to talk shop. She finally took it out when I opened mine. Hers was *Intersection*, written by her father, David Rayfiel (who cowrote *Three Days of the Condor*, *Absence of Malice* [uncredited], and *'Round Midnight*) and was a creative partner of the director Sydney Pollack for forty years. The script she was reading was not yet a Richard Gere–Sharon Stone movie. It was an art film, for lack of a better genre to assign.

I had just been nominated for a Best Supporting Actor Academy Award for *Star 80*, and Rayfiel had just been given the nod for a screenwriting Oscar for *Out of Africa*. Despite my reputation for being under the influence, the day I met Eliza I was as sober as a hanging judge. Tender the cat was a big selling point for Eliza, though I know it bothered her when I turned down a little boy's request to pet my cat. The child walked past me on the plane and asked, "Can I see your kitty?" I don't know why, but I said, "He's *my* kitty." It was fucked up, I know, and I could tell that Eliza didn't think it was so cool either.

And with Tender sitting on my lap during the entire flight,

Eliza probably thought I was gay. That actually worked for me. It gave us a chance to become friends. I didn't have many of those back then—still don't. Later on, when she stopped thinking I was gay, she liked my "bad boy" image, which I seemed to have had all my acting life.

I rushed to take her untouched lunch tray off her table so she could get up to go "freshen up" (and sneak on a touch of mascara, I later learned). It's funny to think about it now. When we fly together, which is often, I pile all my crap onto Eliza's tray, eating my food off her overstocked tray table, and then eating her food too.

Three years and three months later, we were married. And that is a story in itself.

But there's no way to tell our story without telling Eliza's. She grew up in New York City, the granddaughter of your basic left-wing socialists. Very left wing. Her bedtime stories were more about Emma Goldman than Goldilocks. Eliza was what used to be called a "Goody Two-shoes." She was educated at Walden, a private day school on Central Park West. It was the kind of school where students addressed teachers by their first names, and they were encouraged to design their own course of study. I would've loved a school like that. After Walden, Eliza went to the United Nations International School (UNIS), where learning French took up much of the day. The lessons were all in French, so you either spoke the language or you sank like a stone.

By the age of seven or eight, after just two years at UNIS, Eliza was fluent in French. When her family moved to California, Eliza was bewildered to have a French teacher from the South who spoke French with a Southern accent ("Comprendre, y'all?").

Lila, Eliza's mother, insisted that her daughter wear stockings instead of socks to school, even though it got her into trouble with the dress code. But it was her mom's idea. When they moved to California, she got in trouble again, this time for wearing pants to Paul Revere Junior High School, but then she got into even more trouble for saying it was her mom who made her wear the pants.

Eliza would never admit that she wanted to be an actress until she was successful, so from a very young age, she kept telling herself that she was pre-med. She was going to be a hospital doctor—that's what she told everyone. She would also torment her successful, working mother with fantasies of becoming a housewife, that all she wanted was to grow up to be a mom and be very, very kind to her children. It must have driven Lila crazy, as that was Eliza's mother's idea of hell on earth. But it does tell you something about my wife's true obsession: she can't abide suffering in any living creature, and so she started acting because fake suffering is always better than real suffering.

In school plays, Eliza was clearly exceptional. She had gone to Oakwood when she was in senior high school, which is a very progressive, very artistic private school in Los Angeles. When she was fourteen, Eliza appeared in an adaptation of J. D. Salinger's *Franny and Zooey* in 1967. Now, it was widely known that Salinger never approved of any theatrical adaptation of his work, but it shows you what kind of place Oakwood was, that they went ahead and did it anyway. All of Eliza's important people were in the audience: Lila, with her husband at the time, screenwriter Bernie Kahn; Don Garrett, Lila's previous husband with his current wife, who was twenty-three years old and spelled her name Annee; and

Eliza's biological father, David Rayfiel. There were clearly dramas on both sides of the klieg lights.

Eventually, Eliza got her Screen Actors Guild card in 1974, met up with the director John Landis, who eventually offered her the role of Brunella in *National Lampoon's Animal House* and later, *Schlock*. She was pregnant with Keaton during the making of that now classic comedy, the forerunner of everything from *Ghostbusters* to the *Hangover* movies. (I guess you could say that Keaton was the youngest member of the 1977 *Animal House* cast, having been a fetus during the filming.) Eliza's been acting ever since, whereas I've been acting *out* ever since, with a little acting on the side. Not really, but I'm sure by now, you catch my drift.

I was a chronic fiancé. Along the way, I had proposed to Sandy Dennis, Kelly Cunningham, and the actress and singer Dana Wheeler-Nicholson, and probably a few others. (Dana appeared in *Fletch*, *Friday Night Lights*, and *The Night We Never Met*, an apt description of how that relationship turned out.) I might have even given a few of them the same ring. Eliza was kind of a hippie when it came to marriage. She wasn't especially interested in the state of matrimony, although she had been married and divorced before I met her. She was pregnant when she started shooting *Animal House*, and she had no time to get married, but Lila wanted her to. Eliza told her mother she didn't believe in marriage, and Lila said, "If you don't believe in it, as I do after four marriages, get married for *me*!"

So she did.

Here's how it happened. August 16, 1992, was a day I will always remember. I'd woken up with the sun, looked west out of one of the bedroom windows at the very still, half-mile-wide Hudson River.

I looked over to my right at the woman with strawberry-red hair sleeping beside me. Her eyes cracked open as if on cue. I told her I loved her. She said, "I love you, too."

I asked, "Will you marry me?"

She said, "Yes."

"When should we do this?" I asked.

"Whenever you'd like," she replied.

"How 'bout today?"

After coffee we called the local doctor, an older, hard-of-hearing gentleman, to ask about the need for blood tests. When he learned of the immediate nature of the event, he said not to worry, he'd take care of it.

"By the way, where are you two doin' the deed?" he asked.

"Woodstock."

Why Woodstock? Because we loved its Main Street, and I had always been charmed by a swinging sign that read: JUSTICE OF THE PEACE / MARRIAGES / LIQUOR LICENSES.

Before we left to get married, we went downstairs where fourteen-year-old Keaton and his friend, Lisa, happened to be watching *The Pope of Greenwich Village* for the first time. Eliza said, "Eric just asked me to marry him and he meant today, so, do you want to come? You'll be the only guests, though you can't be witnesses because you're both minors, but we'll find a witness."

They were so involved in the movie, and Keaton didn't want to leave Lisa alone, so they opted not to come. Talk about *meta*—Keaton preferred watching me in a movie than watching me in real time marry his mother!

We were the only two people in Woodstock that day who were dressed up, Woodstock being famous for a little three-day concert in 1969 and its general casualness. The husband-to-be (me!) looked regal in my Confederate gray Brioni suit with a monochromatic shirt and tie. My soon-to-be Better Half looked confidently unpretentious in a navy, ankle-length skirt with an off-white blouse, topped off with a blue silk dinner jacket borrowed from my closet.

We said our *I do*'s in the presence of the justice of the peace and his wife, who served as witness and who took the only two pictures we would forever have of the event. But you can see in those photos we looked just like we felt—in love, and proud of each other.

When we returned on the slow drive back along the Hudson, we told Keaton that the deed was done. I was glad to hear that he approved, having told his mom weeks earlier, "Ya know, Mom, I think I love the guy." This was all that Husband-to-Be—now Husband—needed to feel accepted, and for all the right reasons. (I would recall that remark with great comfort and pride many times over the course of my up-and-down relationship with Keaton, but I'll get to that later.) One thing Eliza had neglected to tell me at the time, however, was that she was already married.

She had never dissolved a marriage she'd made with a Canadian guy named Byron Lucas, mostly so he could get a green card and work as an actor in the United States, and she could work freely as a local hire in Canada.

Say what?

Lucas wasn't the father of Eliza's two children—that was her first husband, Jimmy Simons. I knew Lucas only as a friend of

Eliza's; and I have to admit, I was very jealous, but I didn't know that she had married him. I hadn't even known on the day I suggested we get married. In fact, I never knew any of this until I came to write this book, when Eliza decided to tell me that she was a bigamist the day I married her!

So when I said to Eliza that morning, "Go ahead, take a shower, and let's go!" she was probably thinking, *Oh fuck*, but neither of us really knew that much about how you get married. We were babes in the marriage woods of upstate New York.

Earlier, we had been driving around and I had been telling Eliza that if we had a wedding, I'd want it to be on a beautiful estate. Of course, truth be known, if she had said to her family, "Eric asked me to marry him," she would have had lunch dates from here to eternity with people trying to figure out how to talk her out of it. So that morning, she just put on her prettiest skirt, and I put on my nicest suit.

We were so naive! We thought maybe you had to go to a church or a temple or something. There was no excuse, except that we weren't traditional, and we lived on Planet Show Business. I suppose Eliza's mother should have been able to tell her since she was married so many times herself—four legal marriages, one annulment, three divorces, plus seventeen years of common-law marriage—but I'm not sure she wouldn't have known either, as she lived on the same planet as ours.

Before heading to the justice of the peace, Eliza and I went to the Kingston Courthouse to get a license. They entered our names into a computer database, and Eliza just recently told me that she had been terrified that her marriage to Byron Lucas would pop up. How would she explain that? She was prepared to say, "No, that wasn't really a marriage, it was an arrangement so I could work in Canada." But for some reason, her previous marriage never did appear, maybe because it had taken place in Las Vegas.

Apparently, Eliza had already spoken to a lawyer who'd helped her with the dissolution of her marriage to Lucas. Eliza's lawyer warned her against getting married again before that marriage could be dissolved, and Eliza, who hates to disappoint anyone, even her lawyer, said, "Don't worry, I won't do it then." But she didn't mean it at all.

I had pictured a wedding on a vast estate, the most expensive wedding in the history of weddings. Instead it was cheaper than going out for breakfast. Little did I know that, during the entire day, Eliza was waiting for someone to come and arrest her.

Not long after our wedding, Eliza called her lawyer again and admitted, "Well, we did get married."

"Okay," she said, "but the marriage is not valid. So if you want to be married to Eric, we will have to get this other marriage dissolved, and you'll need to do the wedding again."

I should have sensed something when, just a few months later, Eliza casually said, "Let's get married again."

"You mean a big wedding?" because I really wanted that with her.

But she said, "No, let's just go to the same guy." And so we did.

I don't even remember what we wore the second time, and when we got there, the justice of the peace couldn't quite understand why we were back. "We just want to renew our vows," Eliza told him.

"Well," the justice of the peace said, "that usually comes a little later than just a few months after the first wedding." But he married us anyway.

I swear to you, Eliza just confessed all of this to me while I've been working on this part of the book. I asked her how she was able to pull the wool over my eyes so expertly. She said that I'm the easiest person in the world to gaslight, because I can't keep track of anything, that between the drugs and my car accident, it wasn't hard to keep me in the dark. I like to think that it's something of a compliment. She didn't want me to change my mind, and she didn't want me to say, "Let's wait."

And here we are, over thirty-two years later, still married.

I've had cats all my life, ever since I was a little boy, so I know cats. I've never seen anybody better with cats than my wife. Now, I had a relationship with one other cat woman in my past—Sandy Dennis. As I mentioned earlier, when I first met Sandy, she had around thirty-five cats, but by the end of our relationship she had a hundred, so I know what it's like to live in a houseful of cats.

I've always been great with animals but I've never seen anybody better with them than the woman I married. She makes friends with all kinds of fucking animals! There's her Russian Blue, and they communicate. They kiss and they talk, and they share like you would with a two-and-a-half-year-old child. It's the same kind of relationship, and it's mind blowing.

She also has a relationship with squirrels, and I do too, now. They're very used to people, and we feed them walnuts out of our hands. I quickly became fascinated by their delicate hands. Eliza grew up in New York City, where squirrels were practically the state bird (if you pardon the mixed metaphor), and she would say about their hands, "How come I never noticed this before?"

When we realized we had a ton of squirrels living on our property, we began to stock up on walnuts, which they won't touch now, after all these years. They're very picky and just want spoiled walnuts, so one of our biggest panics is not having at least twenty pounds of walnuts in the house. It's even in my will. We've always got nuts in the car (and I don't mean Eliza and myself).

We have raccoons, possums, squirrels, and now, even a few ducks. We had a possum living in our house. He would just hang out part of the year, and we'd see him only once at night. He'd come through from his hiding place, past our bedroom, and kind of tip his hat, as if to say, "Hey dude, hello, just passing through."

In the beginning of our relationship when Eliza and I were having all this wild sex, she told me, "I thought you should know, I get pregnant very easily." Eliza already had two kids—Keaton and her daughter, Morgan, known as Prairie, and we didn't want any more, so I decided to have a vasectomy.

You see, we thought we were old when we got married, but we were only in our mid-thirties. Eliza was such a young parent that her kids were already teenagers, and I already had a baby girl, Emma, though I only got to live with her and her mother for eight months before I blew that whole relationship. By then, Eliza had probably figured out that I was a big baby who would need a lot of care and feeding, so I decided to put my money where my balls were and get a vasectomy.

My doctor was Dr. Sharron Mee, who happened to be a woman.

Dr. Mee's vasectomy room had a lot of humorous art hanging on the walls, like a drawing of an elephant with big balls, and a caption that read "If yours look like this, come and see me." She was being assisted by Manuel, a male nurse practitioner. Throughout the procedure, I was awake but, thankfully, couldn't feel a thing. Nonetheless, I'd asked Eliza to be in the room with me. (I guess I am a big baby after all.)

At one point, we both panicked when we heard Dr. Mee ask for a size 2.3 clamp, and Manuel told her, "We don't have any 2.3's."

"Well, go into the cupboard and look for some 2.5's."

He comes back and tells her they only have 3.5's.

At this point, Eliza starts to sound worried, asking, "Is this okay? Should we come back another day? Would you like me to run down to the pharmacy?"

They must have found what they needed, because they finished up and I tell the doctor that I'm supposed to fly to New York the next day.

"Why didn't you tell me that sooner? Why did you schedule your vasectomy now?"

"Well, can I go, doc?"

"It's a very bad idea, Eric. There's always a slight risk of infection. You need to stay home for a couple of days."

But, as was often the case, I didn't heed her advice. I got on a plane the next day and went back to Rhinecliff, where the nearest hospital was two and a half hours away. The following day, I woke up and looked at my balls—they're as big as two Bartlett pears in a Cézanne still life and they're definitely turning blue. Oh, my God.

I called my wife. "Honey, my balls! They're blue and something's wrong."

I didn't want to talk to Dr. Mee about this, so I asked Eliza if she would call Dr. Liu, her doctor, but he was on call to deliver a baby. God bless her, Eliza got Dr. Liu on the phone for me. He asked, "Eric, what's up?" He probably thought I was dying.

"Dr. Liu, I'm freaking out. I have giant-sized balls after my vasectomy. They're very blue and the closest hospital is over two hours away. What should I do?"

Dr. Liu says, "Eric, do you realize I'm a gynecologist? My patients are all women, and it's not even legal for me to treat a male."

But I was desperate. I said, "But you're a guy, aren't you? You have balls."

Dr. Liu says, "This is true. Okay, how can I help you?"

I explained the problem, and he ended up reassuring me. "It's not a problem. It happens all the time. Just take an antibiotic and you'll be fine."

So I did and I was.

My life with Eliza hasn't all been smooth—far from it—though I never stopped loving her. Of course, what everybody wonders is: were we faithful to each other? After all, Hollywood marriages are notoriously perilous. Or, more to the point, was *I* faithful? Plus there were all those love scenes I acted in all those years, all those temptations, all that fiery passion—how did we handle that?

First of all, I never went after my costars in a movie, no matter how much chemistry there was between us. I know that's a violation of everyone's expectations about actors. In fact, the most romantic role I ever played onscreen was as a gay man playing opposite Gregory Harrison in *It's My Party*, a particularly good, if somewhat forgotten, movie that remains one of my favorites.

But that's not to say I didn't have lots of opportunities. Almost every time I'd go to the airport, I'd get offered sex. Women will say, "I'm very married, but it's okay."

"I'm glad it's okay with you, but I'm *so* married," I'd usually say.

I learned that to sleep with someone because you think it's

easier than saying no turns out to be the worst thing you could do. How can you then turn around and say, "I don't want to be with you" when you've already been with them? When I was a recognizable star in my twenties, I said yes every time. I'm so not that guy anymore, the guy who thinks, "Okay, I have a half hour . . ." I *was* that guy once, but he doesn't live here anymore.

In the beginning, my lost weekends with Eliza were lovely. There was nothing else in the world that mattered. I've clocked so much mileage with Eliza that I feel I belong to her, that I *am* hers. It's like we're conjoined twins. If Eliza were to die before me—boom—I would take a couple days with some awesome drugs and then I would kill myself. I would have no interest in the world, because my world would be gone. The humor, the affection, the disagreements—all the things we have in common as actors and lovers—I could never recover that with anyone else, and I wouldn't even try.

Over the years, there's been a lot of curiosity about how Eliza and I managed to stay together—it's been over thirty years now. Eliza laughs when she hears me tell people in interviews, when they ask about our long-ass marriage, that there are two things that keep a marriage together: sex and honesty. She'll say to me when we're alone, "Honey, what are you talking about, because neither of us are honest with each other." Well, I guess I can say that we both *try*.

Okay. Here's me being honest, though it will probably not come as a shock to mention that I have had a few affairs. That's not unique in Hollywood. There are quite a few celebrated, long-lived marriages in which the wife takes care of the kids and the house, goes to the premieres, etc., but then there are girlfriends or courtesans on the side. Though I always insisted in public that I never had affairs after marrying Eliza, that's not the truth. I'm spilling the beans now, in an effort to be as honest as I possibly can. In terms of how it affected our lives? It created anger and hatred in this otherwise loving situation—followed by healing and recovery, thank God.

I know that as someone who's punched some holes in the marriage contract, I have no right saying this, but sometimes I've found myself jealous of my wife's past amours, men she knew before we were married. At least I hope they're safely in the past. I once asked Eliza to list her past lovers, and to my horror and torment, she did! It included some pretty attractive guys and some heavy hitters, an all-star lineup including George Clooney, David Duchovny, and Roger Daltrey. Sometimes I feel that I'm competing with the past. Though I have no right to don the mask of the green-eyed monster, there he is when I take a long, hard look at this face that's been staring back at me all these years, like a Georgia narcissus.

Sooner or later, you return to your partner and—if you're lucky and they accept you back—you try to be the person they can be faithful to. I think Eliza was wrong to laugh at "honesty and sex," as being a part of how we held on through all these years, because it's true, even if there was some dishonesty along the way. I think there's no such thing as people who are absolutely honest with each other for thirty years, or for a million years, or for two years. It just doesn't happen. As I said, we try, and we keep on trying, because it's worth it.

As I mentioned earlier, besides being my wife and lover, Eliza is also my manager, setting up jobs for me in all kinds of productions, large and small, all over the world. I know Eliza isn't going to tell me all the fucking gory details of trying to cobble together work for me. I know nothing about that side of it—I just go where I'm told, whether it's Casablanca, Calabasas, or Croatia.

That's sometimes hard to do when family members are involved. I was doing a movie in Malta just four weeks after we got married (the first time) and Eliza came with me, but she missed her kids and was worried specifically about her son, Keaton, who was having some kind of problem at school.

Keaton was a young teenager then, and he and some of his friends got hold of a copy of *High Times* magazine (from their parents!) and went to work experimenting in a spare locker at school, to see if a single pot seed could grow into a plant. While the teens were on a school trip to Joshua Tree National Park, someone at the school discovered the locker. When they were questioned, Keaton's friends knew enough to lie, but Keaton, because he's such a straight shooter, such an honorable, righteous, and thoughtful dude, went into a long soliloquy explaining his "science project"—how he and his compadres could coax that seed into a fully grown marijuana plant. At least that was the plan.

The school officials said, "Okay, that's interesting. You're kicked out of school." And he was their prize student! The other kids were given seventh-grade tutoring and desk clean-up duty, but Keaton was out on his keester. (Not for long, as they eventually reinstated him.) But while all this *sturm un pot* was going on, Eliza felt she just had to leave Malta and get back home. I wasn't in such great shape then and needed her, but the kids were too important, and she had to go. I was very sad to say goodbye, but I understood.

I didn't know she'd be gone for over a month, and she didn't know that I would have a fling with Michaela, a French prop mistress who used to obtain cigarettes for me. But she guessed. On Christmas Eve to be exact, the phone rang, and I could hear Eliza speaking French. She's fluent in the language as a result of her parents sending her to UNIS, the United Nations International School, in New York City. I realized she was probably talking to Michaela.

"I need to speak with Eric. Could you please have him call me?"

Eliza told me later that she immediately had the feeling that Michaela was pregnant.

I called her back. As hurt as Eliza was, she took up Michaela's side. She was like, "Listen, you son of a bitch, I disrespect the way you're treating her more than your sleeping with her."

Needless to say, it was a pretty desolate Christmas. It was like living in a snow globe without any snow. Eliza was mad at me because I was disrespectful to Michaela, who wasn't pregnant, by the way. Eliza's attitude was, "She fell in love with you and now you're gonna be a dick? I don't like you."

It's true. I did have a fling with Michaela, and I wasn't used to being busted. I was bleeding apologies all over the rug: "I'm so sorry, baby . . . I just . . . you know . . . you left me . . ." I was a walking, talking, breathing cliché of every sorrowfully unfaithful, abject guy. "I didn't want to, but you left me, went running off to Los Angeles to take care of your kid, and I'm not used to this!"

To add pain to the pain. Eliza was pouring herself a cup of tea while on the phone with me. She forgot to put the cup under the tea kettle, so she ended up pouring the boiling tea onto her foot and got a third-degree burn. She had to rush to the burn center.

I was beside myself with guilt and worry. "It's all my fault, Eliza. Please forgive me."

We healed from that, but it was hard.

It also wasn't the last time. The one thing I've learned from my many mistakes is that I never learn from my mistakes.

But Eliza did learn something. I call it "Eliza's way." Whenever I was in danger of becoming involved with someone, or when Eliza felt things had already gone too far, she would find a way to befriend the person, and she's such a good listener and a fount of empathy that they invariably came back to me and said, "I'm sorry, but we can't be together, because I'm becoming best friends with your wife."

I guess it is kind of Machiavellian, but her philosophy about it all is: if you're going to share with a girlfriend—"Oh my God, you love that book too!!?" or you both love the same movie, or you secretly do Erica Wilson knitting—then why are you suddenly going to hate their guts when they like the same guy as you? It didn't make sense to her. And it turned out to be the best way to handle a rapscallion like me.

Now if I were in Eliza's position, I would be gone, crushed beyond repair, and the other guy would be dead. The classic double standard. But guys are stupid. We always think that women are not fucking around, and we always think that they don't know when *we're* fucking around.

Eliza asked me if there had been others besides Michaela, though if I said one or two, I'm sure she wouldn't believe me. It's like if an alcoholic says I had only one drink today, multiply it by ten. Fact is, I still get hit on a lot, especially in airports, where people are between lives and more open to adventure.

Once we were changing planes in Chicago. We sat with a woman who it turned out was an assistant at William Morris, and the three of us were talking. Eliza had to get up to go to the bathroom. She was happy I had someone to talk to on the flight while she was in the washroom. The William Morris assistant never let on that she knew who I was—and maybe she didn't—but she later told Eliza that she was a fan and was super excited that we got to have a conversation.

"She did a good acting job," Eliza told me later, "but giving you her phone number was dumb" because I was just going to lose it, or absentmindedly hand it over to her. I know it sounds vain, but the truth was (not so much anymore) I used to come back from trips with my pockets stuffed with phone numbers.

Actually, Eliza did try to leave me, at least three times. The first was after she and I were in a movie together that was filmed in Los Angeles at the Ambassador Hotel. If the name sounds familiar, that's the hotel where, in June 1968, Senator Robert F. Kennedy—just minutes after winning the California Democratic presidential primary—was assassinated in the hotel kitchen, a terrible event that changed our country for half a century.

There was an extra in the movie named John. He was crazy about Eliza, and as Eliza had a much bigger role than I did, John asked her if she might be able to get him a small speaking part.

I guess I figured that John owed me for what Eliza had done for him, so I asked John if he would go over to another extra in the movie, a pretty young woman who seemed to be flirting with me, and get her phone number. Eliza found out and was understandably furious with us, and pretty crushed about my ruining this shoot for her.

I remember that there were two older makeup artists, sisters from Bulgaria, who were working on the movie. They had to keep freshening Eliza's makeup because she'd been crying. Finally, they asked her if there was anything wrong, and she told them what happened. They were disgusted, but not for the reason you think.

"Ugh," one of the sisters said. "You want to have sex with the husband you've been with for all these years? Just let him fuck whoever he wants. You're lucky!"

It was an interesting attitude.

I thought Eliza had gotten over it and forgiven me, but I was wrong. We were supposed to go to Lithuania for a movie, but at the last minute, Eliza decided she wasn't going to come with me. I couldn't blame her. At the last minute, just before boarding the plane, I decided I wouldn't leave Eliza, and so I rushed home from LAX and begged her to come with me on the next flight. I had no idea that Eliza was planning on leaving me for real and for good.

She was adamant about not going with me, and so I left for Lithuania without her.

When I got back, there was a thirty-six-page letter from Eliza. It reminded me of those letters I used to get from my father, except Eliza's missive was reasoned, and sane, full of truth and, yes, even empathy for a wretch like me. I found out she had taken an apartment on Dickens Street, where all the divorced ladies go. She even drew up her own property settlement, as she doesn't believe in lawyers. Keaton even wrote a song about it, called "Mama's Song": "Mama is frightened, lost and free."

I looked around the house and saw that things were missing. I called Eliza and said, "I don't understand."

All she said was, "I need time away." (She remembers it a little differently, though, the phone call, I mean. She recalled saying only, "We're done," and then she hung up.)

Her friends all laughed at her because, a few days later, she invited me over to her new apartment. And we spent a few blissful nights there together. I loved every particle of that place—and being with Eliza. I guessed she forgave me after all.

Despite our checkered past and my foolish dalliances, I'm gonna keep following Eliza's lead, because she's smarter than I am. She keeps me honest and she keeps me straight, as much as possible. I have no issues with that. I like hearing what she thinks about everything. Besides, Eliza is my Miss Kitty from *Gunsmoke*—Amanda Blake with red hair, dressed in those big, rustling muslins. (I only watched TV at my grandfather's house because we didn't have one, and he also loved *Gunsmoke.* That was about the only thing Grandpa Thomas and I had in common.) Miss Kitty was strong, tough, and independent, probably the first true feminist on TV. She owned her own business—sure, it was a saloon and a brothel, but it was all hers, and everyone in town knew and respected her.

Well, I grew up and found my Miss Kitty, and I've been in love with her for a long time, ever since I was a little boy.

I soon found out after marrying Eliza that I wasn't the only one dealing with difficult and often selfish parents. Eliza's mother never could find it in her heart to forgive David Rayfiel for his infidelities, and he left her when she was six months pregnant with Eliza. After two years of marriage, Lila had caught him fooling around with Tovah Feldshuh among the piled-up coats at a party in their Riverside Drive apartment in New York. He'd had many other affairs, including with Sally Kellerman, and a flirtation with Barbra Streisand when they were filming *The Way We Were*, a movie Rayfiel cowrote (despite Arthur Laurents getting the writing credit). Rayfiel then ran off with and later married the actress Maureen Stapleton.

Lila could be honest to the point of cruelty. Eliza told me once that her kids had kept a fish tank filled with guppies, and Lila often seemed lost in thought watching the tiny, swimming fish. Eliza made the mistake of mentioning Rayfiel, a forbidden subject with Lila, and suddenly Lila said, "You see these guppies, honey? That's how much he's your father." She took to referring to Rayfiel as "the donor." Eliza never lived with her biological father, or ever spent more than two consecutive hours with him until she was thirty-six. Lila's fourth husband, Don Garrett, adopted Eliza when she was three or four years old.

You can also see in my personality and my pathology, my moods, not listening, my blaming others, that I'm not unlike Eliza's biological father. Rayfiel was a talented man as well as someone who abandoned his family. The comedian and actor Paul Reiser, who along with Helen Hunt were so wonderful in the sitcom *Mad About You*, once told me that Eliza's father and I even look alike, as he too had a lot of thick, gray hair and blue eyes. So I think that I was "home" to Eliza from the moment we met.

But there are fathers—the ones who are fathers of children—and then there are *fathers*—those who are fathers to children. Don Garrett was one of those truly fathering fathers. When Eliza was about three years old, Lila was introduced to him. Don was in public relations and promotion for Screen Gems, which meant that he was in charge of promoting TV shows like *The Flintstones*, *The Jetsons*, *Circus Boy*, and *Dennis the Menace*.

Don was never really suited for those jobs; he would've been happier working for the Sierra Club. He was a healthy, down-to-earth, and outdoorsy type of guy. He loved dogs and sledding in Central Park. Lila and Don married very quickly and soon became pregnant with Eliza's sister, whom they named April. Don was such an easygoing, nurturing fellow that he quickly agreed to adopt Eliza, so he became Eliza's dad in every sense of the word.

Garrett took on the task of becoming a true dad to Eliza. When April was born, he brought home a little nurse's costume for Eliza, to help her feel important and not jealous of her new baby sister. They even built the crib together. It was such a clever and advanced way to think about a second baby coming into the house.

Don even encouraged Eliza to let Rayfiel back into her life—he didn't feel there was any need to kick the guy all the way to the curb, maybe just the nearest bus stop. It was a generous thing to do. Don was one of my most favorite people ever. Eliza and I both loved him, but we lost him to dementia, or Alzheimer's—we were never quite sure which. Who even knows the difference when you're in that situation? It's like crocodiles and alligators. Either one can eat you alive.

In 2011, David Rayfiel passed, as we say down South. He left most of his estate to his third wife, a flight attendant named Lynne whom he met on a TWA flight from Paris, and he left something to Maureen Stapleton's grown kids. The rest went to Eliza, his only biological child, who divided her portion with her two kids,

Keaton and Morgan (Prairie). Remembering, or disinheriting, one's offspring in a will is always the last act of every family drama.

Before I knew any of this, Eliza's father was a cool cat to me. In fact, he was one of my idols in a field I revered. I kept an original, early copy of some of his scripts. They were so artistic. Perhaps Eliza was drawn to me because some of my bad behavior reminded her of her father, and that was something she had already learned to deal with. After all, he had abandoned Lila when she was six months pregnant, and I had abandoned Kelly when Emma was just seven months old.

The second time I almost lost Eliza was after she'd gone to our house in Rhinecliff. We were going to put it up for sale, and Eliza had offered to go and pack up the books and pictures that filled this charming getaway.

Before I drove her away with my cocaine habit, Kelly had done all these thoughtful and beautiful things, like framing a letter from Walter. It was a sweet letter and so Eliza understandably thought, "Oh God, he loves his father so much," so she thought maybe there were other things in the house I would want. We were spending most of our time in California, so we seldom came to the house in upstate New York anymore. But Eliza didn't want precious things left behind, so she opened a trunk where I kept all of Daddy's letters. There were hundreds of them.

Eliza later told me that she went into shock reading them, and yet she couldn't stop. She kept reading them on the plane flying back to Los Angeles. She kept looking at the signature to see who signed these letters, not wanting to believe that it was her husband's father who had written such cruel and vicious things. This wasn't the man that I had taught her to know. She never knew Walter, and only knew the father that I had *wanted* her to know, the man that I had pretended to myself—and to my sisters—that he was.

It frightened her. These letters were the memoirs of an abuser. Eliza began to think, *What other secrets does this man that I've married have, what other darkness is he carrying around within him? Who is he really?*

So when the plane touched down in Los Angeles, she didn't come straight home. She was too afraid to see me. She pretended she wasn't back in California. She stayed at a friend's house with her two kids, just sitting there, reading more and more of the letters. There were so many, she couldn't even get through them all. She couldn't confide in anyone what she was reading. In fact, for a long time she was afraid of me. I kept calling our friend's house to speak with Eliza, asking, "When are you coming back home?" She was only five minutes away from our house.

Later, after she returned, we went out on my friend Mike's boat, and I could see that she was keeping her distance—a hard thing to do on a small boat. A long time later, I asked her why she was so frightened, explaining that my father's letters were not *me.*

"I thought you were planning to kill me. Oh God, Eric," she said, breaking down, "I had just decided you were serial killers, you and your dad."

Eliza had sent copies of Walter's letters to her father. Though

Rayfiel didn't raise her, Eliza still turned to him from time to time when she needed advice.

Not long after receiving them, Rayfiel phoned his daughter. He described one letter as reminding him of a scenario in the Elizabeth Taylor and Montgomery Clift movie *A Place in The Sun*, based on *An American Tragedy* by Theodore Dreiser. It tells the story of a poor boy (Monty Clift) who plans to drown his pregnant girlfriend, played by Shelley Winters, so he can marry his beloved, an heiress played by Elizabeth Taylor. But once on the water, he has a change of heart and realizes he can't murder her. However, their boat tips over and the girl drowns anyway, though he tries to save her.

Walter's letter, in David and Eliza's view, seemed to be asking me to help him drown Eileen.

I explained to Eliza what really happened that day on Lake Lanier, but I, too, was haunted by the guilt of not being able to save my stepmother and my own doubts about Walter's intentions—conscious or unconscious. His letters had revealed his contempt for his young wife, and his interest in her will and her estate, and he had already enlisted me in the phony psychic scam to defraud her.

What, actually, had been in Walter's heart and mind?

Today—after years of the distortion of cocaine abuse—I try to walk a straight and narrow line. If I slip up and mistreat someone, say something unkind, or seem ungenerous, Eliza will come after me. "You're not allowed," she will say to me. "You have absolutely zero room to hurt anybody's feelings, to be rude, to insult anyone—that is your penance for not stopping whatever happened out there on Lake Lanier." I guess that's Eliza's brand of tough love, and I guess I needed it to finally get straight and stay straight. If this book addresses my yearslong cocaine addiction, it's also about my recovery, which would have been impossible without Eliza.

Before meeting her, I found myself sinking deeper and deeper into the abyss.

VIII. No Beast So Fierce

Runaway Train—1985–1987

Hope is still ahead of you—but someday it will be behind you.

—*Eddie Bunker*

The part of Buck McGeehy was offered to me, so I read the script for *Runaway Train*, which was being produced in 1985 by the Israeli producers Menahem Golan and Yoram Globus of the Cannon Group (they made action movies like *Enter the Ninja*, *The Delta Force*, and *Death Wish*). I was told that Jon Voight was already cast in the lead role, Oscar "Manny" Manheim, a mean motherfucker who breaks out of jail in a heroic but doomed escape attempt. The producers offered me the second lead—a dumb, uneducated loser from New York who's in jail for rape.

The movie depicts a great adventure that I wanted to be in, but I didn't want to play the character as written. The script called for two guys essentially of the same ilk escaping from prison together. But that didn't feel right to me, so I objected. I asked the director, Andrei Konchalovsky, who is very Russian and has no ear for American accents, if I could make some changes.

"Even though Jon and I are different people, with different acting techniques and different personalities, we're gonna play two different types who are really the same character?" I asked. I just didn't like that my part was so similar to Jon's, only not as strong.

I can't help it. Once I have a vision for how a character should be, I kick over the traces until I get my way. That's what almost got me fired from *The Pope of Greenwich Village.*

So I said to Andrei, "My character is in for rape. Can we put me in for statutory rape instead? And can I be from, like, Memphis, Tennessee, or Ardmore, Oklahoma—someplace that ain't famous for education? That's got an accent? And can I make my voice higher, so it's not this low, dangerous man's voice, but it's a stupid kid who's in for statutory, right? You know—'Oh, I didn't know she was fourteen. I thought she was sixteen or seventeen at least.'" That kind of kid.

"Eric, you do what *you* want. *I* want you in this movie."

Okay, great. So I made this tough, dumb New York rapist into a dumb, likable hick who was in for statutory rape. Hell, I knew people like that from growing up in Georgia, and that made him very different from Jon's character, who was a stone-cold killer.

So Buck McGeehy—complete with Georgia-born charm and a certain vulnerability—is quite different from Jon's desperate convict, Manny Manheim. Manny is brutal, but Buck is capable of tender feelings for Sara, a railway worker (played by the wonderful Rebecca De Mornay), stuck with the two escaped convicts on a train that has gone completely out of control and is barreling toward a spectacular crash. McGeehy just wants to survive, but Manny's desperation is over the top. There's no way he's going back to prison. When Sara calls him an animal, he answers, "No, worse! *Human.*"

Runaway Train is set in a frozen Alaskan landscape that must have reminded Konchalovsky of the Russian steppes, though it was filmed mostly in Montana as well as Alaska.

Another aspect of the movie that I found appealing was that it had a great provenance. The original script was written in 1966 by the legendary Japanese screenwriter and filmmaker Akira Kurosawa. His movies, like *Rashomon*, *Seven Samurai*, *Throne of Blood*, and *Ran*, were hugely influential and brought him a Lifetime Achievement Academy Award. He'd wanted to make *Runaway Train* for Embassy Pictures, but it was never to be. Fast-forward two decades, when three screenwriters were brought in to rewrite Kurosawa's screenplay, originally adapted from a 1963 *Life* magazine article.

I have to say, though it didn't get great box office, it was a thrilling movie that got good, solid critical reviews, earning Voight and me Best Actor Academy Award nominations. If Mickey Rourke became a rock star in France, I can humbly say that I became one in Russia, mostly because of *Runaway Train* and the 1989 martial arts movie *Best of the Best.* Those two testosterone-fueled films were among the most popular in the former Soviet Union. Whenever I'd go to Russia, I was greeted like Elvis Presley. Russian women used to grab me on the main streets of Moscow. I even needed Russian bodyguards, but they were so mean, I'd have to tell them, "Be nice to people," and they'd say, "No, I protect *you*."

But every silver lining has a cloud. Besides bringing me adoring fans in Russia, *Runaway Train* brought me Eddie Bunker, the charismatic, jailbird novelist and screenwriter who would introduce me to heroin.

He was one of the three screenwriters brought in to rewrite Kurosawa's script, along with Djordje Milicevic and Paul Zindel, and like Doug Kenney and others before him, he picked me right out.

Eddie Bunker was born in 1933 on New Year's Eve in Hollywood. Eddie was an actor and a helluva good writer. His novel *No Beast So Fierce* (inspired by Shakespeare's *Richard III*: *No beast so fierce but knows some touch of pity / But I know none, and therefore am no beast*) is to armed robbery what William S. Burroughs's *Junkie* is to drug addiction. If Eddie's name doesn't ring a bell, his face will. Quentin Tarantino—may the gods of cinema bless him for birthing so many great films—put Eddie into *Reservoir Dogs*. Once you've seen and heard Eddie Bunker, you can't quite forget him.

Whoever said biology *isn't* destiny was never held up at gunpoint by Eddie Bunker. He was built like a cement truck and had a voice like an unpaved road—you'd think gravel might come flying out of his mouth any minute. He led a life of crime before he took up his pen. At one time he made it onto the FBI's Ten Most Wanted List. He was once convicted of robbing a bank and was the youngest person doing time at San Quentin State Prison, home of California's only death row for males.

But Eddie Bunker was my friend. He reminded me of some

of the ex-cons I used to work beside at the Jory Concrete Company, back in Atlanta.

I was certainly rattled by his past, which included smashing a neighbor's backyard incinerator with a claw hammer when he was only three, setting fire to a neighbor's garage at four, and jamming a fork into a boy's eyeball when he was fifteen. By seventeen, Eddie's arrest record, including robbery, assault, and the stabbing of a prison guard, had earned him a residency at San Quentin, all expenses paid.

Eddie also wrote some terrific movie scripts, including cowriting *Runaway Train*. Jon Voight's desperate character, Manny, was actually based on Eddie himself. I met him when I was costarring in the movie, and I began to hang out with the convict-turned-writer.

I remember one such adventure we shared. We were driving north in his little Alfa, and he put the top down. We headed up the coast, and it was a great trip. Suddenly, I saw a castle looming ahead of us in the fog.

"What's that, Eddie?"

"That's Hearst Castle. You haven't been to Hearst Castle?"

I said, "No."

"Want to go?"

"Sure."

So we planned to make a weekend out of it. A few weeks later, Eddie told me, "I'm making a score and got to get away from the house, so you and I are gonna go to Hearst Castle."

By the time we got to San Simeon; however, the place was closing, so we just rode around until it got dark, and we drove to a Holiday Inn down the road from the castle. We got a room, as we planned to spend the next day at the Hearst mansion.

But once we were settled in, Eddie took out his heroin, his "Mexican Brown." He boiled it in a spoon and drew it up into a hypodermic. Without saying a word, he tied me off until my arm felt like it was going to break in two, and then he stabbed me with the needle. As he untied my arm, he asked in that cement-mixer voice of his, "Do you hear the call?"

Flushed with heroin, I did hear the call. I threw up right away, but I've never felt better after throwing up in my whole life.

Then he shot up. Even a tough hombre like Eddie could, after shooting heroin, become as sentimental as a Chopin nocturne. I learned why he wanted to show me Hearst Castle—as a little boy, when the newspaper baron William Randolph Hearst was still alive, Eddie would swim in the pool there.

With heroin, you remember the tenderness you feel about everything, though it's a fleeting feeling. I just knew I wanted to feel that way about everything again. I always smoked pot because it killed my anxiety, but I discovered that heroin not only kills pot, it puts it in a casket in the ground. It gives pot a funeral. And then, when you come down off the drug, you sleep like you've never slept in your whole fucking life.

Strangely enough, I never became a heroin addict, but that time at Hearst Castle was the most incredible thing I've ever done. I slept a hard nine hours. Then, *bang*. I woke up clear as the most perfect day that ever was. I was in God's country from being high.

I did it again, not long after that, with a friend of mine named David Agresta. We were in *Best of the Best* together. He also had some Mexican Brown, but you just can't keep going back there. First of all, it's hard to find. You've got to spend your whole life getting it and you can't live like that. I'm talking about Mexican Brown, dude! It looks like a Tootsie Roll. It's dark and has the same consistency, and then there's China White, which is often mistaken for cocaine, because it's white and powdery. But it's heroin—you can't powder a baby's ass with it. That was something special. But even if you're a billionaire, you're not gonna stay a billionaire if you keep getting fucked up on China White. It's expensive, it's illegal, and so you have everything working against you, just to enjoy yourself.

David has since died—complications from diabetes—but why do so many heroin users die of an overdose? That happens often because it's the most incredible high there is. And once you do it, every time after that, it's not as good unless you keep adding to it. The highs diminish the more often you return to it. If you do it two or three times a week, you're on your way to being an addict. You learn to handle it, but then you fuck it up, and by then you're intoxicated, dude. You're fucked.

All in all, the Eddie Bunker era was very mixed for me. We were a bad and good influence on each other.

There was an incident when I was drunk and probably high on other things, and I was walking up Beachwood Drive, breaking off car mirrors. This was much later, because I was with Eliza by then, and she called Eddie to pick me up. He arrived with his friend, the actor and former San Quentin inmate Danny Trejo, who had made his acting debut in *Runaway Train*. Eddie had gone through a methadone program, and Danny had gotten sober through a twelve-step program, so they performed a kind of an intervention on me. I mean, tough love.

They slowly drove alongside me at my walking pace, trying to talk me down. I didn't even realize they were there at first. They were like, "Hey, hey, get in the car!"

"I don't need a car!" God knows what else I said.

They were determined to get me into the car. They started off kind of making sure I did it voluntarily. Frankly, I can't remember exactly how they got me in the car, because I was really belligerent.

Finally, Eddie said, "Hey, it's your dad. Hey son, I'm your dad."

"My daddy's dead."

But it worked. And I did often refer to Eddie as my dad. He was another in the conga line of father figures, for good or for ill, that I found throughout my life. He did this kind of dad-son thing with me, which he believed saved more cars from being damaged and saved me from losing my freedom, and my wife.

Eddie Bunker should have died of an overdose long before, but he died in 2005 after surgery to improve the circulation in his legs. It had gotten hard for him to stand up straight. He was always hunched over. I think he also had cancer. He'd had it for a long, long time. Heroin wasn't Eddie's long goodbye. Cancer was.

I don't know how I didn't get fatally hooked on heroin, but I reverted to my drugs of choice—cocaine and weed. I felt they were the only way I could handle my runaway train of anxiety. You should probably know just how bad it really was.

IX. To Bedlam and Part Way Back

Sleep and Drugs—1987–1994

If you're gonna save a life, maybe it should be your own.

—*Keaton Simons, "Beautiful Pain"*

To Bedlam and Part Way Back is a book of poetry by Anne Sexton from 1960, and though I read it much later, the title knocked me out. It's about the poet's time served in a mental hospital and her attempts at recovery, but it reminds me of my own attempts to get clean and stay that way. Sometimes, part-way back is the best you can do, but always with hope for the future.

Drugs have brought out the best and the worst in me. It's like a love-hate relationship, and it was all getting processed through me like the water filter in a fish tank. It's great while it works, but when it stops or gets backed up, all the fish die.

It might help to know what my addictions were.

There was weed, there was snorting and shooting cocaine, there was heroin (briefly), and there were speedballs (shooting a mixture of cocaine and heroin). Mostly I was a cocaine addict. All day. Every day. For years. In 1995 I stopped the hard drugs for good. I was still offered coke, because, frankly, it permeated the industry like a toxic mold—mainly in the seventies and eighties—and it's still very present. It seemed to have gone away for a while, but now it's back.

This may seem like "the Elvis defense," but it's true even if you don't happen to be Elvis Presley. When you reach a certain level of success, real loneliness can sink into you. You don't have friends, you have admirers masquerading as friends, and in their eyes, you can do no wrong. And then the drugs come. Sometimes "friends" will join you in this long, sad slide, and if you're smart enough, you come to realize these people don't really give two shits about you, because they're helping you to commit suicide on the installment plan. My drug abuse was partly what sabotaged my relationship with my sisters, what brought such serious harm to the love we felt for each other. Lisa and Julia, who were so much younger than myself, just didn't know what to do with me when I was high, which was most of the time back then. I don't blame them for keeping their distance.

I'm sure they thought I was going to die any second. I think the overriding fear was that they couldn't watch my demise—even now, if it takes the form of saying the wrong thing or flipping a mood from sunny to dark. God knows, I'm no psychiatrist, but I wouldn't be surprised if they suffered from PTSD from when it was dangerous to be around me. It didn't help that when Daddy died and they really needed me to be the man of the family, I was falling in love with drugs. I did try to take care of them, just as soon as I began to make some serious money, but I had little or no control over my cocaine addiction. Lisa and Julia needed my love and protection—instead they got fear and uncertainty and, at least when I could, a check in the mail.

Okay. Let's start with the beginning of my drug use. Let's start with August 1969. I was fourteen, and we were ending a summer season of Theater in the Park in Atlanta that Walter had set up. He'd patterned our workshop after Joe Papp's Theater in the Park, and we held it every weekend. During the week, we'd tour the underprivileged areas of Atlanta. It really amounted to repertory theater.

I was ending a summer season in the park. It was one of those evenings in Georgia when the sun is still out and everything is bathed in a kind of dark golden light. Standing next to me, as the scenery was being taken down, was a tall, cool nineteen-year-old chick named Stephanie. She asked me, "Have you ever been stoned?"

"No."

"Would you like to?"

So we got in a car, in the back seat. Somebody was driving, and we were riding around, smoking a joint. I didn't even know I was stoned until we stopped at a mini-mart because I had the munchies. For the next two years I was a severe pothead, missing school, my home life falling apart even more than ever. Because I didn't have my sisters to be responsible for—I only saw them every other weekend—I was just fucking off. I wasn't acting in Walter's classes either. I was playing soccer in high school, running track and cross-country, but not all that well. I would see Daddy in the stands because he would come and see me lose.

That was when he gave me one of his "life lessons." He'd tell me, "If you're gonna talk about athletics, don't talk about the fact that you suck. Tell them that you were great, because you're only two feet tall anyway, it's going to be impressive."

I was going through some horrible anxiety, about my parents, about my own stability, about my place in life. I discovered early on that weed is a great drug for killing anxiety. I was fifteen, which is a hard road whoever you are. I would go up to Peachtree and Fourteenth Street in Atlanta, where all the dealers hung out back then. They had street bags—nickel bags—which were five bucks in those tender days, and you'd come back with a bag the size of your fist. Armed with my first nickel bag, I officially became a pothead.

I always avoided pills. I had a lot of friends who were into uppers and downers, and I had heard about LSD, but no thanks.

When I first got to New York City, I didn't do any drugs except occasional pot, until I was cast in Joe Papp's *Rebel Women*. That's when I met Doug Kenney, whose girlfriend, an actress named Kathryn Walker, was in the play. Doug was something of a comedy genius, and he'd almost become something of an urban legend. I mentioned earlier that he wrote *Animal House* (which Eliza, my future wife unbeknownst to me at the time, would be in) and *Caddyshack*, with Bill Murray and Rodney Dangerfield. I looked up to him, as he was an older guy. I was just a kid, nineteen, and he was maybe thirty.

Doug picked me out of the group of young actors and took me under his broken wing. As wickedly funny as he was, there was something deeper going on with Doug. Under that speedy brilliance I sensed a slow, churning unhappiness.

It was Doug Kenney who led me by the nose to cocaine.

I remember that afternoon very well. Doug and I were across the street from the Public Theater at a restaurant on Astor Place; it was just after a matinee. Out of the blue, Doug asked, "Have you done coke?"

"No. Should I try?"

"Sure."

And he put it right out there in the middle of the table, in the middle of the afternoon, in the middle of an after-theater restaurant crowd, and he rolled up a five-dollar bill and we snorted cocaine right then and there, and my nose began to burn. I didn't even realize I was coked up, but I just started talking—yammering was more like it. Half an hour went by in a minute or less and then it was "Everybody back to the theater." I was just coming down off the drug by then. As time went by, the lines of coke I did with Doug got longer and longer.

Doug was a lunatic, an apostle for coke. He always had coke with him, and he loved to turn people on. Which is the reason why he's dead. I forget who first told me, but I got the news from somewhere that Doug was in Hawaii making a big coke deal. The seller saw all his cash, took it, and pushed Doug off a cliff. I don't know if that's true, but I do know that Doug died on that trip to Hawaii.

Eliza told me that when she was making *Animal House*, it was everyone's job to keep Doug from completely distracting cast and crew on the set, because he could be so creative and crazy at the same time. They were also trying to keep John Belushi from using. Considering the collection of characters on that movie—though most of the cast and crew were pretty straight—it just blew everyone away that it was such a runaway hit. Was it in spite of the drugs that *Animal House* became a hit, or because of it? Or do good drugs make for a bad movie, which has often been my experience?

Once I was hooked, for years I had the same dealer, a Frenchwoman named Simone who lived on West Eighty-Sixth Street. She was very petite and always dressed in black, like she was in mourning for her entire life. In the ten years I knew her, her shoulder-length hair went from brunette to blond. She would leave the cocaine under a bicycle seat in the hallway, and with one quick gesture, I'd grab it and leave the money under the seat. That was her arrangement, unless she was home. Then she would open the door and she was, "Ereec, soooo good to seeee you." As you handed her the money, she'd go, "Thank you verrry much." She was verrry French. That was all there was to our relationship—it was either the doorway or the bicycle seat.

When did I realize I had a coke problem?

One day, just after scoring, I got into the elevator in Simone's building, which had a chrome railing, and I put out a long line of coke. I basically snorted the entire gram on the way from the penthouse to the lobby. When I got to the lobby, I see I'm outta coke. That's when I realize I have a problem—I'd just snorted a gram of coke in an elevator on an eighteen-floor drop. *What the fuck? I better go score some more.* I went back to Simone, got some more, and that was the beginning of the end for me.

Cocaine addiction has a shelf life of about ten years: either you're going to die or you're going to quit. Marijuana, in its own way, is more insidious, the way it weaves into your life. Norman Lear's ex-wife—she's since passed—thought for a long time that she was bipolar and was on all kinds of psychotropic drugs, but it turned out she was just an incredibly dependent marijuana addict who finally got sober in her sixties. But cocaine quickly turns you into a jerk. You start treating people badly, to everyone's detriment, especially your own.

I often treated my fellow actors badly, stepping on their lines. The hair and makeup folks were usually my true buddies on a movie set, but I treated them like shit sometimes too. It's painful to think about it now, because when I wasn't high, we loved each other.

The nadir of all that cocaine, though I'm sure people will remember other nadirs—there must be dozens—occurred in Rhinecliff. I was coming down a very high ladder from a loft and I missed a rung and fell.

Eliza's son, Keaton, was there. Eliza's children had sort of adopted me, and Keaton saw me fall and came running over.

"Are you okay?" he asked.

I answered in a nasty tone of voice, "Of course I'm not. What do you think!"

Eliza and Keaton left shortly after that, but they eventually forgave me and came back. For a time, Keaton and I stayed in the house in the country by ourselves. I was still a fucking mess, though. At some point a neighbor came by and saw me practically wearing my clothes inside out. In that little community of Rhinebeck, New York, word got around that Eric Roberts was living there, followed by "He's a great actor, but we saw him being weird, peeing in the parking lot."

My love affair with cocaine had a dramatic Hollywood ending. I was in my bathroom. It had a beautiful standing marble sink, something out of the Gilded Age with brass legs and a big old mirror hanging over it. As I put out the line of cocaine and snorted it, I had what felt like a heart attack.

I grabbed the sink and looked at myself in the mirror, thinking, *Wow, this might be goodbye to yourself, dude.* I said out loud, "If I live, I'll quit this shit," and I passed out and woke up on the floor. I had practically pulled that beautiful sink down with me. I brushed some of the mirrored glass out of my hair and looked long and hard at myself in what was left of the mirror, and that was the end of it. It was only then that I realized how cocaine had altered my behavior so incredibly. I was another person on that drug.

I quit cocaine forever.

But I went back to my drug of choice—weed.

Scoring pot in Hollywood was always easy. There are so many people like me who are in some fundamental way totally incompetent in their life, but they know how to score their drugs. Even now, when my only substance is pot, I couldn't find my way around L.A. if my life depended on it—but I know where every cannabis shop is in the city and I can get there blindfolded.

We tend to think of pot as relatively benign, especially now that's it's been legalized in so many places, and especially when compared to hard drugs and alcohol, but Eliza has always been against it. I have a harrowing example of how pot can enslave you—an example that my dear wife never lets me forget. It happened not far from our house when we were living in the Silver Lake section of Los Angeles.

Eliza and I were getting dressed up to go to the Emmys, which is a fairly big deal in this part of the world. If memory serves, and it rarely does anymore, the TV drama *In Cold Blood* was up for a couple of nominations, including a nomination for me as Best Actor in a TV Drama.

We headed out for the Emmys in my little two-seater when I turned to Eliza and said, "I badly need to score some pot." At that moment, I was convinced I couldn't live without it. I certainly couldn't go through the evening at the Emmys without it. Someone had told me that there was a place on Vermont where I could go—not a particularly pleasant area, and certainly not so great when you're in a tuxedo.

Eliza looked beautiful, all dressed up in a dazzling gown. So we're driving around, circling this seedy neighborhood, but I have pretty good dealer radar, so I see some fellas who are gently loitering, clearly there to sell drugs.

They recognize me, so I pull up to the curb.

"Hey man, you got anything?"

But these dudes aren't at all interested in selling marijuana, they wanted to sell coke and other hard drugs. When I asked for pot, they told me to fuck off.

We drove away, but I was still looking. I finally found a guy who said he can get me some weed, but first, we have to go to Echo Park, and it's not anywhere near where we are. So I look over at Eliza and ask, "Would you mind if this guy gets into our two-seater and you sit on his lap while he directs us to this park?"

Poor Eliza. The guy was kind of creepy, and she was all dressed up, but she did it, with one reproach: "This says it all, dude." The detour made us late for the Emmys, but with the pot. At least for me, it didn't really matter.

I've taken pot with me everywhere I've ever gone. It's always in my bag. The only time I got into trouble was in Canada, of all places. I got popped there, at the airport, when I was heading home from a shoot.

I was doing a movie in Toronto, and there was a guy who kept hanging around me at the airport who wanted to sell me some pot.

"I'm fine, dude," I told him. "I'm okay. I have pot."

But the guy was insistent, telling me he had the best pot in Canada and that it would blow my mind and he didn't want me to miss out. So he handed me an ounce.

"I want you to have this, because this is the pot that I grow."

I was already packed, but not wanting to insult him, I took it and shoved it down my pants.

So I was standing in line to check my luggage when a man in uniform showed up walking a German shepherd. As they walked past me, the dog stopped and smelled my crotch. He immediately sat down in front of me.

That's all it took. The man in the uniform said, "I need you to step out of the line."

He took me to a private room where I took out the bag of pot and handed it to him. But that didn't end it. He told me that there's a procedure that has to be followed, even if they don't believe you're still hiding any drugs. "We have to do a strip search."

"Really? Okay, dude."

It's the most humiliating experience you can have in your whole life. They look at everything. They're like, "We have to do this, buddy. Bend over. Gotta do it. Sorry. Spread your legs."

They fined me 650 bucks. They kept my dope, but I made my flight. By then I had appeared in something like thirty movies in Canada, but no matter where I go in Canada now, they pull me out of the line and go through all my shit with a fine-tooth comb.

Looking back, I've never been scared of anything, except for those dogs. They kept finding more and more. I would say, "That's it, officer," but the dog would sniff out something more. One of the last times, it was in my sock.

Somebody taught me to put it in a large jar of Noxzema. But the dogs always found it anyway. You get this invisible mark on your passport, so the second I show it, they take me out of the line. It got to the point that whenever I saw one of those dogs, I would involuntarily back up, like Pavlov's dog in reverse.

Another time I was busted in the airport was when I went into one of those private bathrooms reserved for diaper changing and breast-feeding, and I brought my little pot vaporizer in there with me.

One of the mothers who went in after me must have complained that someone's smoking pot in the breast-feeding room, and these large officers came toward me. Eliza was with me at the time, and she was allowed to board the plane, but I was detained. She gets claustrophobic on flights anyway, and so she's sitting there alone, and the flight is about to take off, and she's probably thinking, *Fucking Eric, goddamn it!*

They finally let me on the plane after scolding me and telling me not to do it again. It didn't take long for Eliza to chide me as well. She reminded me there are countries I go to for movies where carrying any kind of drug is a death sentence.

For at least seven years this kept happening, then suddenly, the searches and seizures stopped.

I feel badly for Eliza for being handcuffed to someone who lied to her all day long, because it's so hard to live in the world without lies.

Eliza and I did a movie called *Babyfever*, and all the women on the set would get together and talk, and there was one woman there in particular whose husband was a very well-established director, and she was thinking about leaving him. They had been married for a very long time, and she said it's the pot—his dependency was such that it altered his personality, so now he's a total dick unless he's stoned. Not to mention that it destroys your abilities, it weakens whatever your strengths were.

"Cannabis-induced dementia" is Eliza's phrase for it. I'm afraid it's a real thing. For example, it came down to me and Nicolas Cage for *Raising Arizona* back in the day, but for some reason I got all fucked up for the audition. I went to the last callback and, of course, I mumbled my way through it. The Coen brothers were disappointed, and Frances McDormand, who was in and out of favor back then, was pissed. (They gave her part to Holly Hunter.)

That wasn't the only time I lost a great role because of being high. I should have realized much sooner that I had a problem because I continued to lose great opportunities to work with some of America's best filmmakers. I managed to piss off Woody Allen, who let me know he was insulted by the fact I would show up high to audition. Oliver Stone was a little different. "What the fuck is your problem, guy?" he asked, but there was at least some understanding because he told me, "Hey dude, I've been there." But he made it clear that "there" was not a good place to be.

I bounced this off my shrink at the time. How do you deal with stuff that's so precious to you? His advice was so simple. "You should always shave and be presentable, and don't show up high."

"But I'm an artist," I would say.

"Yes, you are, but shave and wear a clean shirt."

I don't go to work stoned anymore, but back then, as soon as I got home, I'd get stoned and go through withdrawal the next day. At the time, it was a pattern that worked for me.

Even when I wasn't stoned, I was prone to sabotaging myself, especially if Eliza wasn't around. When there was something I wanted, when the stakes were high, there was an entire thought pattern that ran like a loop through my brain. It went something like this: *I really want this. I'm going to be really angry if I don't get it. I deserve this, goddammit. I've paid my dues*, segueing to *I don't fucking deserve this at all. I will feel bad having something good happen because I'm just a piece of shit.* By the way, that's the other thing I say in my sleep a lot: "What a piece of shit. I hate myself."

I think the best example of this would be my encounters with Quentin Tarantino, the great director and cinema savant who made *Reservoir Dogs*, *Pulp Fiction*, *Jackie Brown*, the *Kill Bill* movies, *Inglourious Basterds*, and *Once Upon a Time in Hollywood.* If you're reading this book, you know who I mean.

The first time around with Tarantino was for the part of Big Daddy in *Django Unchained.*

I got called in to audition by Vicky Thomas, an incredible casting director who casts all of Tarantino's movies.

I always prefer to self-tape an audition because in-person auditions make me nervous, but I felt that with Tarantino, it was going to be different. It was going to be more like a get-together, more like a workshop than an audition. I had a kind of backdoor connection to Tarantino because at one point, Eliza and I had talked John Travolta into doing *Pulp Fiction*. At the time, she and I were doing a movie with John's wife, Kelly Preston, and Travolta was mulling over the offer to be in *Pulp Fiction*. "Do it, dude!" was our advice.

Tarantino has another aspect to his work—he is the Resurrection Man of careers. Robert Forster, Pam Grier, even Travolta at the time, and quite a few others. Just what I needed!

I think it comes out of his love for actors and for all sorts of movies, going back to his days as a video store clerk with a knowledge of cinema as deep as the Mariana Trench.

The word got back to me, through Eliza and Vicky that Tarantino really dug me, which I was so happy to hear. But my reputation showed up before I did, and Eliza had to warn me that Tarantino has *his* vision, and his actors listen to *him*. Tarantino directs them, not the other way around.

So Eliza and Vicky set up the audition. A limousine picked us up and took us to one of the offices that Tarantino and Vicky used to audition actors. I threw a suitcase into the car because I was supposed to go to Germany to make a movie right after, and I needed to catch that flight.

We arrived in plenty of time. Vicky greeted us and told Eliza how sorry she was to hear about the death of her father, David Rayfiel, who had just passed and who was something of a legend in the movie business for having written so many fabulous scripts. It was a kind and thoughtful thing for Vicky to say.

Then I went into the room with Tarantino, and as I went in, Vicky gave a reassuring glance to Eliza, as if to say, "This is gonna work." Vicky looked happy that this was finally happening. She told Eliza, "Everybody's been waiting for Eric to work with Tarantino, even Tarantino's been waiting."

Eliza and Vicky were just outside the door so they couldn't help but hear what was going on inside the room.

Tarantino started to give me direction about a line in the script; he kept asking me to make it louder . . . Louder . . . LOUDER! He really was asking me to yell. But I was used to doing things more subtly. I should have listened to Eliza. Her mantra is: "Do what they ask. You can always figure it out later. This is an audition. Say yes to everything." But I got thrown off by Tarantino's energy. I just got thrown.

Eliza listened to all this unfold, and she panicked. There was so much at stake. She asked Vicky, "It's just the two of them, should we go in? Can I talk to Eric?" She was like a baseball manager wanting to go up to the mound and talk to the pitcher who was having a shaky start, to calm him down.

It came down to the fact that I just wasn't prepared to be in the room with Tarantino. I think you might reasonably say that I was intimidated. I'm not particularly quick-witted. I know a lot of quick-witted people and I'm not one of them. Eliza says I live in a space of regret—that's what I know and I do my damnedest to get myself there, so I sabotaged myself with Tarantino. I don't totally disagree, but I think that's only part of the package.

Eliza asked Vicky what we should do.

"Let them work it out."

Eliza said, "Just have him come out and I'll talk to him, because I know exactly what happened."

But Tarantino comes out of the audition room and says, "This is great. It's fine."

Eliza is not sure, however, so she tries to save the day by reassuring Tarantino that I love to take direction. And so I went off to Germany.

Don Johnson ended up getting the role of Big Daddy.

What the hell.

Germany was cold that time of year.

I did have another chance to work with Tarantino, though. Sometime later, Tarantino was preparing *The Hateful 8*, but this time the audition was at Tarantino's pad, which is like a movie fanatic's idea of nirvana, including a playroom like a king's treasure cave filled with movie memorabilia. It's beautiful and crazy. You can get lost in all the memories it triggers of movies you've seen and where you first saw them, and with whom. I felt like Rod Taylor sitting in *The Time Machine*, in the H. G. Wells classic, going back through the years as things flickered and changed.

Vicky was there as well, but Tarantino and I spent most of the time alone together. Again, Tarantino seemed very encouraged, very excited about the possibility of working with me.

"We've gotta make this happen sometime, dude," he told me. "We just have to make it happen. We've gotta work together."

We were having a good time, and the sap was flowing. I left on a hopeful note. Eliza and I flew back to Toronto, where I had landed a recurring role on *Suits*, a cable series that happened to have a working actress by the name of Meghan Markle, the future Duchess of Sussex and wife of Harry, prince of the realm.

Before I even had the chance to unpack in Toronto, I was called back to meet with Tarantino. So we got on the plane the very next morning, flew back to L.A., and I went straight to Vicky's office at the studio on Gower Street. We didn't even tell anyone we were back in town. They would have thought we were crazy.

But it felt good to be there and to be called back. The lights seemed to be turning from red to green. I went in and we immediately started working where we had left off. I was still a little resistant, but I was trying to follow direction and do what Tarantino was asking of me.

I was pretty sure it was better this time, but after we leave the office, while we're walking toward the car, I said to Eliza, "I don't even know if I want to play that part."

"Eric, in the big picture of your life and your career, trust me, you *want* to play that part. It's Quentin Tarantino!" she replied.

I had to cross the country again and go back to work on *Suits*. We flew back to Toronto, but guess what? Tarantino wanted to see me the next day. Eliza was adamant: "We'll do it!"

This time the door was wide open and Tarantino asked if we'd mind if Vicky and one or two other people sat in with us. Maybe it was the effect of my having to row against the jet stream back and forth, or my ambivalence about having to go through everything twice, but whatever the reason, I started quarreling with Tarantino about the part he'd written. Tarantino explained patiently how he envisioned the character, and I'm saying, "Dude, I really don't see it that way."

Tarantino acted like a prince about the whole thing. He said, "Okay, let's see what you do with it."

Out of the corner of my eye, I saw Eliza trying to send me telepathic waves. She had a look that if I had to write a caption for it, would be "Dude, your gun is aimed right at your fucking foot and you will not be able to walk once you pull the trigger." I thought she was going to lose her mind right then and there.

Needless to say, I didn't get the part.

I had come so close. Privately, Eliza told Vicky, "I know

you're not going to want to try this again, but I just don't know what comes over him." Vicky told Eliza that Tarantino was just worried that it would be like that on the set.

"He's dying to put Eric in something, but Tarantino's the director, he's got the vision, and Eric's got to play along."

I read somewhere that Tarantino is thinking about hanging up his megaphone and not directing movies anymore, that he wants to devote himself to writing. I hope he changes his mind about that, and about me. I believe that he loves me as an actor, but he needs to know and feel that I respect him as a director, which of course, I do. I just didn't show it.

Who knows what the real cause of our self-destruction is. I don't even think of it as self-destruction. It's more like wanting to have control over your own demise.

Of course, the biggest consequence of my drug use was losing Emma. I was still impossibly coked up when she was born, which explains everything. (It's ironic that Emma's first movie role was in *Blow* in 2001, the Johnny Depp movie directed by Ted Demme about the American cocaine kingpin George Jung.)

The question has been begged, forever it seems, whether Julia and I had a giant falling out over custody of Emma. I'd like to clear the air about that, once and for all, so let me begin by defining custody.

There's physical custody, which means that a parent petitions the court to have the child live with him or her. There's also legal custody, and if it's joint legal custody, all that means is that you share decision making over things like whether to go to private or public school, whether to get a driver's license at sixteen or eighteen, that sort of thing. When parents separate, there are discussions about child support, visitation, and legal custody. I never saw myself as someone who deserved to have physical custody of Emma, not in a million years. We both knew better than that. Kelly never claimed I was trying to get physical custody of Emma, so therefore, Julia never sided with Kelly in a custody fight. There really was no custody fight. I'm very happy to be straightening this out right now.

When Kelly and I separated, we needed to arrange for child support and visitation. The legal fees were incredibly high, and I paid for Kelly's lawyer and my own as much as I possibly could. Thankfully, Julia helped, for Emma's sake and because she could afford to. I deeply appreciated it. Naturally, Julia and Lisa were distressed that I couldn't keep our little family of three intact, that Kelly and Emma and I couldn't make it as a family. My sisters were hoping that my having fathered a child that I loved with the woman I was with would maybe calm me down and make me more stable as a person. Unfortunately, the stability has to come first. It's not a child's job to make you stable.

And so Julia and Lisa sided with Emma and her well-being—but so did Kelly and I. The difference being that I just couldn't raise Emma on my own. We were a nice little family for a while, but it didn't last. I was in too much trouble.

Since my devastating car accident, I've had real worries about sleep. I only manage a couple of hours a night. Now some people say that's the effect of drug dependency, and having to dose every few hours, like a baby nursing, so your body wakes you up because it's feeding time.

I also talk in my sleep, and that's probably another reason I sleep fitfully. Eliza once recorded me talking in my sleep because

I didn't believe the things she said I was saying. When she played it back to me, it was like sleep was a truth serum. I kept repeating, "What a shame, what a shame. I really need to kill him, oh, what a shame." Was I dreaming about Walter? Then I'd wake up talking to myself, thinking it was somebody else talking. But mostly I connect my sleep problems with my drug problems. It changes your brain, dude!

Another thing I learned the hard way was how difficult it is to wean yourself off prescription drugs. Here's a case in point that landed me in jail. In the mid-1990s, I was taking prescription Jalyn, prescription benzodiazepines, and over-the-counter sleeping medications, all of which were a disaster for me. I was probably smoking pot and maybe even doing coke on top of it all, so I was pretty much of a nightmare.

Eliza, Keaton, Prairie, and I were living in a salmon-colored castle of a house on Ivanhoe Drive in Silver Lake. It was a falling-down kind of castle, but we loved it—it even had a moat! It had four stories, with one or two rooms on each floor. There was a funky little apartment above the garage where Keaton was staying, and Prairie was in the bedroom on the top floor.

There were always kids coming over; they liked hanging out in the little apartment over the garage. The other person staying with us was Tina, a young assistant we'd hired while we were doing a movie in Malta. She's British and we were all very fond of her and happy when she came back with us to America.

In an effort to get me off illicit drugs, my doctors had put me on psychotropic drugs—head meds, but I had what they call a paradoxical reaction to those drugs. If something was supposed to prevent anxiety, it would only make me twice as anxious. If something was supposed to calm down any violent tendencies, I would become an angry bear.

I was starting a movie that meant the world to me—*It's My Party*—but the problem was, *I* didn't mean the world to me at that time, so my instinct for sabotage was at its zenith.

On this particular evening—this was around 1995—I was supposed to go to the home of Randal Kleiser, our director, for a table read with the full cast. It was scheduled to begin around six p.m. Randal lived up in the Hollywood Hills, where we eventually filmed some of the movie. But around ten o'clock in the morning, I began the day in an extremely agitated state. I decided to get into my Corvette and just drive to Randal's house, eight hours early.

I had my script bag in my hand, which is really an old, scratchy Swiss Army bag. Tina and Eliza were in our home office doing some work when, suddenly, I was just running up and down the stairs of our three-story house, freaking out. I could see Eliza was becoming concerned, so I decided to get the hell out of there.

Eliza had had to vouch her head off for me to even get the role. The producer, Joel Thurm, knew Bill Treusch very well and thought of me as a brilliant actor who was difficult. Creatively, he and Randal wanted me in the role but they were very wary and skeptical. So, in an agitated state, I went upstairs and said, "I'm going to rehearsal."

Eliza, in her very gentle way, tried to distract me. She said, "Honey, the rehearsal's gonna be great, but at six p.m. tonight, so do you want to run the script with me?" She had all these nice, calming ideas, but I was insistent. She was afraid for me, and what really frightened her was for me to drive the car in the state I was in, and to show up so absurdly early, because that would mean the end of the job.

At a certain point, Tina managed to take my car keys without telling me or Eliza. It was a very smart thing to do, but it infuriated me at the time. I remember I was out in the garage, bellowing. Eliza came outside to put a stop to this tantrum, but I pushed her aside and kept on walking.

She came up behind me and put her arms around me, and I swung my hand back with my heavy script bag. In trying to get her out of the way, I shoved her into the corner of the garage wall. And in swinging my hand back, the script bag tore the skin on her leg. She was only slightly injured, but it was violent and it was scary.

Tina was concerned enough to call the police, so she dialed 911. This was right after the O. J. Simpson debacle and trial, so the police were quick to investigate any reports of domestic violence.

Meanwhile, Eliza kept saying to me, "Let's call Dr. Podell," my psychiatrist at the time. "Perhaps you're having a bad reaction to your medications," she said, still trying to calm me down. "Believe me, Eric, you don't want to show up at rehearsal in this way."

My answer then was always the same: "What way?" We didn't have that mutual ground where we both acknowledged my addiction problem.

The next thing we knew, the cops pulled up. At the same time, so did the kids, who'd been on a one-day skiing trip for Prairie's birthday. They go, "Cops at the house. What else is new?" But they did ask their mom, "Are you all right?" She reassured them that she was fine, but with the cops there, it wasn't reassuring.

Into the house walked a female police officer, accompanied by an extremely large, male officer. They sat me down on the couch, and I immediately felt the way I feel when I see drug-sniffing dogs. I was humbled, to say the least. They asked me, "Mr. Roberts, tell us what's going on here, because we have a report of a physical assault."

The female cop took Eliza and Tina into Prairie's bedroom, and Tina said to Eliza, "Tell the truth." And she said the same thing to me.

The female cop saw the scrape on Eliza's leg, but Eliza said, "All I want is for you guys to get Eric's psychiatrist on the phone."

The policewoman said to Eliza, "You can tell me anything you want. You're injured, and you're also a witness, and here's how things are now, because they've changed in the last few months. We're photographing what happened to you, and you don't have an option."

Eventually they did call Dr. Podell, and he was pretty amazing. He said, "Eric, I'll talk to you as long as you like. I'll even come down to wherever they're going to be holding you." He told the police, "It's not atypical to have a psychotic reaction to getting off meds, and that's probably what was happening."

And off I went to jail.

I was allowed to make a phone call, so of course I called my wife, to tell her, "Honey, it's horrible here. I'm in a holding cell with people who are fans of mine, and they just won't leave me alone."

Eliza consulted two lawyers, Ron DiNicola and his younger

partner, Jeff Frankel. Jeff, who didn't know me well back then, was more tenderhearted about my being locked up and wanted to spring me from the pokey as quickly as possible. But Ron DiNicola was more concerned about protecting Eliza, so he told her that he thought I should stew in jail awhile longer. Eliza agreed at first, but she did come downtown to bail me out, though Ron tried to talk her out of it. She really wanted me to make it to that rehearsal!

This was something of a pattern for me—and I've done it since then—when I would quit pot on the day of filming or taping and then be in full withdrawal, agitated as hell, on the very day of the performance. I just didn't understand what I was like in those days, off drugs, as compared to being on them. For years, I resented the hell out of my wife and Tina for the whole incident that day.

The paparazzi and the press listen to the police radio—at least in Hollywood—so pretty quickly a gaggle of photographers showed up on Ivanhoe Drive. The kids complained, "We can't leave the house—we're prisoners here!" They came up with a scheme to wrap themselves up in bandages and come outside on crutches, telling the press, "You guys have no idea!"—just to give them more than their money's worth. Thank God they didn't do that.

I can't remember if we had to cancel rehearsal that night, or if I actually made it, in an entirely different state. Dr. Podell told me, "I will taper you off the meds, but you need to take a pill."

Oddly enough, Eliza's mom called her, not to commiserate but to say, "How did you let that 911 call happen? Don't you know what that can do to his career?"

In spite of all that, *It's My Party* turned out to be one of my favorite experiences of my movie life. Though it was one of the bridges I nearly burned, my wife managed to douse it before it went up in flames.

I wish I could say I quit all substance abuse, but there was no way I was going to give up my weed. Even if I had to go on *Celebrity Rehab*, with the amazing Dr. Drew, but that was much later.

X. *In Cold Blood*: From *The Specialist* to *Fatal Desire*—1994–2006

The whole time we were all wishing that . . . the Clutter family could come back to life.

—Eric Roberts

The better the material, the less it paid. I remember right before filming Luis Llosa's *The Specialist* in 1994, for which Sylvester Stallone did some writing. I was doing what they used to call a straight-to-video B movie—I can't remember the name, they all blur together like when you pass small towns on a speeding train. But these producers really wanted me to be in their movies, and Eliza, whose memory isn't as fractured as mine, tells me those kinds of movies usually paid us somewhere between $250,000 and $750,000, and then *The Specialist* came along and I made only about $7500, a little over scale (minimum pay), and they owned me for months and months and months. Not that the movie didn't have its peculiar charms, including working with Sharon Stone and the incomparable Rod Steiger, who played my evil but lovable dad.

Sly Stallone had offered me a couple movies in the past, and then he finally got me for *The Specialist*. Shooting it was so cool, like a paid vacation in Miami. Once there, I thought it would be fun to show up one night, like all the fans do, and just watch Stallone shooting a scene with Sharon on the street. So Eliza and I were watching the shoot among all the fans when suddenly Sly sees me and goes, "Yo, Eric."

"What's up, Sly?"

"Eric, I realize we don't have a scene in this movie together. I'll write it so it's really slick. I'm gonna turn it in next week."

I didn't believe him, but a couple days later, I got the new scene from Sly where we have this confrontation on the street and I put a knife to his eye. It's kind of a cool scene 'cause I'm such a badass in it. We shot the scene, and it was a really good experience.

So I got the best script, playing this bad guy that Sly had written for me. He plays an explosives expert trying to right a terrible wrong, and I play the shady, pampered son of a Cuban crime boss. Oh my God. Those monologues were unbelievable—language and character! But, sadly, it turned out that we shot only the big stuff, but not all of the good stuff. By the time the movie was released, a lot of my best scenes were gone, including a love scene with Sharon.

Similarly, when I was shooting the film *The Expendables*—also with Sly Stallone—I had some of my scenes cut. So, we're in the home stretch of the movie, with five or six days to go. I asked Sly, "When are we gonna shoot my stuff?"

He goes, "What are you talking about?"

"The scenes and the monologues you wrote for me."

"We're not."

"Why not?"

"Time and money," he says. "Time and money."

I was heartbroken. Sly had actually spent time with me in Rio, on the patio outside our hotel rooms, writing those scenes. We rehearsed them over and over again, but we never shot them! It just broke my heart, we went from "Hey Eric, we have a big scene together" to "When are we gonna shoot my stuff?" If you have to ask, it's already over.

Except for that disappointment, though, all my experiences with Sly have been really good. After *The Specialist*, he offered me *Judge Dredd*, but the studio said you couldn't really use the same two costars in a row like that. I was upset. Sly had really wanted me.

I especially loved working with Rod Steiger, who played my father, a crime kingpin with a strong Cuban accent, and I found out that we were born just two days apart, separated by thirty years. Though Steiger's role was as a criminal, his character really doted on his son. You can tell by the way I call him "Papa" that there was real affection, and admiration, there. It was an intense, father-son bond, the kind I wish I'd had in real life.

When I knew Steiger, he was deeply sober, but he'd once had a major prescription drug and alcohol problem. When Rod and his then wife, Paula Ellis, said to Eliza and me, "Let's go to dinner," we accepted immediately.

At that first dinner, in an Italian joint on San Vicente in West L.A., Rod suggested, "Why don't we go to dinner once a week, or even more often?" I was like, wow, that's incredibly nice. Then, when he brought up his own addictions, it dawned on me that he really was being a dad. He recognized that we both suffered with addictive personalities—though Rod also had serious depression that once caused him to hide himself away in his apartment, watching football, for nearly a decade. Such a tragic waste, because in my view, he was one of the greatest, most versatile film actors of the twentieth century, winning an Academy Award for *In the Heat of the Night*. As unforgettable as Marlon Brando was as Terry Malloy in *On the Waterfront*, it was part of Rod Steiger's greatness as Malloy's older brother, Charley, to let Brando shine.

Speaking of acting, during *The Specialist* I was one of the few who supported Rod's extreme Cuban accent because I've done some extreme accents myself, and certainly some extreme characters. I encouraged him to keep it, and so we bonded, like father and son. Another father figure, onscreen and off.

The first time I'd worked with Rod—we were together in a few little, independent movies before *The Specialist*—Eliza told me she knew Steiger because her mother had had a mad, passionate affair with him back in the day. So Eliza knew him before I did. Whenever Rod spoke about Lila, it was as if she was the woman he had never forgotten. And he had five marriages, so she really was the one that got away. That's Hollywood for you—city of nets that connect you as well as ensnare you.

By the way, I totally enjoyed working with Sharon Stone—she was cool. I totally approve of her. She likes my wife and my wife likes her—that seals it. Sharon, in my experience, is the opposite of the femme fatale she played in *Basic Instinct.* There is a Yiddish word that Eliza taught me that describes Sharon to a T: *heimisch*. It's defined as having qualities associated with a homelike atmosphere—simple, warm, relaxed, cozy, unpretentious. She is the least "actressy" person I've known.

I'm very fond of Sly Stallone as well, but Sly is a bit of a body shamer when it comes to women. And men, too, I suppose. He's worked so hard on his body, I can kind of understand that, but Sharon is so beautiful, and she felt so flawed during the making of *The Specialist*, which is completely crazy. For example, the love scene between the two of them. His naked body hogs the whole scene. In fact, if I remember it correctly, it's just him in the shower. They might have been in there together, but it's him you mostly see.

When you think about actors being too modest to do nude scenes, it's not true. Actors who think they look good do not have a problem with taking off their clothes on camera. It's not like the nude scene has to have "meaning"—that's just the biggest lie there is. The only reason for modesty, really, is they don't want to look like shit. Everyone wants to be naked if they think they look great. I remember reading that Norma Jean Baker—Marilyn Monroe—used to have dreams of walking naked into a church full of people, and it was a happy dream! She was an exhibitionist, and why not? She was completely beautiful. Her body was her temple.

I read an interview with Sharon once in which she said she was unhappy during that shoot, that she would stop at Roscoe's Chicken and Waffles in L.A., on the way home, to make herself feel better, even though she was worrying about her weight. I didn't know what the hell she was worried about—the woman is gorgeous all the time. I love her! I'm only mad that my love scene with Sharon was cut out of the movie, though I probably did as much posing as Sly. I've been known to do that also. We are all actors, after all.

The only other time I was nearly that naked was for *The Odyssey,* a 1997 miniseries based on Homer's epic poem. It was directed by my friend Andrei Konchalovsky, who'd directed *Runaway Train* more than a decade earlier. We filmed it in Malta, and Turkey, and other places around the Mediterranean, where the story takes place. Francis Ford Coppola was one of the producers, and it had an amazing cast—Armand Assante was Odysseus, Greta Scacchi was Penelope, the great Christopher Lee was Tiresias, and Isabella Rossellini was Athena. I played a character named Eurymachus, one of Penelope's suitors. Even in the ancient world, I was cast as arrogant, disrespectful, manipulative, and deceitful. I'm finally killed by Odysseus when he returns home to root out Penelope's obnoxious admirers.

I have a niece named Arielle who doesn't like show business. She's the daughter of Eliza's half-sister, April Garrett. Arielle came home one day from high school, very upset. She explained that the class was so happy when they were told they didn't have to read *The Odyssey* and were just going to watch the movie instead. But then she was sitting there with all her friends, watching the epic, thinking how lucky they were that they didn't have to read the stupid book, and here comes her uncle on camera wearing a very short skirt, like the kind ice skaters wear, with a goat in tow, and she was praying that nobody knew that was her uncle Eric. But then one of the kids was like, "Isn't that your uncle, Arielle?" She told her mother that it was the most horrible day of her life. She said, "I would rather read that thousand-page poem instead of having to endure the humiliation, and I don't want to go to school tomorrow."

So much for art.

Getting back to *The Specialist*, there were tensions on the set. Eliza felt that each of the key actors thought that everyone *else* was the problem. She sat with Jerry Weintraub a lot during the shoot, and she said that he was like a dad with five impossible, crazy kids. Besides me, he had Jimmy Woods, Sly Stallone, Sharon Stone, and Rod Steiger, the best thing in the movie as far I'm concerned. I guess we were all pretty needy.

Though I wasn't paid a lot to be in it, *The Specialist* was what we used to call a "money movie," as opposed to a movie you do just for the credit. It's what comes after the comma that counts: "Eric Roberts, from *Dark Knight*." All the Lifetime movies that I've been doing in the past ten years or so used to pay $250,000 or $350,000. Now I'm lucky if they pay $40,000, even if I have a starring role.

Glamour is the myth Hollywood uses to sell itself. I play along as best I can, but the reality of it always makes Eliza and me laugh. Here's a good example. Let's say we have to go to a premiere of a movie that I'm in, like Damien Chazelle's *Babylon*, which came out in 2023. I played Margot Robbie's father. Brad Pitt was the star. Well, to go to the premiere, a lot of times they don't pick you up at your front door anymore. So we'll literally be all dressed up, I might even be wearing a tuxedo, and Eliza's all dolled-up in what looks like a ball gown, and we're both sitting in our living room asking ourselves, "How do we get gas in the car, and once we get there, what do we do about tipping the parking attendant?"

When we finally arrive, after pulling a few bucks together, I notice the free popcorn and drinks, and you don't want to eat popcorn in front of everyone at the premiere because it always gets stuck in your teeth, but we're thinking about the raccoons that nest in the nooks and crannies outside our house. (They'll probably end up taking over the house like something out of a scene from *Grey Gardens.*) They would love the popcorn. There's one raccoon in particular I'm concerned about, as he looks slightly undernourished to me. But first we have to figure out how to take the popcorn to the car without anybody noticing?

Here's another example. I remember just before the trip to Barbados to shoot *Blackbird* for Michael Flatley, I asked our business manager about the flight, and he reminded me that producers don't fly you first class anymore, because SAG—the Screen Actors Guild—no longer makes it a requirement, which I'm sure the producers and studios are thrilled about. But when he told me that I've also got to pay for my checked luggage, that's when it dawned on me that I might not have a working credit card, at least not then—and to be honest, not that often. But I had a way around it that I've used before. Sometimes it pays to have been raised by a grifter. Thank you, Walter! I wait in line and, if my credit card is declined, I offer to pay cash, knowing they don't accept cash—so rather than hold up the line, I ask the person behind me if they would mind paying for the luggage, and not wanting to be late for their flight, you'd be surprised how often people will step up to the plate and bail me out. If they happen to recognize me, my face can become my bond, and I'm home free. Of course, I'd rather be able to pay for it myself, but sometimes you're just up against it and the clock is ticking.

While I'm on the subject of money, I never thought I'd look upon the 1970s as the golden age of anything, but in a way, it was. You didn't see families of different generations having to live together out of economic necessity, not like today and not since the 1930s at any rate. I didn't realize how comfortable the seventies were.

Eliza's mother was an incredibly lively, outspoken, and funny woman. She was one of the first great female sitcom writers in television—*Car 54, Where Are You?*, *Get Smart*, *The Addams Family*, *Bewitched*—and she directed episodes of *Archie Bunker's Place*, the sequel to *All in the Family*. Lila used to say about her life as a writer and actress, "When I was living in New York, I used to pray, I just don't want to be an old lady stealing apples from the A&P. And then I moved to California and started praying, I don't want to be an old lady stealing apples from Ralphs."

No matter how much I work, it seems as if the studios or independent producers have arranged it so there isn't quite enough to go around. One of them recently said to me, "We can pay you through Venmo or PayPal," which to me means low wages! I asked Eliza, "I know what PayPal is, but what the hell is Venmo?" And then I thought, crabbily, money isn't real anyway, and all it's doing is ruining people's lives. That, and the lack of it.

I remember when Julia was on *Oprah*, and Oprah said, "I hear you're learning to sew and make clothes and knit," and Julia said, "Yeah, I am, because the kids grow so fast and they keep outgrowing everything and you know it's expensive." But then she stopped herself. She probably realized most of Oprah's audience can't afford high-end clothes for their kids, and that she was beginning to sound like an asshole. But the fact is, it doesn't matter who you are, it's always possible—even if you're Julia Roberts—

that whatever you've been able to reap, you could go broke, and need the clothes you sew.

I was in between movies while were living in Rhinecliff, New York, in 1994, so when I was invited to appear on Howard Stern's controversial radio show, I said yes.

Howard's show was really early in the morning, so we had quite a trek ahead of us. It's really hard to park in New York City, so we decided to take the train from Rhinecliff, and once we arrived in Manhattan, walk to the studio at West Fifty-Seventh Street. There was no Uber in those days. The trains ran early, and somehow we managed to get to the city in time.

We decided to walk from the train station to West Fifty-Seventh, when a cop suddenly appeared.

I was very popular with the New York police in 1994—I guess they liked my bad-boy image. The car pulled up to us and the officer rolled down the window.

"Hey Eric, hey Eliza! You on your way to Howard?"

If you're walking in that direction, and if you're a celebrity, you have to be on your way to Howard's at that time in the morning. Besides, his show was the highest-rated morning radio show in the country, so everybody knew about it, whether they listened to it or not.

We were like, "Yeah," and the officer was like, "We'll give you a ride. We give people rides all the time." So that was a cool way to arrive at the studio.

Once there, the staff made us really comfortable while we waited to go on. Howard wanted us both in there, but Eliza was unsure about it, worried whether he was gonna get super lewd, knowing that her kids, especially Keaton, listened to the show.

It was a radio talk show then, only audio with no visuals, and we were assured that there were no hidden cameras.

Eliza usually doesn't turn stuff down, and she likes to be there to save me when I put my foot in my mouth, but the kids come first. Nevertheless, they convinced Eliza to go on the show, and she decided to trust Howard, so we both showed up and are about to go on.

The first thing we noticed was that someone was touching up Howard's makeup.

Eliza said, "Wait, if there are no cameras, why is there a makeup artist? Is he doing a photo session afterwards?" Nobody answered her. We didn't know until we heard weeks later that he had begun taping the show live and airing it on television. We found out when a friend said, "Hey, we saw you on Howard Stern!" You can actually see it on YouTube now.

We started out with the usual back-and-forth banter, but the whole ending of our segment was all about my sister Julia. He was obsessing about her. Howard kind of goes from bold honesty—speaking marginal thoughts that no one else will verbalize—to just going too far in a hit-and-miss way. And a lot of it really isn't connected to anything. His sidekick, Robin, was very comforting and supportive throughout—they were sort of playing good cop–bad cop, a dynamic I was familiar with.

Still, it's hard to keep your head above water. I'm so quiet and don't really like to talk, so I didn't mind all his interruptions—let him talk the whole time, as far as I was concerned. Of course, you look back and there're a million things you wish you had said or had said differently—or had not said. But overall, it was the beginning of a kind of quasi-friendship with Howard Stern. Howard did his usual, you know, saying things like, "You're gorgeous, you're a knockout." And when Eliza said thank you, Stern replied, "I'm talking to Eric."

Later on, I was on a TV sitcom called *Less Than Perfect* that lasted four seasons, and Howard's wife at the time, Beth Stern, was on one episode, so our paths crossed again. He was so proud of her and excited that she was doing the part and wanted her to do well. In that context, he was a mensch—not misogynistic or vulgar in the slightest. He was a good guy, unlike "Howard Stern," that character he plays on his own show. He gave me a signed copy of his book. I love books, especially when they're signed by the author.

The last time I made a lot of money was for the TV miniseries *In Cold Blood* in 1996, when I played the killer Perry Smith, but that was because they had a popular TV star, Anthony Edwards from *ER*, playing Dick Hickock, Perry's psychopathic sidekick. They paid me $350,000 for an eighteen-day shoot. As far as I was concerned, *In Cold Blood* was both a money movie *and* a credit movie. I'll explain why.

We shot *In Cold Blood* in Alberta, Canada. I was honored to be given that role. I was scared, too, just like I was when I was offered the role of Stanley in *A Streetcar Named Desire*. I turned it down 'cause I felt that role had been played by the consummate performer, Brando of course, and there was no touching him. I feel the same about playing Perry Smith, a role that Robert Blake had made his own. But the director, Jonathan Kaplan, was so compelling. He told me he wouldn't do the movie without me. I'm sure that wasn't true, but it was flattering coming from an incredible director like Kaplan. It was a plus that Anthony Edwards and Ryan Reynolds were in it. Ryan had a small role—it was local casting as he's Canadian.

I never felt I quite reached the level I wanted playing Perry. For one thing, my character is often shown playing a guitar, and that was hard for me because I have a screwed-up finger on my left hand so I can't make chords. So we had to do slide guitar, and the music guy really worked hard with me. He was great, and I did the best I could.

In fact, the cast was amazing. We had a nice kickoff dinner hosted by Edwards and his then-wife, Jeanine Lobell, who was a makeup artist and an entrepreneur who created Stila Cosmetics. The next day Anthony and I shot a scene on a boat. I'll never forget it because everyone was seasick. We tried all these natural remedies. Eliza brought us lots of ginger, but nothing really worked.

To make it worse, I was still in a pretty obnoxious phase at that time due to my drug use, and it was hard for me to fit into the kind of camaraderie on the set. Edwards was especially put off by me, thinking I was too "actory." Edwards and Clooney were costars on the TV series *ER*, so they were very good friends and played basketball together. Even though Eliza had dated Clooney and they'd been friends forever, around them I sometimes felt like a three-day-old fish out of water. Clooney was very open to me as an actor and as a person, but I think maybe he kind of soured on me a little bit, under Edwards's influence.

Basically, the vibe in the makeup trailer was very family. People passed around pictures of their kids. It was so Canadian—kind and nice. And even though I was so proud of my stepdaughter—Eliza's daughter, Prairie—who had just turned fourteen and who I thought of as my "bonus daughter," I guess I was so concerned with myself that I didn't participate. I think the young parents and the new parents were put off by me, and I was very hurt when I realized that.

A strange feeling hung over that production the whole time because we were all wishing that somehow, by playing those scenes, we could change the outcome, and the Clutter family could come back to life or avoid being murdered in the first place. Those killers came so close to chickening out of doing that horrible thing, and we so wanted it not to happen. In the scene where I murder the smart, pretty daughter, Nancy Clutter, played by Margot Finley, Perry tells her in a sweet, comforting voice that soon everything would be all right. You believe him—hell, I believed him—up until the point when I pulled the trigger. It was traumatic for every single person on that set.

I got offered a Lifetime TV movie in 2006 called *Fatal Desire*, also shooting in Canada with the late Anne Heche. That was a shock, hearing about her recent death. She was only fifty-three, and from where I sit, that's young. Too young. I'd seen Anne in a couple of things very early on, and back then I didn't think she was great; but after working with her on this movie, I thought she was amazing, and terrific to work with. It was also a plus that Eliza and I love filming in Canada. I think it was Nova Scotia, so it was someplace wonderful.

My wife, in her role as a casting director, had a couple of actresses on her "I don't think they're that good" list. Anne used to be on that list. I guess she'd given some performances that Eliza saw and just didn't like. But the nice thing is that she ended up at the top of that other list—excellent actors. When you think about it, Sharon Stone got those terrible reviews for the remake of *King Solomon's Mines* in 1985, and Jessica Lange didn't exactly get raves for *King Kong* in 1976, but then they turned out to be among our most prized talents. I think, fortunately, that I was always thought of as a good actor. I say that because I don't know if I could have come back from what happened to some of them. All I can say is, thank God they stayed with it.

When Heche and I did *Fatal Desire*, I thought, not to mince words, that she was fucking brilliant. I loved working with her. Anne was such an interesting character. One day, she initiated kind of a dance that she and my wife did onstage at one of our locations. It was pretty wild. She was very, very free, and free speaking. A lot of the things she talked about in the makeup room could make you uncomfortable. She would talk about sex toys, and sex, and I'm much more of a prude than people think I am. I'm convinced that it wasn't because of the character she was playing in *Fatal Desire* or the nature of the story—it was because that's who she was. Like Mickey Rourke, she's another actor who reminded me of the Visible Man/Visible Woman, those plastic model kits we used to have back in the day. Anne really turned herself inside out. You could see her guts, though you couldn't always tell with her what was real and what was fantasy. Maybe that's why we got along so well, to say nothing of the fact that she had been through some rough stuff, and she was scarred by it.

Fatal Desire was based on the 1999 real-life murder of Bruce Miller by a fortyish ex-policeman named Jerry Cassaday. I played that guy, renamed Joe Bird for the movie, and Anne played the murdered man's wife, Sharee Miller, who had seduced Joe online and then goaded him into the doing the killing. I knew that character—a vulnerable, lost soul who gets manipulated into committing a murder. In fact, Joe's wife and the mother of his child tried to get in touch with us just to say that he was a good guy. I think I played him as fundamentally a good guy. The producers didn't want us to speak with her, but I really wanted to. I felt that it was a perfectly fair request on her part. I was playing her husband, for God's sake, but it was not to be, and I never heard from her again.

It was horrifying the way Anne's life ended, losing control of her car and hurtling into a stranger's house. It was like a metaphor—Anne just crashed into your life, and if you let her, she could blow it up. I can say that Anne, and *Fatal Desire*, really got to me. I feel about Anne Heche the way Marilyn Monroe felt about Monty Clift when she first met him on the set of *The Misfits*. At last, I'd met someone more screwed up than I was. But what a talent!

R.I.P., artist.

ABOVE LEFT: Here I am, around age fifteen, in your typical school yearbook photo from Henry W. Grady High School in Atlanta—forty years before Justin Bieber stole my haircut. (Credit: Roberts Collection)

ABOVE RIGHT: My first breakout movie, *King of the Gypsies*, scar intact. Pretty awesome makeup. (Credit: Snap/Shutterstock)

BELOW: Brooke Shields as my sister in *Gypsies*. Later she played my wife in *The Hot Flashes*. (Credit: Alamy)

ABOVE: I loved hanging out with my two amazing sisters. (Left to right: Lisa, Eric, and Julia.) We were young once! (Credit: Roberts Collection)

RIGHT: A visit from Lisa, still in high school, not long after I moved to New York. I loved those visits and took pride in showing her my adopted city. (Credit: Roberts Collection)

BELOW: A moment as Paul Snider in *Star 80*. It took a long time to shed the skin of that deeply disturbed character.

ABOVE LEFT: Yours truly as Paulie Gibonni on a cigarette break during the making of *The Pope of Greenwich Village*, but still in character. (Credit: © MGM/Everett Collection)

ABOVE RIGHT: Paulie and Charlie Moran, aka Mickey Rourke, in *Pope*. I showed up on set having fully memorized the entire script, but Mickey showed up and just winged it to great effect. (Credit: MGM/UA/Kobal/Shutterstock)

BELOW: Here's another one of my favorite leading ladies, an Arabian mare we named Silk. She was a gift from Wayne Newton, and I rode her in *It's My Party* and *The Long Ride Home*. (Credit: United Artists/Kobal/Shutterstock)

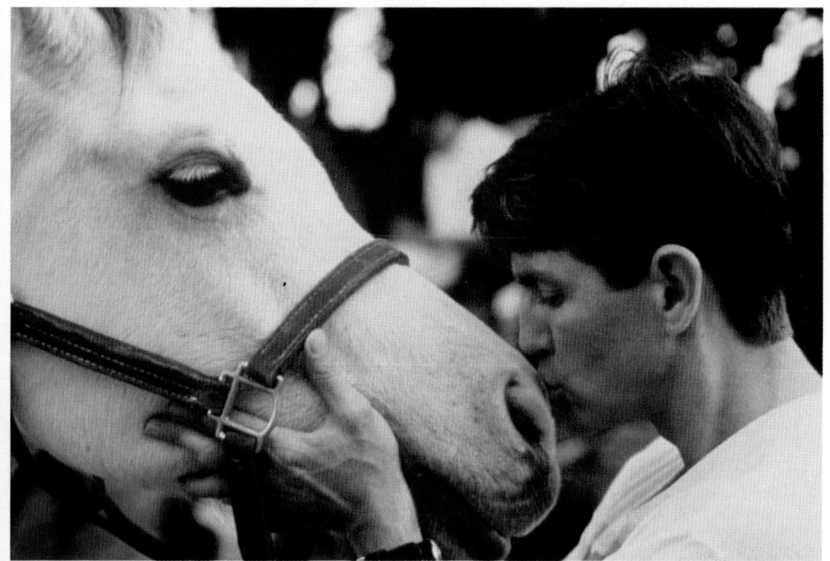

LEFT: On the cover of Andy Warhol's *Interview* Magazine in 1986. Warhol once said that in the future, everyone will be famous for fifteen minutes. My fifteen minutes has lasted—one way or another—for almost fifty years. (Credit: © *Interview* Magazine)

RIGHT: The Greg Gorman magazine photo of me with Cindy Crawford. Magazine shoots can be like small movies. It's all acting, even for the still camera. (Credit: © Greg Gorman)

BELOW: The 1984 Golden Globes with Ali Sheedy, Tom Hanks, Melanie Griffith, and me. The Golden Globes have always been kind to me: I was nominated as New Star of the Year in 1979 for *Gypsies*. In 1984, nominated for Best Performance by an Actor for *Star 80*. Two years later, I was nominated again for Best Supporting Actor in *Runaway Train*. (Credit: Ralph Dominguez/MediaPunch/Alamy)

ABOVE: Emma and me, playing in the sand—an all-too-rare happy memory of being her father. (Credit: Roberts Collection)

LEFT: Kelly Cunningham (the mother of my child, Emma Roberts) and me. Though Kelly always shunned the limelight, she's still luminous. (Credit: Ron Galella, Ltd./Ron Galella Collection/Getty Images)

ABOVE LEFT: On the set of *The Immortals* with movie legend Tony Curtis and my wife, Eliza, with her glorious red hair. (Credit: DMI/The *Life* Picture Collection/ Shutterstock)

ABOVE RIGHT: Eliza and me on a muggy day in Louisiana during the filming of *Heaven's Prisoners*. (Credit: Roberts Collection)

MIDDLE LEFT: In the center, my mother-in-law, Lila Garrett, surrounded by Keaton Simons; my sister-in-law, April Garrett Laub; Eliza; yours truly; and my bonus kid, Morgan Simons, whom we call Prairie. (Credit: Roberts Collection)

BOTTOM LEFT: Me with my costar in *The Pope of Greenwich Village*, Mickey Rourke, and my stepson, the gifted musician Keaton Simons, at Grauman's Chinese Theatre. Instead of a cement overcoat, Mickey gets his moment—and his footprint—on the Hollywood Walk of Fame. "They're gonna walk all over you, Mickey," I told him. (Credit: WENN US/Alamy)

ABOVE: With Sharon Stone, one of my favorite leading ladies, even though I did kill her entire family in *The Specialist*. (Credit: © Warner Bros./Cinematic/Alamy)

MIDDLE LEFT: The remarkable cast of *It's My Party*, one of my favorite movies. I was proud to play a gay man dying of AIDS who throws himself a party. (Credit: Robert Zuckerman/ United Artists/Kobal/ Shutterstock)

BOTTOM LEFT: Richard Dreyfus, Anthony LaPaglia, and me on the set of *Lansky*. I played Bennie Siegel, another gangster. Seeing a pattern here? (Credit: Ron Batzdorff/ HBO/Frederick Zollo Prod/ Kobal/Shutterstock).

TOP: With my dear John Goodman in a moment from *The Righteous Gemstones*. I loved playing Junior Marsh and it broke my heart when that character was written out of the show. (Credit: Ryan Green/HBO/The Hollywood Archive/Alamy)

BOTTOM LEFT: 1992. A memorable moment in *Final Analysis*, with Richard Gere, Kim Basinger, and Uma Thurman. I played a gangster married to Kim Basinger's character. (Credit: © Warner Bros/Everett Collection)

BOTTOM RIGHT: I've gotten twisted up a lot in my life, but this was for the martial arts movie *Best of the Best 2*. (Credit: Twentieth Century Fox Film Corporation/Photofest)

XI. Works Hard for the Money—2000–2015

Stop pointing out mansions and complaining about our house when we're being chauffeured to the airport . . .

—*Eliza Roberts*

People want to know, why do you sabotage yourself? Why do you work all the time? Why are you still smoking dope? It's ruining your brain cells. Is it important because it's all part of what makes you a compelling actor, because you can go into these characters?

Maybe you *do* have to be crazy to play crazy.

One of the things I would learn from Dr. Drew when I was on his show, *Celebrity Rehab*, in 2007 is that I do have an addictive personality, which means the best I can do is to switch out harmful addictions for more benign ones, like work. So I became a workaholic, which meant taking just about every acting job that came my way, no matter how slight, silly, undignified, or harmful to my career it might have been. They tell me it won't be long now before I'm in the *Guinness Book of World Records* for having appeared in the most movies in America—I'm credited with 750 film and television appearances so far—gaining on Kanneganti Brahmanandam, the Indian actor who's credited with 857 screen appearances. It helps that Eliza is a casting director, and she agrees with me that if you must be addicted to something, addiction to work is the safest bet. Besides, I love acting! I need to be engaged in that way all the time, every day, every week of the year. And I am.

Sometimes I'm showing up on the sets of three different movies in one day—on an indie set for two hours to say a few lines, then off to another set, another location, another movie. I acted in Chris Nolan's *Dark Knight* the same day as Larry the Cable Guy's *Witless Protection.* You might say, I'm in front of a camera—whether for movies or TV—nearly every day of my life. I've been in *Grey's Anatomy* and *C.S.I.: Crime Scene Investigation* as well as "straight-to-video" movies like *Sorority Slaughterhouse*, *Hansel and Gretel: Warriors of Witchcraft*, *Cowboys vs Dinosaurs*, *Sicilian Vampire*, and *Snow White: A Deadly Summer.* As I mentioned earlier, I played Margot Robbie's father in *Babylon*, a very high-profile film about the dark history of Hollywood. I could've been a consultant on that one!

These days, feature films have pilots. They're like short versions of what's to come if the movie ever gets made. You can get actors to work more cheaply that way.

So I'm on the set for one of these in L.A.'s Chinatown with Michael Madsen, Steven Bauer, Tom Sizemore—the usual suspects, all good actors. We're going to be shooting all night. Eliza's daughter, Prairie, a genius baker and chef, is catering the shoot. We wrap the Chinatown shoot at four or five in the morning. Eliza always drives me if the location is close enough to our house in the Valley. We catch a little sleep, but before hitting the sack, I have to pack a suitcase and then return to the Chinatown set later that night.

I haul my luggage because, when the shooting stops, Eliza drives me to LAX at six in the morning to fly to Chicago for a film festival. They're not even showing any of the movies I'm in, but for some unfathomable reason, they want me there. I don't know why I'm going, but I go anyway. Once there, I'll do a bunch of podcasts and some press in Chicago, still not knowing why I'm supposed to be there, then on Sunday fly back to L.A.

After I get back, I have a date with a dentist chair. On the ride home, Eliza gives me the schedule for the next week—some personal appearances, a few cameos in movies that no one but the director's in-laws will ever see, some voice-over work, a quick appearance at Moby's vegan restaurant, Little Pine, where all the proceeds go to animal rescue (Eliza and I are both vegans), and then we fly to Barbados for a movie called *Blackbird*, written and directed by the Lord of the Dance himself, Michael Flatley.

That movie has long since come out, and some have described it as one of the worst movies ever made, a vanity project in which the mirror cracked. I felt so badly for Michael, a lovely guy. For a lot of folks, F. Scott Fitzgerald was right—there are no second acts in American life, only first acts and endings.

Oh, and whenever we're not filming, Eliza has me recording an audition tape for someone who wants me to play a casting director.

Living and working like this leaves you in a kind of dream

state, not knowing if it's day or night. You have to wrap your head around the idea that as soon as you get home it's already the next day and time to pack and do the audition and bring that suitcase to work. When we wrap in Barbados, we'll go to Sonoma and then San Francisco for publicity for the Lifetime movie series *Stalked by My Doctor.*

The movie *Inherent Vice*, based on the novel by Thomas Pynchon and directed by Paul Thomas Anderson, is a good example of this way of working, this way of life. At the same time I was in this movie, I was doing something called *Starcrossed*, playing this outrageous former rock video star with the marvelous name of Rommel Lazarus, so it involved a lot of makeup and hair (his hair having to be beautiful and long). Eliza and I panicked because they kept changing our call time on *Inherent Vice* when I still had *Starcrossed* to finish. So we jumped in the car, washed all the makeup and glitz off with baby wipes, and then drove back to the set of *Inherent Vice*, where the look had to be grungy despite my being in a suit. But at the same time, I was also shooting something called *The Opposite Sex*, so Eliza kept calling them, saying, "We'll be right there, we'll be right there."

In addition to movies and television, I've also appeared in a lot of music videos—good ones! I came up in a time when there was no such thing as a music video, though music has always been visual for me. I believe that's true for Eliza as well. She once worked for *Don Kirshner's Rock Concert*, but that was music on television, even before MTV. So this was a whole new world for me.

I think the first music video I did was for the rapper-songwriter Ja Rule's "Down Ass Chick," along with Clarence Williams III, the actor who was so cool in *Mod Squad* on TV. It was like a little movie we shot at the beach for a few days, with dialogue. Then, in 2004, I was offered a video, "Mr. Brightside," for a group called the Killers. I remember I was on the set of the TV sitcom *Less Than Perfect* when I got a call from a casting director who was a friend of Eliza's, saying, "Sophie Muller is going to be directing a music video for the Killers, called 'Mr. Brightside.' The only problem is they're doing it today!"

We were supposed to drive there on our way home, but nobody could even tell me what the story was about. To be perfectly honest, I didn't want to do it. My thing was, "I'm tired. I just wanna go home." Plus they were only paying me $150.

I instantly said no, but Eliza countered with, "Of course you're doing it. The Killers? They're huge."

Eliza wasn't taking no for an answer, so off we went to this location, a kind of multiple-story warehouse, where I met with the fascinating British director Sophie Muller. She explained the concept and what I would wear, a kind of smoking jacket. On the way home, I asked Eliza, "Do you have any idea what this music video is about?"

Eliza said, "Frankly, no. But that's the nature of music videos."

I remember complaining to a friend, Zach Levi, that I was offered this music video that the Killers were doing, but that it would be exhausting doing that and the TV series at the same time. Zach, who, unbeknownst to me was a big Killers fan, said, "You're gonna do it, man, and by the way, can I be in it?"

I got the same reaction from Keaton and Prairie and my daughter, Emma. It looked as if I couldn't say no. They all wanted to be on the set for this, but I don't think they were. Still, I never understood what I was doing, because Sophie would just guide us into these moments—that's the only way I can describe it. But I was amazed and impressed by how much presence the band had, and the fact that this was one of the first songs they wrote, years before it became a hit.

I was so glad I took Eliza's advice when "Mr. Brightside" reached number ten on the U.S. and U.K. singles charts. So I did "Smack That" with Akon next. That went to number one in the U.K. Then two videos for Mariah Carey in 2005—"It's Like That" and "We Belong Together," which also went to number one. I think the first half-dozen music videos I did all went to the top of the charts, so I was like a lucky charm for a while, and it brought me a whole new audience.

The two Mariah Carey videos were genuinely fun to do, mostly because I always thought she was a great and powerful performer. On the set of "We Belong Together," directed by Brett Ratner, production had set up all the trimmings fit for a diva, but I quickly realized that wasn't Mariah at all. She made sure we met first and talked. She had this luxurious and beautifully outfitted trailer, but she mostly just hung out with us. They even had a parasol waiting for her every time she took a step, but while she was very gracious about all that, she wasn't demanding in the slightest. So often, when you do a music video you have to hear the song over and over again, so that even your favorite song becomes like fingernails across a blackboard—but that didn't happen with Mariah's music.

In 2015 I appeared in Rihanna's video for "Bitch Better Have My Money," which was apparently based on a true thing that happened to her, when a business manager lost a lot of her money. The video was Rihanna's fantasy of how to get the money back—by kidnapping his wife to hold for hostage, then finding out he really didn't care to get her back. (One of the best uses of the song was as a prank when Rihanna and her team woke up Jimmy Kimmel singing the song in his bedroom.)

I was in Germany when we got the call, and Eliza gave an immediate *yes*. They explained the storyline to her. I was to play the husband of the kidnapped woman, who's killed in the video. Even though I was in Germany, Eliza didn't want us to lose this one. They tried every configuration of travel to get me there on time. Meanwhile, Eliza was talking to other people about the part, including her good friend David Duchovny, because it's an article of faith with us that if *we* can't do it, at least it could go to a friend or someone who's creatively exciting, and hopefully both.

But I managed to make it to Los Angeles in time. We had the wardrobe fitting at a beautiful hotel in L.A. Rihanna was there, and the first thing she said to Eliza was, "He can't be the husband because I can't kill him. He's too fine to kill." So they came up with another role for me: a clueless cop who flirts with the women floating over the tied-up wife at the bottom of the pool.

Now, Eliza remembers this quite differently—that it was a scheduling problem that caused them to offer me the part of the policeman, not because I was "too fine to kill." But I'm afraid vanity isn't always fair or faithful, so I prefer my version. In any event, it was a great shoot out in canyon country and then on a boat in the marina. Rihanna was very gracious and invited Keaton to come down to the set as he was living in Venice at the time, very close to the marina where the boat was docked.

I know it sounds like I'm blowing show-business smoke up everyone's bum, but Rihanna is an absolute doll, a sublimely gifted songwriter and performer, genuinely and intensely interested in people. Even the makeup trailer had the gemütlichkeit of a local barbershop, just jokes and teasing and thoughtful opinions about everything in the world. It was a kind of haven, really.

Around 2014, we got a call from one of our agents who asked if we wanted to meet with the director Jessie Hill about appearing in a music video for the singer-songwriter Chris Cornell, lead vocalist for Soundgarden and Audioslave. The song was called "Nearly Forgot My Broken Heart." We all gathered at a vegan restaurant near the Farmer's Market in Los Angeles. The director explained the concept of the video, and, again, I didn't quite understand what she was talking about, but I agreed to take the part, even though the money wasn't any good. ("Brightside" had paid just $150; "We Belong Together" paid $300—less than the makeup artist was paid—though "Smack That" for Akon paid $25,000, so that was nice.)

In "Nearly Forgot My Broken Heart," set in the old West, Chris and I were to play prisoners about to be hanged. Tragically, it would turn out to be one of the last Chris Cornell videos ever made.

Cornell had an amazing solo career, and was what I call a transcendent person, but he lived with depression—until the living part became too painful. In 2017, he was found dead in a Detroit hotel room, just hours after a Soundgarden concert at the Fox Theatre. He had hanged himself.

Chris's wife believes a combination of prescription drugs may have contributed to a violent mood swing that night. I'm no stranger to that form of suffering, which is why—though we never became close friends—I'm still trying to process the loss of this beautiful soul.

I'll try to blow past this cobweb of grief to tell you something about being in Chris's video. First of all, he insisted on doing his own stunts, but the filming of the prisoners' hanging didn't go so well, and Chris was forced to do it several times. I wonder now if that had planted the idea. Some type of chemical on the rope rubbed off on Chris's neck, leaving him with second-degree burns on his shoulder.

Many of us found it too realistic and too painful to watch that video after his death. I heard that there was talk about removing it from YouTube, but I believe it's still there. We all grieved with Chris's three kids, whom he adored; his wife, Vicky; his first wife, Susan; and his brother, Peter. But Chris's death was particularly shattering to Keaton. I'll tell you why.

It was a very warm day, and we had a little break from shooting Chris's video. They were resetting a shot when Chris came flying out of his trailer waving a CD in the air, saying, "Oh my God, who is this guy? It's my dream to play guitar like that." And we realized he was talking about Keaton. I had forgotten that I had given Chris one of Keaton's CDs, just in the hope that he'd listen to it.

I wish that we had a video of that moment because we thought Keaton was never going to believe it. But a few weeks later, Keaton got a phone call from Chris's manager, who said that Chris was looking to book Keaton to come on tour with him. For Keaton, it was a dream to play guitar and sing backup for Chris Cornell! So Keaton began touring with Chris. I think they even had the same birthday, different years. There are some photographs of them together where they even look alike.

While we were all hit very hard by the suicide, it must have been unimaginable for Keaton. I don't recall what the scheduling conflict was that had kept him from playing that final concert in Detroit with Chris. But I do know that when the news reached him, it came down like the blade of a guillotine. He and Chris had had big plans. Some people are just so good—their hearts as big as a washing machine—you wonder why they are taken from us too soon. Don't they deserve our love? (Maybe I don't want to know the answer to that.)

Poor Chris, poor Keaton, the poorer all of us.

Fade out. Fade in. Years after shooting "Mr. Brightside," I'm on location somewhere in Michigan and Eliza gets a call from somebody who says, "Oh, we're doing a prequel to 'Mr. Brightside.' It's called 'Miss Atomic Bomb.' Would Eric be available?"

Of course, Eliza says, "Sure, he'd love to do that." And, once again, they said something along the lines of "Great, see you tomorrow."

Through Eliza's genius at pulling all sorts of rabbits out of a hat, she found a green screen studio in a small town in Michigan run by a wonderful fellow who pulled it all together in the middle of the night.

I couldn't rightly end this soliloquy about music videos without mentioning that the one artist whose music videos I've never been in, by the way, is Keaton Simons's, my stepson! All kinds of well-known people have been in Keaton's videos, but not his bonus old man. Hmm.

So why do I even do it? As I said, I didn't grow up with this kind of mini-genre, the music video. But it all feeds the lake. A movie generation is only four years long, so every four years or so, you have to reinvent yourself—and if you don't, you're left on the side of the road, dude! I've seen a lot of actors suffer from a condition I call "fame-lost"—the misery of having once been famous, once been in demand, but now overlooked and discarded. I'm not gonna be that guy. That's just how it is. So Eliza and I have built a career where I'm here to be used. It's exhausting, but I kind of love it. It's made me the hardest working actor in America.

Of course, that's not the only reason I work all the time. Besides loving the work, we need the money. There are these websites where you are supposed to be able to find out the net worth of people. I would have believed it until I checked mine and saw that it was so ridiculous—in the millions. I think someone needs to tell the truth about actors and their money.

I understand the public's curiosity very well, especially because of what's going on in the world these days—everyone is struggling, even in our business, the movie business. It used to be that a movie star could achieve a high per-movie price and that would give her or him the freedom to go out and do a labor of love, or do something risky, just for scale, or for nothing. That was then. Now you have to figure out where that basic income is going to come from, because if you wait for the high-paying dream project, it's likely you won't be able to earn a living.

The truth is, Dear Reader, I work all the time, and Eliza works just as hard, because we need to. We are often overdrawn, broke, and scared. I'm not alone in this. I know people who were in the cast of *Titanic*, actors who have children who've worked with some of the wealthiest people on earth, and they can't pay their rent and they're living with friends. You have your name splashed on the cover of a magazine and people assume you're building a house in Malibu. It's just not true.

Look what comes out of a single job—you're paying 10 percent to an agent, 5 percent to a business manager before you even wake up in the morning, then 5 percent to a lawyer and then, often, to a publicist. Eliza says it's anywhere from $4,500 to $12,000 a month. And let's not forget, 45 percent in federal and state taxes! Eliza is basically running a management company with a single client. Me.

Now, we don't have a publicist. Eliza does it all because we can't afford one. I don't have an outside manager or an attorney, so we can cut those commissions as much as possible. Actors I know who were making 10 percent of what they used to make, are now making 1 percent of what they used to make.

Even the people who are making money or who used to make money in this business—movie stars, mega stars—most of them have ancillary income. They've either invested in restaurants, spirits, or they're doing high-end voice-overs or commercials. So it's not like you can be a big fish in a small pond anymore. Now everybody is in the same crowded koi pond.

An actor who is a fifth or sixth lead on a show like *CSI*, the guy whose name nobody ever knows, gets people stopping him on the street saying, "I love you on *Law & Order*." They don't know even know what show the guy is on! They know the face, but it's all a blur, really.

But if you can work your way up to $350,000 an episode, if you find yourself securely on a series that runs for years, you can get safe and comfortable. But if you're going from job to job to job and you have no steady anything, you just worry all the time.

That's why our house is falling down around our ears. We bought it a long time ago; we'll hang on to it, of course, but I don't know how much good it's going to do for our kids. Most of Eliza's job is finding the next job, but by the time we find it, the money is already spent.

Is it exhausting? You bet it is. Here's a sample of my schedule for just one week:

Tuesday, November 8, 2022

Austin, TX for PROTOCOL-7 Continuation
Home for G.O.D.TECH "Angel"
Toronto for PAROLE "Parole Officer"
Back to New Jersey for HERE'S YIANNI Continuation
Edmonton, Canada for RED PINE CITY "McGill"
Home
Vegas for THE COMIC SHOP "Hamford"
SCRIPTS to have with you:

1. HERE'S YIANNI "Jim Hopper"
2. PROTOCOL-7: Block 2 "Errani" (not that they've sent it to me)
3. G.O.D.TECH "Angel" Sc 38
4. PAROLE "Parole Officer" (awaiting new script)
5. RED PINE CITY "Mick O'Neil"
6. THE COMIC SHOP "Hamford"
7. SCARS "Dr. Thomas" Suzanne De Laurentiis
8. EMERGENCE "Luther Latimer" Paris Dylan
9. DEATH PAYS FLORA A VISIT "Death"

Wardrobe:
What you have in your suitcases:
Casual clothes packed for HERE'S YIANNI
Your suits
You'll retrieve those Nov. 22 at wrap likely
Packed for G.O.D.TECH
But you will have time at home now on Nov. 16
To pull these from your closet:

Black shirt (as for INSANE), black trousers
Black jacket (I think you've packed?)
White silk tie (they will provide)

Saturday, November 12, 2022

8:40A Pick up to go to set with Bourke
Possibly rehearse w Joe Cortese who's playing "Yianni" & producing
You've worked w a lot of the YIANNI crew before, including Tonie on THE ELEVATOR
w Matt Rife & Elliot
Shoot YIANNI Scene 112 right after lunch

Sunday, November 13, 2022

8:30A Leave for Newark Airport, United Airlines
12:31 Fly United #1973 to Austin with a stop in Houston
Seat 28A, 4-hour flight
3:29P Land Houston
4:20P Depart Houston on United #461 for Austin
Seat 23F, 1-hour flight
5:20P Land Austin
Your helper for Zoom & maybe car pickup in Austin
will be Donald.
7P or so Austin Time ~ Donald will get Zoom set up
with director
Ti West about doing a truly fantastic project with him:
Be sure I prep you for this!

Whew! It's a good thing I love acting.

But I do feel that with all the work I've been doing—more than a hundred movies a year on average—it's as if I'm on a kind of artistic apology tour. I'm doing penance for how difficult I was to work with and to be around. Something has changed, though, and I feel as if—thanks in no small part to Eliza—we've flipped the ratio, so that for every producer, director, or casting director who seemed reluctant to hire me, Eliza tells me there are now dozens who are "dying to work with you, Eric."

So now we can forget about the people who can't shake off the image of the old Eric, who refuse to even consider me, and we can move on to the others who are willing to give me a shot. I guess you can call it the algebra of forgiveness. It's almost as if my IMDb page is an expression of pure gratitude—mine.

I realize that it's a whole new industry now. Sadly, movies are mostly over as a shared experience in theaters, and while that breaks my heart, at the same time I realize that it's given me even more opportunity to work. There are so many films being made—people are green-lighting projects like crazy—and Eliza tells me that it's a whole new Hollywood, a whole new crop of people with whom I haven't had a difficult history, who are only familiar with the work I did and not the woe I brought with me.

XII. *Celebrity Rehab*—2011

Addiction is a family disease.

—Dr. Drew Pinsky

There's a joke about actors going to AA meetings just to make connections with people who matter in the industry. It's true. I went to meetings with folks like Oliver Stone and Sean Penn, but I would go stoned. I did that for about ten years. Even though I didn't get sober, I *was* asking for help, saying, "You see where I'm at, now help me, because I'm worth helping." I get it now; I just didn't get it when I should have.

I was high on cocaine most of that time—back then, cocaine ran through Hollywood like a contagious rash. It was everywhere. You'd arrive on the set in the morning, and they'd send you to the prop truck where there'd be bowls of cocaine. Everybody from executives to craft servers were doing it. I was doing tons of it, to the point where Eliza finally said, "It's me or the coke." Eventually, I gave it up, though I went back to pot.

* * *

It was Eliza's idea. *Celebrity Rehab* has been variously described as a "humiliation machine" and "sanctioned voyeurism." It also seemed to me a kind of elephant's graveyard for former stars—not the kind of thing that would inspire future directors to hire me. The idea behind Dr. Drew Pinsky's TV series was to bring together a handful of celebrities who were struggling with substance abuse. Appearing on a show like that was considered the kiss of death for a working actor, but most of the addicts on his show had long ago given up their careers, or had been given up on by the industry.

I was on the fence about going on the show, for like a minute. Actually, we jumped in, even though nearly everyone we told about my decision was aghast.

Boy oh boy, did we get some serious flack! Everyone—from family members to agents—was adamantly opposed to the idea. The general theme of their reactions was something along the lines of, "He'll never work again."

But a funny thing happened on the way to Dr. Drew's show. Eliza began calling producers and casting directors she knew to ask if they simply stopped considering people once they'd appeared on shows like *Intervention*, or *Celebrity Rehab*.

It was unanimous. Across the board, everyone she asked said, "Absolutely not. If anything, we look at them more supportively. Why would we want to vilify someone for sharing their struggle?" To say nothing of the fact that it gave them the chance to boast about their own hard-won sobriety. So instead of abandoning me, producers and casting directors were even more welcoming. Some of the best things I've done have all been after appearing on the reality series.

So I said yes, but what I needed for the show was to come up with a problem. The irony in all this was that, except for smoking pot every day, by 2010 I'd given up cocaine and I felt I no longer had an addiction problem. Unlike my wife, I never considered weed a problem. In fact, the thinking today is that pot is not addictive—although both Eliza and Dr. Drew disagreed with that assessment.

So it was as a pothead that I entered the world of reality television in 2010 by appearing on *Celebrity Rehab.* I was on season four, along with supermodel Janice Dickinson, the musician Leif Garrett, and Jason Davis, grandson of the billionaire industrialist Marvin Davis. We were a motley crew, and that, I guess, was the point. Anyone, anywhere, could become addicted to anything. The hook of Dr. Drew's show was that he brought together all kinds of celebrities—or former celebrities—struggling with substance abuse.

During my first interview with Dr. Drew (as he's known) at the Pasadena Recovery Center, I admitted to the good doctor that I smoked pot virtually every day of my life, the equivalent of a joint and a half. In fact, I'm kind of your standard asshole when I'm not dosed, but if I'm dosed, I listen, I'm patient, I'm kind, I have a sense of humor.

I honestly told Dr. Drew that, looking back, anything bad or negative that had happened in my career and life had to do with the abuse of drugs. When the camera was on, I was able to launch into my litany of disappointments and missed chances. "Now I'm more famous for being the brother to a very famous sister and the father of my famous daughter," I complained. "I was nominated for best newcomer by the Golden Globes for *King of the Gypsies*! I lost. I was nominated for Best Supporting

Actor for *Runaway Train*! Lost that, too. I was in the biggest movie of the year—*Batman*—but in the smallest role." I polished my woe-is-me act until you could see it shimmer in the dark.

Pinsky—Dr. Drew—is a tall, good-looking fellow, prematurely gray, with more charisma than many of his famous clients. Really a sweet guy who deserves his success, but he didn't deserve what I did to him. I really wasn't feeling the torment that I portrayed on his show. Having long ago kicked everything but weed, I just wasn't into it.

Eliza noticed. The patients aren't supposed to communicate with family while they're being treated, for all the obvious reasons. Family might be part of the problem, for one. But Eliza did manage, somehow, to place a call in to me.

"Eric," she said, "I've been watching the show, and you're not giving them anything. You're not showing any true emotion, not a single tear."

Well, I always take my wife's advice. During the last session with Dr. Drew, the camera following me as I walked toward his office, the whole time I'm trying to think of something that will make me cry—something that will really open the valve and let the tears start to flow. Then it hit me. I started to imagine that I'd just gotten word that Eliza is dead. Little did he know I was drawing on it big time to help me start crying. It worked. The sobs came, and they were real.

I was also touched by Dr. Drew's concern and genuine affection, and that worked as well. At one point, he took me aside and explained, "It's a small percentage of pot smokers who get addicted, but it's a common syndrome and it happens rather fast. They start messing with other things to try to correct how they're feeling, and they lose their insight into how it's affecting them. My feeling is *that's* the reason you didn't get the jobs," he reassured me, "because you have a very deep well from which to draw. In you is a rich, flourishing guy, whom drugs make less." No one had ever talked to me like that.

Another insight he gave me was recognizing that I was a workaholic, and he even had an enlightened view of workaholism as a more benign substitute for other kinds of addictions. Dr. Drew cited several studies that suggested that workaholism—insofar as people are engaged and fulfilled by their work—doesn't have to be purely negative. I was certainly relieved to hear that.

On the other hand, one of the more significant problems Dr. Drew has found in treating celebrities is the trap of returning to work too quickly. It's not just the patient's desire to get back on the road or stand in front of the camera, but pressure from the people around them who want to see their meal ticket back in the saddle. The poster child for this is the sublimely gifted actor Robert Downey, Jr. He kept going back to work after being in rehab, and he kept relapsing until he famously disappeared for a couple of years—prison!—and that's when he was finally able to get—and stay—sober.

One of Eliza's grave concerns, besides the effect of the cannabis on my ability to work, was that I seemed to have shut down emotionally. That all changed when Keaton showed up on *Rehab* on my last day. You would've had to have been made of stone not to be moved by what went down.

Keaton and I hadn't spoken for the longest time—something like sixteen years. (More about that later, Dear Reader.) A few attempts had been made through therapists and so forth to get us back on track with each other, but it was not happening. He was scared to see me, and I don't blame him. I was dying to see him, and nervous about a possible reunion. So there I was, sequestered at the rehab facility in Pasadena, along with Dr. Drew, counselor Bob Forrest, the other patients, and a pretty great team of specialists, looking forward to seeing Eliza when she visited on Family Day.

I was told that I was gonna have a special session with Dr. Drew that day, but I don't remember if they told me why. I wasn't even sure if Eliza was going to show up. It was in episode six of the fourth season, and it turned out to be extremely emotional, in part because it was a surprise.

I was with Dr. Drew and Eliza when Keaton was suddenly brought in.

I was shocked, but so elated that I asked Keaton if I could hug him. He nodded and we hugged. The last time I saw him he was just a teenager, and now he was a thirty-two-year-old man. I blurted out, "I missed you so much!" After sixteen years—half of Keaton's life by then—I was in the same room with Keaton, many of whose songs, by the way, I knew by heart. Apparently, he didn't believe that I listened to his music and was quite flabbergasted when he saw me singing along, knowing all the lyrics, when they played his music on that episode.

Here's how it happened.

Eliza had submitted some of Keaton's songs from his album, "exes & whys," because they were relevant to many of the addicts' stories. One of the creators of the show, Damian Sullivan, listened to the songs and flipped out immediately. He called Eliza and asked if they could use his songs on the show, and it was his idea to have Keaton join us on Family Day and perform one of them. Eliza, afraid that Keaton would not want to see me, asked if it were possible for him to perform on a different day, to avoid me. But Sullivan took a chance and brought us face-to-face.

Why did Keaton agree to show up? I guess it's time to tell you why we'd been estranged for so long, as much as I've tried to repress the memory of it. Of course—big surprise!—it really was all my fault.

In the mid-1990s, we were living in that pink castle on Ivanhoe Street. I'm a terrible sleeper in the best of times, but back then, I was on a lot of prescription meds, all kinds of stuff that turned me from Dr. Jekyll into Mr. Hyde. On that awful night, Keaton and a friend of his were playing guitar, three flights up from our bedroom on the ground floor. It wasn't especially loud, Eliza tells me, but I was such a fitful sleeper, their music woke me up. Enraged, I stomped up the stairs, pushed open the door, and shouted, "What the fuck are you doing?"

The boys apologized, but apparently that wasn't enough for me. I must have continued to rage because Eliza got up in my face like a mama bear and said, "Eric, get out of this house." But it was Keaton who left, not me, and for sixteen years he stayed away. I deeply regretted it.

He had apparently been living in fear of me, I'm ashamed to say, but he eventually realized that it wasn't a healthy way to live. He was familiar with Dr. Drew's work, trusted and liked and respected him, and he believed the assurances he'd been given that this would be safe. In fact, Keaton and Dr. Drew had had a private session before our reunion. He told Dr. Drew that he'd been working on our estrangement in his own therapy and wanted to make some greater steps. He understood that there was no guarantee of any breakthrough. Even then, Keaton didn't make a commitment to seeing me. Eliza told Sullivan, "Keaton has not felt safe seeing Eric for half his life. They are completely estranged."

But Sullivan answered, "I'm talking about Family Day. This is the day that families shattered by drug addiction come together to heal." Dr. Drew had often said, "Addiction is a family disease," but you need your family's support to get sober, whether it's the family you were born into or the one you created. "True sobriety cannot be achieved alone." I knew that my drug use was the bottom-line cause of my rift with Keaton—my relationship to drugs, the effect that drugs had on my behavior, my mood, my perspective, my personality, my life. Keaton was one of the casualties of my being an addict.

It was time to heal that rift.

Our reconciliation was one of the most incredible experiences of my life. I felt real support, and real love, and real movement in the right direction. It had all come about because of Keaton's music and his willingness to take a chance. As much honesty as is humanly possible went down on this show—a show that some people think was staged. I didn't experience it that way. I liked Dr. Drew a lot, felt he was legit, and felt helped by him. Everything I experienced on the show was 100 percent real. Nothing was planned or rehearsed. There was no second take.

I remember learning that it had been a nightmare to clear the licensing of Keaton's songs from CBS Records for that episode of the show. Eliza had to really fight for it, just to allow Keaton to play his own original songs on Family Day. But it was worth it. Everyone gathered around him as he played and sang, and I mouthed the words as he sang because I knew all the lyrics. It blew Keaton's mind because he had never believed that I knew and loved his songs.

Eliza was twenty-four when she'd become pregnant with Keaton, and he was about fourteen when Eliza and I married. I tried to be a substitute father to him. Having Keaton reunite with me that day brought back the early days when he had felt affection for me. Now I think he saw how much I'd always loved him. Eliza tells me that I sometimes mistreat people I love, that I'm a borderline narcissist, but I *am* capable of love. I love Eliza's kids and their kids, even if I couldn't always show it.

Keaton's performance that day was amazing. He had walked out of the house when he was sixteen—driven away by my behavior—and we came back into each other's lives when he was thirty-two. Our days of estrangement were over. I never thought I'd see the day.

Since then, I've kicked all my addictions except pot, which I will probably use for the rest of my days. But to me, it felt like sobriety, which—as Dr. Drew always said—could not have been achieved alone.

XIII. The Best and the Worst—2008–2015

I was just a hired hand who had a good time.

—*Eric Roberts*

When I was first given the script for *Stalked by My Doctor* (under a different title), I didn't want to do it. I found the part of the psychopathic Dr. Albert Beck just too disturbing. It's a character study about a dude who has issues about his age and who keeps trying to sleep with much younger women. He ends up creeping out all those women, though he's not a bad guy. He just does bad things. There's a lot of men like that, I think, especially in Hollywood. There are certain parts I won't take—a pedophile or child abuser, for example. With *Stalked*, I had no idea what I had on my hands. *Who are these guys who wrote this?* I wondered.

But I took the role and it ended up being a fun shoot and then a surprisingly popular series. It was actually a good script, about a teenage girl who barely survives a car crash who is then saved by Dr. Beck, a respected cardiologist. However, he becomes obsessed with her and starts stalking her. It was so popular that *Stalked* spawned four sequels, but each new movie became more like a slasher film.

In the first sequel, *Stalked by My Doctor: The Return,* Dr. Beck has assumed another name and moved to Mexico. He rescues a young woman from drowning, and, naturally, becomes obsessed with her. This incarnation begot *Stalked by My Doctor: Patient's Revenge*, which begot *Stalked by My Doctor: A Sleepwalker's Nightmare*, which begot *Just What the Doctor Ordered*, in which the unfortunate Dr. Beck escapes from a psychiatric prison hospital.

I think part of *Stalked*'s popularity was that the guy I played was so over the top that each movie felt like both a psychological horror film *and* satire—not so easy to pull off, but I think we hit the sweet spot. Credit for the success of the series should go to its creators, Ken Sanders and the director Doug Campbell, by the way.

I and II were the best of the lot, which is usually the case. Part II was rough to film, though, because I was still on drugs at the time (this was two years before I got mostly sober), which meant I started to bully the crew, and the crazy character I was playing was seeping into my soul. With me, always an occupational hazard. By the time we filmed the last movie, in Atlanta, the crew complained about me. This was during the Covid era, and they said I was not being careful enough, and that I was unpleasant to be around. I got quite a letter from the crew explaining why they couldn't work with me anymore.

I was sent home before the shoot was over.

Poor Eliza! She had driven to Nashville to visit Keaton, who was living there at the time, so my being grounded cut her trip short. But as often happens in Hollywood, several months later,

Stalked had a different crew and I was invited back. Filming went well this time, and we finished the last few days of the shoot.

One reason it went so well was that, in Atlanta, I was able to spend time with my cousin Adam, and we even got him a small role playing an orderly. The production company set us up in a house, and Adam was with us a lot, assisting us in all kinds of ways, such as getting the wardrobe person to fit me with the right size scrubs and taking pictures on the set. He made friends with everybody in the production, so it was really great to reunite with him.

The house we stayed in had one of those stupid, voice-activated, Wi-Fi devices—must've been Siri—that's supposed to read your mind or something, and instead it just didn't work at all. I couldn't figure it out. Adam couldn't figure it out. Even Eliza, who has learned to figure stuff out by default, couldn't figure it out. We hated that thing!

This was early in the Covid pandemic, so there was a lot of virus testing going on. Adam had to test in order to be around anybody, which meant a long drive in his truck to the testing site. He never complained, though. He's the kind of Southern guy who can look tough and scary, but he's really very tenderhearted. He mostly gets sad for other people if they're in a bad way, and he desperately misses his mom, who died some years ago. He's the last of my original family that I'm close to, and he means a lot to me.

It was a good shoot for another reason. I met one of the sanest, kindest people I know while I was working on *Stalked*, a prominent cardiologist named Dr. Rico Simonini who is also an actor who consulted and then played a doctor later on in the series.

In the tradition of the playwright Anton Chekhov, the writer

Somerset Maugham, the poet William Carlos Williams, and Arthur Conan Doyle, Rico Simonini remained faithful to medicine while following the siren call of the arts. Just a year earlier we had acted in another movie together, *Frank and Ava*, in which Rico played Frank Sinatra, Emily Elicia Low played Ava Gardner, and I played Columbia Studio boss Harry Cohn. The late, great character actor Harry Dean Stanton was also in the movie with us and became both a close friend and a patient of Rico's.

Rico practices medicine at Cedars-Sinai Medical Center in Los Angeles and has many prominent patients—including famous actors, though I can't name them here. Trust me, Rico keeps them going, and Eliza and I had a role in getting Rico involved in *Stalked.*

I've always thought the world was divided into "thems who do" for others, and "thems who don't." Eliza's mother, Lila Garrett, did for others, for example, but her father, David Rayfiel, didn't—not even for us. Eliza and I love giving parts to other actors. If I'm not available for something, Eliza will obsess about it, and if she's able to cast a friend or someone she believes in who wants the part, then she's just as happy. Doesn't matter.

As a result, many of our projects have been friends-and-family affairs. Prairie catered our shoots, and a lot of the music was by Keaton. Medical consultants were needed for *Stalked by My Doctor*, so we felt lucky to have Rico available to us—a doctor who was also a friend and an actor.

One night we were shooting Part IV of the series in Griffith Park, and the actor who was cast to play dean of the medical school was unable to do it. We needed to recast it really fast, but up there in Griffith Park there was little cell or internet reception. And it was freezing. Thankfully, Rico was already on hand.

So producer Ken Sanders and the director (who had not listened to Eliza when, earlier on, she'd begged them to use Rico) ended up using him. They were so glad they did. But first they made him audition, so we didn't wrap that shoot until two o'clock in the morning, freezing our asses off. But we were elated when they cast him in the role, and Rico was happy because it was a big part with several scenes and several wardrobe changes. He was really, really good, and I hope they bring his character back if they reboot the series.

We'll do anything for Rico. In fact, he saved both of our lives. Eliza's primary doctor was retiring because he was losing his hearing, so he wasn't aware that she had developed a leaky heart valve. Rico caught it and has monitored it ever since, handling everything beautifully. After she aced her echocardiogram, I said, "I want one." Rico arranged it, but I didn't do so well, even though I'm a gym rat who works out all the time.

I was sent across the street to nuclear medicine, and next thing you know, I'm checking into Cedar-Sinai Medical Center and having two stents placed in my blood vessels to remove some blockages. That saved my life.

Although I should say I've not been asked to do another *Stalked* movie since then—I don't know if Sanders will ever revive the franchise, which has been cryogenically frozen since 2021. It was a good run while it lasted, an improbable series that somehow found its audience, and I'm grateful for the chance to play Dr. Beck in all his pathological glory—my specialty!

In 2008, Christopher Nolan cast me as Salvatore "The Boss" Maroni in *The Dark Knight*, the second installment of the Batman trilogy. Sal Maroni is a mob boss who has taken over the

Falcone crime family in Gotham City, and he's an archenemy of Batman. This is the one with Christian Bale as Batman and Heath Ledger, RIP, as the Joker, in his last role before his shocking death at the age of twenty-eight.

Looking back over the movies and TV shows I've made over the past fifteen years or so, I can say that the best experiences happened when the cast and crew came together to form a family. Dr. Drew said, "Addiction is a family disease," but he also said you need your family's support to get sober. If it can't be the family you were born into, it can be the one you gathered together in your life and work.

That was true of *The Dark Knight*, which had the best people all around. Filming it was like going to summer camp—really wonderful. Most of the cast occupied a hotel, which meant there were a lot of families there. Gary Oldman was there, and Christian Bale with his kids and their mom, and Chris Nolan was there with his wife, Emma, and their kids, so there were a lot of little kids running around. The hotel staff got used to us and we'd just run into each other everywhere or we would call each other's rooms. It was really a fun shoot. We shared Keaton's music with everybody, and he got a lot of genuine fans out of the experience. One day, just about the whole cast was on the call sheet. We were shooting at a huge courthouse or city hall, and everybody was in their chairs waiting for shots. Anytime one of us got up to go to craft service, we'd say, "Hey, does anybody want anything?" It was that kind of set.

I later read some of the stories about Heath Ledger staying in character all the time, but I did not witness that. I just saw an actor who had taken on a tough role. He got a lot of accolades for it, but those kinds of villainous roles are not always the most fun to play. Take it from me, who has had more than my share in my checkered career. Sometimes those roles are just too far from reality. Who—or what—is the Joker, really? Where does he organically come from?

It's all challenging stuff, but in real life, Heath was just a sweetheart. His performance was fantastic, adding to the tragedy of his early death from a potent, self-administered accumulation of prescription drugs. Heath had trouble sleeping when he was in the grip of an all-consuming role—I was a fellow sufferer—so he dosed himself up good, just so sleep could slip into his exhausted soul. It did, permanently.

In my view, and in the view of much of the world, Chris Nolan is a brilliant director. You can see his hand on every frame of *The Dark Knight* and in his other movies, like *Memento*. He had a rule on the set: no cellphones. But then, if he was trying to get something he needed from one of the department heads, they would have to go up to him and say, "I can't really do that without a means of communication. I didn't know you wanted it, because how was I supposed to know?"

Chris sometimes seems like a person without humor because he's so focused. He doesn't miss anything. It was hard when he asked me not to be funny in my funniest lines in *The Dark Knight*. When my character, Maroni, is with a woman in a club, she says, "Let's get out of here. It's too loud. You can't hear me talk." And I have to say, "What makes you think I want to hear you talk?" Even though it got a laugh when I rehearsed it with Eliza, and it got a laugh the first take on the set, Chris said, "No, no. I don't want it funny." I—who am terrible at comedy—was suddenly given the task to take the funny out of the line.

I must say that when Eliza and I were sitting next to him at the premiere of *The Dark Knight*, it was the first time I saw Chris take his foot off the gas. He's a very different guy when he's relaxed.

Michael Caine played Alfred, Bruce Wayne's loyal butler in *The Dark Knight*. I can't believe I was lucky enough to be in a movie with Michael Caine! I mean, this dude should be president of the universe. If he were in a beauty pageant, he'd be Miss Congeniality. Everybody loved him.

Here again was another guy who just loves his wife. It's inspiring. He can't go wrong the second he does a scene. He's just one of those people who had to be an actor—you don't even know what it is that he's doing that fascinates you, but you can't get enough of him. Which, by the way, I also think is true about my sister. Julia is immensely watchable, whether it's her best work, or work that she didn't love that much. I've said before that I thought Lisa was the true actor in our family, but Julia is just beyond watchable. She just had to come up somewhere.

Two years later, in 2010, I teamed up with Sly Stallone again for *The Expendables.*

I was in particularly good action-hero company when I was cast to be the villain in this story of a group of mercenaries based in New Orleans. Headed by Sly, of course, they take on the mission of overthrowing a cruel Latin American dictator who turns out be the puppet of a corrupt ex–CIA agent, James Munroe—that would be me.

I don't think it's spoiling a movie released in 2010 to tell you that, after many explosions, the Expendables crew eventually catch up with my character and kill me as I attempt to escape. Mickey Rourke was in the movie, as was Bruce Willis, Steve Austin, and Dolph Lundgren, so there was a lot of testosterone on that set. Stallone co-wrote the screenplay and skillfully directed all those weight-lifted egos. I loved my role and thought Sly was a phenomenal director, even though there were times he wanted me to go more overt, bigger, angrier, and I wanted to do something more insidious and subtle. Finally, when Sly wanted my character to yell in certain in scenes, I wouldn't do it. If you watch that movie, you see that my character is very controlled, even soft-spoken. He's not a screamer. Eliza was mad at me: "What the fuck are you doing? Why are you fighting your director? Just so he'll never hire you again?" She was right, of course, but that's how much being true to character meant to me.

We ended up shooting those scenes both ways. You'll have to watch the movie to see which way made it in.

I enjoyed playing that part so much that I wanted to come back for the three sequels that followed, but after they killed me off at the end of the first one, there wasn't a convincing way to bring me back. I pleaded, but it was a lost cause. Arthur Conan Doyle brought Sherlock Holmes back from almost certain death in the Reichenbach Falls, but Stallone couldn't quite find a way to put me back together after his character cut me to ribbons in a hail of gunfire (while I'm holding a beautiful hostage on a bridge). Such is movie death as opposed to the printed word. As it turned out, I guess I was the expendable one after all.

I flew to Toronto to appear in two projects, the movie *Lost Girl* and the cable series *Suits.* I was offered the role of Charles

Forstman, a shady, billionaire banker with a bad reputation, in the most well-dressed role I've ever played, and it turned out to be the most fun I've ever had on a TV shoot. I loved the scripts and I loved the directors and the cast and crew. Their support was enormous. Eliza and I had the best time in Toronto, with the added bonus of Keaton's song "When I Go" (written with Smith Carlson and Laura Goldfarb) included in the soundtrack.

We watched the numbers for that song go through the roof—there're now around ten million downloads. I credit a lot of that to the popularity of the show itself, to Meghan Markle (aka the Duchess of Sussex), who played the paralegal Rachel Zane, and to the dramatic way Keaton's song was featured in a montage that highlighted Meghan's storyline with the lead actor, Patrick Adams, who played Mike Ross, a college dropout who becomes an unlikely lawyer. The show ran for seven seasons on the USA cable network and had a great cast. Patrick Adams was nominated for a Screen Actors Guild Award for Outstanding Performance in a Drama Series. The superb actor Wendell Pierce, of *The Wire* and *Treme* fame, played Robert Zane, a star lawyer and Rachel's father. Pierce was recently nominated for an Olivier Award for his groundbreaking performance as a Black Willy Loman in *Death of a Salesman* on the London stage. And Meghan? World famous.

But I knew Meghan before her astonishing fame, and fate. I remember her as warm, friendly, and hardworking throughout the filming. Once we did a table read that she couldn't be there for, so she read her lines on conference call, very apologetic about not being there in person. I thought she was dazzling—focused, talented, and graceful. She was already a kind of a princess, long before Prince Harry entered the scene. But she was also a team player. I wish I had gotten to know her better.

While my family was finally coming together after *Celebrity Rehab,* my mother's second family was coming apart.

Nancy Motes was my half sister, born to my mom and her second husband, Michael Motes. As I've mentioned before, he was no picnic. Nancy was only five years older than Keaton. Nancy and I weren't close—how could we be? We grew up in different places, we had different dads. There wasn't much of a framework for a meaningful relationship. But I knew Nancy and I was very fond of her.

Look, it's not always easy being a fame-adjacent family member. I should know. I'm one myself.

The way our relationship began, though, was through my mother. It was back in the day when we all had AOL accounts, at least those of us fortunate enough to have computers. I felt like I had to do something with this giant box on my desk, so I started to correspond with my mother.

I think she was truly happy that we were in touch again after all those long years in exile. I could tell from her emails that Betty was proud of Nancy. After all, Julia was out of the house living her famous life, Lisa and I were long gone too, and my mom's husband had passed, so it was just the two of them.

Nancy had worked with dogs, and she also did some teaching. Betty and Nancy—they seemed happy in each other's company. We even got to the point where we were all exchanging Christmas gifts, but we still hadn't seen each other. That would come in time. When we finally did meet, I was nervous and so was Nancy. We were intimate strangers, and I confess, I'm not particularly good at those stressful moments. If things don't quite go as I imagined them, I'll do something to break the box I've put myself in.

Apparently, I said a few uncharitable things about our mother. I could tell right away it was making Nancy uncomfortable.

"You really should give her a chance," Nancy explained. "She's different, she's not the person you knew. She's become very loving."

Thank goodness Eliza was around. She took Nancy for a long walk, and they had a heart-to-heart talk about all of it.

Nancy struggled to be happy. It wasn't very long ago that the world felt perfectly justified expressing their displeasure—really a vicious prejudice—against people of size. Back then, there were no full-size models on the cover of magazines, there were no spokespeople to take pride in not being sylphs, and no one was called out for fat-shaming. There was just huge disrespect, especially for women. So, in the funhouse mirror of Hollywood, Nancy saw a distortion of herself, and being referred to as the sister of America's darling probably didn't help her self-esteem.

At some point, Nancy lost a lot of weight and she did a paid interview for an overseas tabloid. She got paid $1500 for it. She needed the money. The tabloid reporter asked her what motivated her weight loss, and she told them that people were often unkind. They asked if her siblings were ever mean to her about her weight. She said no, that they were only concerned for her health, but she did confess that she felt a little out of place growing up in a family with a very slender sister, who many people considered the prettiest woman in America.

Nancy was a very emotional person. I know that she had a fiancé that her family disapproved of, but she forged ahead, going so far as to plan for her wedding. I'm sure Lisa, Julia, and Betty were just feeling protective of Nancy, but she took it as disapproval, as if she couldn't do anything right—she couldn't even get married right.

Eliza was taking a bath when the call came.

It was Julia.

"Don't worry," she said, "Mom is all right." Back then, Betty was being treated for cancer. "It's about Nancy. She's dead, and they think it's drugs."

Nancy was only thirty-seven years old! Apparently while housesitting for some friends, she had gone into their bathroom and taken an overdose of pills.

Everyone was staggered by the terrible news of Nancy's death. What is it about some people? If it wasn't for bad luck, they'd have no luck at all. But I feel that because we are responsible for each other, it's easy to see someone else's despair as *our* failure. I'm sure that's not the right way of looking at it, but it's hard to see it any other way when it's your sibling.

Eliza's first thoughts and mine were for Betty. She had loved her daughter so much, and she had cherished her company. Burying a child—there can't be anything more terrible in life than that.

There was a memorial for Nancy in Los Angeles where a lot of people from the TV show *Glee* attended. She had worked for *Glee* as a liaison, arranging personal appearances, and they all loved her. The actress Jane Lynch, who starred as coach Sue Sylvester, was especially fond of Nancy.

Eliza and I were asked not to attend. The excuse they gave was that there was going to be a lot of press loitering there, but that didn't keep other people from coming, so I never quite believed that was the real reason. It didn't matter. I went anyway, with Eliza. We didn't go inside, but drove there and sat outside in our car, just quietly thinking about Nancy. I felt I should have treated her more like a sister from the moment she was born—that would have been the right thing to do.

I'm comforted by the fact that she had so much love from my mom and my sisters, but still, the fact remains, you can always love a little more.

In 2015 I appeared in a movie some people think was the nadir of my career. I disagree. In *A Talking Cat?*, I was the voice of Duffy, a cat who can speak to humans. Duffy is a cool cat who dispenses advice, gives guidance, and instills confidence in the lives of several families. Oh, I forgot, he also has a magic collar. The movie went straight to DVD. Who cares? I like doing offbeat and sometimes silly things, and I also love cats. Besides, it's the kind of movie my grandkids will love. And without variety, how can you sustain a career such as mine?

Created by Danny McBride, *The Righteous Gemstones* is a dark comedy series on HBO that follows a renowned but dysfunctional clan of Southern televangelists. It premiered in 2019 and is still going strong. Great cast—John Goodman as Dr. Eli Gemstone, the widowed patriarch and mega-church preacher; Danny McBride, Adam Devine, and Edi Patterson play the feckless Gemstone offspring. They're all low-rent but rich as Croesus, thanks to the donations of their gullible flock.

From the first time I auditioned for the part of Glendon "Junior" Marsh in season two—a professional wrestling promoter who shares a criminal past with Eli—I immediately saw this dude in my head. I saw Junior as whippet thin, only partially educated. I started working out like a madman, ripped myself up and practically stopped eating. I dropped 20 pounds. I got so skinny, my wife got pissed.

"You look horrible," she told me.

"I'm Junior," I said.

"But you've got to do other parts, and you can't, looking like this."

"Jesus, Eliza, I'm Junior!" That's all I cared about—becoming Junior.

Eliza wasn't having it. "Eric," she said, "you're too old to give yourself to just one part anymore. You've got to do other things. Just look at your face."

I did get a little ragged. My face got lined up. I have old skin now. So now I know that when I get skinny, I look old.

Eliza continued to read me the riot act. "People think you're weird anyway," she said. She jumped all over me.

"But I'm Junior," I kept on telling her. I knew that character and I wanted to be him. I grew up with bubbas like Junior. I wanted audiences to look at me and go, "Is that Eric Roberts? Oh my God."

I was very proud of what I accomplished with that role, so when I didn't get to stay on the show, it broke my heart. I loved that guy, and visually, I knew I *was* that guy. It was like I had him in a butterfly net. He was mine—but I didn't get to keep him, so I put the weight back on. It killed me, but I had to put Junior in a grave.

I had a much different task ahead of me when I was recently asked to play the part of William Faulkner in a new docudrama about him, *The Past Is Never Dead: The Story of William Faulkner*, directed by a young filmmaker named Michael Modak-Turan. We shot in 2022, not just in the town in which Faulkner lived—Oxford, Mississippi—but in Rowan Oak, the very house where he lived, wrote, and died.

You might think it an unlikely casting, but in many ways, it was perfect for me. After all, I come from people like Faulkner's mean-spirited, rural Snopeses. I grew up around rednecks and racists and good ole boys, and also among men with certain codes of honor who were storytellers with colorful ways of speaking. And I loved being in a literary work, just as I had loved being in Willa Cather's *Paul's Case* at the beginning of my career. As an actor, I've always been drawn to biographical material. Because of my reverence for Faulkner's writing, it was a true honor to be asked to portray him in this film. I was prepared to take a deep dive into this brilliant, sometimes drunken Nobel laureate, and I wanted to do justice to this controversial genius who had actually lived during my lifetime.

William Cuthbert Faulkner was born in New Albany, Mississippi, just thirty-four years after Robert E. Lee surrendered to Ulysses S. Grant at the Appomattox courthouse to end the Civil War. Faulkner—though now thought of as racist by today's standards, due to troubling remarks he'd made at the end of his life (cautioning the North to "go slow" on desegregation)—is still considered one of America's greatest writers. He was maybe the first white writer to explore and expose the South's cruel past of systemic racism, building their civilization on the backs of enslaved people. I'm not certain about this, but I think the term *Southern gothic* was first used to describe his brooding—but all too accurate—vision of the dark and deep South.

Always in need of money, Faulkner worked in Hollywood for a time, writing screenplays for *The Big Sleep* and *To Have and Have Not*, now both considered classic films, but he also did some work on *Land of the Pharaohs*, a camp classic starring Joan Collins about the ancient Egyptians. He made some real money that allowed him to keep up Rowan Oak, the plantation home he'd bought in order to fit in better with the aristocratic families of Oxford, Mississippi, but he didn't much care for Hollywood.

In the decades since his death, a lot of terrific and well-meaning actors and filmmakers have tried to bring Faulkner to the big screen, but in my view, most of those movies only managed to shrink him, to make his unforgettable characters and powerful stories smaller, flattening them out like a country road paved over. Paul Newman and Orson Welles in *The Long, Hot Summer*? Despite the brilliant Joanne Woodward, I remember the movie being long, but not very hot. There was a loose adaptation of *The Sound and the Fury* made at the end of the 1950s with Yul Brynner that just couldn't capture the rich and complicated layers of Faulkner's aristocratic Compson family. Curiously enough, I think the best of the bunch was James Franco's adaptation of *As I Lay Dying* ten years years ago. Whatever you think of Franco these days, his movie is probably the truest capture yet of any of Faulkner's novels.

I did read a while back that the writer-director David Milch had signed a deal with Faulkner's estate and HBO to develop a television series based on all of Faulkner's novels and short stories. I don't know what became of that marvelous idea, but a lot of wonderful plans in Hollywood are like oysters in a neap tide—they just never get harvested.

I hope this isn't as conceited as it sounds, but I identified with Faulkner, for a few reasons. Because of the vivid, accurate way he explored and exposed the racism he had grown up with, Faulkner was a controversial figure from the South. *I* was a controversial figure from the South, but for different reasons. Like me, Faulkner had serious addiction problems, mine with drugs, his with alcohol. He didn't drink when he was working, but once finished with one of his many novels or stories, he'd go on a bender that often landed him in the hospital. His daughter, Jill—whom he doted on and who appears in the docudrama—once asked him, "Daddy, please stop drinking." But he could not. As Jill recalled, "He drank until he was ready to quit."

We filmed during a long, hot summer, but I still got chills when we began shooting in Faulkner's white-columned Rowan Oak. Eliza and I couldn't stop taking pictures of everything—the old kitchen implements, the coffee pot, the old-fashioned bedroom, the capacious stone fireplaces. From the moment Eliza and I arrived at the airport, and on the drive into Oxford, past the old schoolhouse, past the cottonwoods bending and swaying, I felt Faulkner tiptoeing into my soul, saying, "Welcome home, you crazy son of the South."

It was an amazing shoot, and the documentary is probably the most honest and evocative one you'll see on the great writer. On set, the craft services table made me laugh. That's where all the food and beverages are laid out for the crew and the cast during those long set-up breaks in the action that make moviemaking seem interminable. In Los Angeles the craft services table offers things like hummus and seaweed, and stevia and soy milk for your coffee, but in Oxford, Mississippi, the craft services table was overflowing with Ding Dongs, potato chips, chocolate milk, and Doritos. The words *gluten free* or *low sodium* never came to the table. Not even a Diet Coke.

I narrate the film and play Faulkner as an older man. My dialect coach, Rory Ledbetter, was tough on me. He was so specific about what Faulkner sounded like. It wasn't just "You've got to have a Southern accent" (which I had hidden away inside me all these years), he was adamant about my having a *regional* accent—not just Mississippi or Oxford, and not just from the town square, but from the very block Faulkner would have walked his dog. This carried over into post-production when we had to loop in some of the lines. It had to be pitch perfect. I mean, Rory was a bulldog about it, and I'm so glad he was.

I just loved all the people involved and adored this role I got to play. It's a fact of actorly life that the most fun parts to play are the tragic scenes, the angry scenes, the flawed characters—people who would make you cross the street if you saw them coming.

I knew what that felt like.

XIV. The Golden Joining

This can be a long process, so patience is key.

—*From* Kintsugi: A How-to Guide

I don't know why Eliza has stayed with me all these years. It can't be fun for her, saving my ass again and again, organizing my life, living the same hectic schedule, having to watch me lose plum roles—first because I was fucked up, then because I was bullheaded, or anxious, or both. I'm not a religious man, but maybe it's a kind of grace that a woman with her strength and insight and huge heart fell in love with my needy soul.

While we were driving in Los Angeles recently, we passed the house where we used to live, and I said to Eliza, "I'm no less in love with you now than I was at the beginning. I may even be more in love with you."

Eliza thought for a minute and said, "Well, that's because we got through the stiff years."

At first, of course, I thought, she meant the peak sexual years.

But no, what she meant was that now all the touchy subjects that she once had to build up her courage—find exactly the right time—to have "stiff conversations" about, she can now bring up at the drop of a hat. Kelly once gave Eliza the advice to bring up my drug use "when he's stoned." But today, she can even make jokes about it all. The "stiff years" are over. It's a great stage of a relationship, though you've gotta be in it for a very long time to get there.

Eliza often describes living with me as a game of badminton in that she keeps batting away all the crap I throw at her. The question keeps coming up: Why does she stay?

For one thing, we're still attracted to each other after three decades together, and our lives are so enmeshed, we work together whenever we can. She might as well be married to me as not, because even if she weren't, she'd still insist on taking care of everything! In fact, this "business"—as actors and entertainers like to call it—is all Eliza really knows. She's tried relationships with people outside of show business, but it didn't really work that well. She certainly never worried, "Oh my God, he's an actor, he'll leave me for a younger woman." None of those kinds of stereotype ever took hold of either one of us.

In her attempt to make whole our fractured family, not long after she and I married, Eliza wrote a long and tender letter to her estranged mother-in-law, Betty Roberts. They had never met, and she knew that Betty and I had never completely repaired the rift that opened up after my parents' divorce, when she took my sisters to live with her and left me to Walter. During the last ten years of her life, Mom did write me some very loving emails, but she never apologized or even acknowledged her abuse during my early childhood.

One thing Eliza tried to do in her heartfelt letter was to correct some untruths about me that many, including my mom, apparently believed.

Here's some of what she wrote:

> I am your daughter-in-law. I am writing to you for reasons that will become obvious as you read this letter . . . but basically just to make contact.
>
> I may seem like yet another foolish person attempting in vain to bring some peace and understanding to this family . . . I know that you and all three of your daughters . . . have given Eric a thousand second-chances in the face of unacceptable behavior. I am married to your son. I don't profess to know all the accurate details of his family—of his origin life—but I do know a great deal about living with him.

Eliza goes on to set the record straight about unfair ways that she's been labeled for marrying me—like being a victim or being "co-dependent"—and she asks for a coming together for the sake of Emma. She writes:

> You are all Emma's family. For her sake, peace has to be achieved between all of you. I know that Eric has been the catalyst for things being in the state they're in now. . . . Eric suffers from a

> combination of very serious depressive disorders. People like that can be unbearable to be around.
>
> The difference in . . . his behavior is so marked since he's basically stopped using everything. This is something that will hopefully, quite simply, make him easy to love again.

She goes on to quote her mother, Lila, as saying about me,

> "He is truly a great actor. These truly great artists rarely grow up to be human beings."
>
> He's come so far, Betty, and this is not foolishness talking. . . . I am not claiming that he's a changed man. He's a work-in-progress, like all of us.

Eliza reminds Betty of all the support I've shown for Julia's career and Lisa's talent, and she passes along compliments from young actors she's met regarding Betty's role as their acting teacher. She concludes with:

> I appreciate your patience in listening. I feel kind of silly going on and on like this. . . . We all have very little to work with. . . . just a bunch of lopsided stories, most of them probably largely subjective, some totally inaccurate—phantoms really. It's a shame.
>
> Be well, Eliza.

Sadly, my mom never answered Eliza's letter. Betty passed away, never having met the woman who loved and married her only son.

After she passed, there was a funeral in Georgia for Betty that Eliza and I weren't invited to. I heard about it only when Adam told me about it afterward. Some lame reason was given why I wasn't invited, though you can guess why. The rest of the family were probably afraid I'd say or do something inappropriate, something that would push the envelope, something anxiety causing.

There was, eventually, a second memorial for Betty that took place at a church in Malibu, and Eliza and I were invited to that one. In fact, when Julia found out I would be coming, she asked for Morgan—Prairie—to cater it. That blew my mind for some reason. It was such a loving and lovely gesture—and quite a spread it was! It would have made my mother happy, I think, to see us all together, all that blood under the bridge at last.

As memorials go, this one was splendid. Dermot Mulroney played the cello, and they showed a badly put together video of Betty's life. The video seemed endless, but probably only because of all the emotions it stirred up in me. Nonetheless, it was quite moving, even if, for me, it was a visitation of ghosts.

For some reason, I remember staring at the shoes Julia was wearing. They were these blocky, black executioner's boots that were in style then, but she was wearing them with a flowery summer dress. The contrast was so much like life itself—the lightness of the flowers weighed down by those black, heavy boots.

Whoever delivered the eulogy at the memorial (I didn't recognize him) spoke of Betty's love for us all, including Eliza, whom Betty had never met, and all the beautiful lies you tell on such an occasion that you secretly hope might be true. But to the best of my memory, it was a festive day—plenty of laughs and warm embraces. Julia's kids were there with their nanny, who did her best to keep them from running amok.

After Julia and Lisa spoke their eulogies for our mom, I left my seat and went over to the section set apart for family members, where I hadn't been invited. Eliza was nervous about it, thinking I would say the wrong thing. I put my arms around both my sisters and brought them close to me and told them I loved them.

I left right after that.

The memorial seemed to hold the promise of a future of continued contact with what remained of my original family, but for some reason, that never really happened. It did make me regret that I didn't go to see Mom at the end of her life. There's no imagining what that might have done for us both, like Lee surrendering to Grant at Appomattox. Maybe she would have even let me go home with my horse.

At her memorial, I was able to say goodbye to my mother, but my father was a different story.

I finally came to terms with Walter Roberts on the day of the 2022 Super Bowl. Eliza and I were driving home from the set of my current picture. It was one of the sets where we figured so low in the ladder of importance, that not only did we need to drop off the wardrobe we'd brought from home, then drive six miles to a UCLA parking lot where we had to pay the $9 parking fee (which was the price SAG used to have to pay you to bring your own wardrobe). From there, we had to be shuttled to the set by whoever had time to come fetch us. Not only was it a shuttle-to-set, Eliza ended up being the shuttle driver for the rest of the day.

However, I was elated to have wrapped in time to get home to watch the Super Bowl. Eliza is always on guard when I'm elated, in case my mood suddenly drops without warning. Driving home between interruptions from our GPS (telling us in essence to stop talking so that she could stop correcting), I was suddenly struck by how great my stepdaughter Prairie and April's family is. Here are two people who knew what they wanted, wanted it at the same time, and did it. They'd wanted to create a family, a little family of four female humans and two female canines. You know why it's working? They have two great kids, they knew what they both wanted, and they did it. And was also working because there were no men! I told Eliza, "We're such a disappointment to you all. So undeserving." Does that surprise you? Sometimes when you expect a misogynist, you find a feminist instead.

Back home, I put a snack in the mini oven while Eliza went across the street to feed a squirrel. Suddenly, I felt sad. Was it just a mood swing?

I knew I had done two things right in this life. Become a working actor, and be with Eliza. But I wondered if, in seven to ten years, I would still be standing. Would I be passed off as an actor, or a person of any value? Maybe, but something else was turning my mood blue.

Suddenly, I realized where that sadness was coming from. It was coming from one thing—a secret I had clung to most of my life. Of course, that secret was my father, who couldn't be *friends* with any of the good people who'd crossed his path, such as the King family, the Abernathys, maybe even his own sisters—because he wouldn't let anyone get too close. I think I was the only one who saw the truth about Walter. But the kicker was, I also knew that I loved him. I couldn't live down the shame of loving him or of who he was, someone capable of terrible things. I was ashamed of being so much *of* him and so much like him.

So if there's a reason for writing this book, for sharing my life with strangers, it's this: If you've ever loved a parent, a friend, even a child with a cruel nature, it's never too late to begin to recover from the shame and pain of it all. Don't shy away from the cruelty in yourself. Look in the mirror, stare it in the face, and do something about it.

You're taught in school that there are fifty states in the US, but there are really fifty-one—the alpha state—it's where I wish I could live most of the time. You should visit. It's a kind of paradise, a place where there's no self-judgment, no regret. Eliza tells me that I often flip down the car visor and look into the mirror when we're driving, which for me somehow triggers an alpha state. I see myself without any prejudices—not the "beautiful man" others saw in me (which I never felt), or the opposite extreme, the drug-addled fuckup. I feel free.

So, if there's another reason for sharing this saga with strangers, it's this: I'm hoping to exorcise my father from my life, for once and for all. And, if you feel, like me, as if you were born broken, you *can* be mended.

One way I know I've mended is how much love I have for my grandchildren. They are my life right now, and I can't stop thinking about them—Emma's son, Rhodes (my only biological grandchild), and Prairie and April's kids, Magnolia and Georgia. I miss them so much when they're not around, and I can't get enough stories, videos, and pictures of all the kids. I never thought I would say this, or even feel it, but I'm overflowing with love for my extended family.

It *is* all about family, wherever or however you can find, or create one.

So this brings me to *kintsugi*, the Japanese art of repairing broken things, aka "the golden joining." It's basically repairing a broken ceramic vessel with glue mixed with gold dust, or silver or platinum, so there's no attempt to hide that fact that the piece of ceramic was broken and put back together again. The seams where the breaks occurred are now actually illuminated—they glow with silver or gold. It makes for a beautiful pattern. I think it's a good metaphor for people like me, who have been mended and mended again and, with any luck, remain imperfect but somehow still beautiful, but in a different way.

I've come to love my life like I love my forbearing wife, but I live broken and always will, probably until the moment when that dude in the black hoodie who carries a scythe comes calling, like in Ingmar Bergman's *The Seventh Seal*, and Death and I walk the same empty beach together. (At least I would have finally ended up in a great movie.) I think I'm a better actor now. I'm ready for my close-up, Mr. Tarantino, or Ms. Bigelow, or the Brothers Safdie. What wasn't quite true forty-five years ago—the tag line for *King of the Gypsies*—finally feels right to me: "It's Almost His Time." I may have been born broken, and I'll never be a perfect man, but thanks to Eliza I'm mending, shot through with silver and gold.

ACKNOWLEDGMENTS

One thing that may surprise you about this saga you hold in your hands (or on your "device") is how much I love books. I've been an avid reader since I was a boy, and one thing I can thank my tormenting father for is that he introduced me to many classics of the theater—*The Member of the Wedding*, *Othello*, *The Taming of the Shrew.* So please allow me to quote a writer I've always admired, Isak Dinesen, who wrote, "All sorrows can be borne if you put them into a story."

So, dudes, that's what I've done here—I've put all the glory and all the misery of my life into the story you've just read. I could not have done it without Eliza, my partner in triumph and in defeat, who helped me to remember, who offered perspective, who filled in the details in her own eloquent way. Eliza, my one and only wife, thank you for running away with me.

Thanks also to my other partner in crime, Sam Kashner, who forced me to remember at the point of a tape recorder when he first interviewed me years ago for a *Vanity Fair* story, and who shaped my meandering tales into the chronicle you've just read. Thank you for running away with us in our sidecar! And thanks, too, to Nancy Schoenberger, who helped keep it all going through the dark days of Covid, and beyond.

Kudos to our ever-patient editor, the legendary Charles Spicer at St. Martin's Press, who quietly encouraged me—and waited for me—through the Covid shutdown and through all my insecurities and delays. Thanks also to the irreplaceable Hannah Pierdolla, editorial assistant at St. Martin's, and the incomparable photo director Ann Schneider.

Emma, my one and only daughter, thank you for being just that.

Here's a list of family, friends, and organizations that helped me along my way that I'd like to thank: Cindy Leong (you must know you're family simply from the way I drive you nuts), Jeffrey Frankel (I hope I'm your favorite runaway client because you're certainly my favorite runaway lawyer), David Duchovny, Helen Cifuentes, Keaton Simons, Lisa Gillan, Morgan aka Prairie Simons, Georgia, Magnolia, and Nurse April—thank you for the loan of your mom/Fama/mom-in-law, respectively. Thanks also to my literary agent, Alan Nevins (thank you for the Renaissance). Speaking of Renaissance, a great debt is owed to Spike Carter, writer and documentary filmmaker. It was Spike's idea to have *Vanity Fair* magazine profile this black sheep of cinema, which eventually led to this book and the film Spike's been working on about mi vida loca.

I'm represented by Sovereign Talent Group, Peter Young, and Tracy Michaels, and I love them all (I couldn't afford a copy of this book without you guys and the team). Hats off to R&R

Business Management, for keeping us going for years on end, sometimes on fumes alone.

People I forgot to mention, because we often neglect those we feel safest with, know that I love you. If I could conjure up every person to acknowledge, this page would be a hundred times as long as the entire book.

Thanks also to Dr. Drew, who believed in me and helped me hold on to sobriety, and I thank the ghosts of that Romanian couple who visited me in the hospital and told me how I could restore my memory—one of an actor's greatest assets.

Hell, I'll take all the help I can get, even from the astral plane.

INDEX

ABOUT THE AUTHORS

Eric Roberts has appeared in more than seven hundred films during his five-decade career, from *King of the Gypsies* and *The Pope of Greenwich Village* to *The Dark Knight, Inherent Vice,* and *Babylon.* He's been nominated for an Oscar and three Golden Globes, and been celebrated at film festivals around the world. He's brother to Julia Roberts and father to Emma Roberts.

Sam Kashner is currently writer-at-large for Graydon Carter's *Air Mail.* He was a longtime contributing editor at *Vanity Fair* magazine. He is the coauthor of two *New York Times* bestselling biographies: *Furious Love: Elizabeth Taylor, Richard Burton, and the Marriage of the Century* and *The Fabulous Bouvier Sisters: The Tragic and Glamorous Lives of Jackie and Lee.*